JAPANESE FROM ZERO! 4

George Trombley
Yukari Takenaka

Japanese From Zero! Book 4
Proven Methods to Learn Japanese with integrated Workbook

PREFACE

Japanese From Zero! is a Japanese language book series built on Japanese grammar that makes sense! Each book is crafted page by page and lesson by lesson to have relevant (and sometimes fun) Japanese conversation and sentence structure patterns that enhance the Japanese learner's ability to speak Japanese faster and understand the small nuances of Hiragana and everyday Japanese speech.

DEDICATION

This book is dedicated and made for:

Japanese culture lovers, Japanese language learners, Japanese anime and drama watchers, Japanese beginners, JPOP music fans, people of Japanese heritage connecting to their history, and anyone planning travel to Japan!

I lived in Japan for 9 years and have been married to my Japanese wife, Yukari, for 20 years. When we began writing the Japanese From Zero series, it was out of frustration with current Japanese books on the market. I felt they were either too fast, too slow, or too complicated. Japanese has enriched my life so much and writing this series was a way to express my sincere appreciation to all that the country of Japan and the Japanese language can offer.

All of us on the Japanese From Zero! team wish you success on your road to Japanese fluency and hope this book is a solid first step!

COPYRIGHT

DISTRIBUTION

Distributed in the UK & Europe by:
Bay Foreign Language Books Ltd.
Unit 4, Kingsmead, Park Farm,
Folkestone, Kent. CT19 5EU, Great Britain
sales@baylanguagebooks.co.uk

Distributed in the USA & Canada by:
From Zero LLC.
10624 S. Eastern Ave. #A769
Henderson, NV 89052, USA
sales@fromzero.com

Thanks for the nice comments! We love feedback!

These books and this website remain my nihongo bible!
Ray_San – YesJapan.com

The books are great! I like the way everything is explained, the examples, the lessons and the reviews.
Eijioo – YesJapan.com

Japanese From Zero Book 1 and 2 are amazing books for beginners! Having tried other ways of learning Japanese from the beginning, I find that the Japanese from Zero series are incredibly user friendly.
Kurisuti.Chan – YesJapan.com

I love JFZ, because it's so so so easy to use compared to others I've tried! It's clear you put a lot of work into it and I'm very grateful. Even though I lead a busy life and can't find too much time to learn, JFZ makes it easy for me to pick up where I left off and revise what I might have forgotten. THANKS!! ☺
J. Brooks – Facebook

THANK-YOU JFZ!!!!!! I think Everything JFZ does is wonderful! It is the most helpful book I've come across!
Rukia Kuchiki – YesJapan.com

Thank you, I just finished the 2nd book and can't wait to start with the 3rd! Soon am getting my hands on the 4th!
religionflag – YesJapan.com

JFZ! is perfect. If you're a complete beginner, this book takes you through the bare basics and really helps you progress quickly. I highly recommend this.
F. Morgan – Good Reads review

The perfect Japanese textbook for young learners. One of the benefits of this book, which also slows it down, are the tangents it takes to explain the nuances of Japanese that a beginner might encounter.
Michael Richey – Tofugu.com

You really learn Japanese from zero – no prior knowledge at all required. The grammar is easy to understand.
Karl Andersson - karlandersson.se

As someone who owns the first three books, I can say the books are great.
Mastema – YesJapan.com

feedback@fromzero.com

Japanese From Zero! Book 4
– CONTENTS –

Japanese
From Zero!

Welcome!
Moving forward

 ## Introduction

Welcome to Book 4 in the "Japanese From Zero!" series (JFZ). Congratulations on sticking to your learning! Coming this far is something to be proud of!

Any student reading this book should already be able to read and write all of the hiragana, katakana, and the first 80 kanji taught in Japanese schools and book 3 of the JFZ series. It's okay if you have to look up a character from time to time.

Try not to be hard on yourself for occasionally forgetting some of the words you have learned. It happens to the best speakers, including myself, that a common word slips the mind. Even after over 20 years of interpreting and teaching Japanese, I find that the brain works in mysterious ways! Remember that no matter how much you study you will forget some of what you have learned.

The more that you speak and use your Japanese the more it will become a part of you. There will be days when you impress yourself with your ability, and days when you wonder if you can speak any Japanese at all. If you have come this far, you CAN speak Japanese.

When will I be fluent?

This question, "When will I be fluent?", is on the mind of many students studying any language. Becoming fluent isn't like a marathon where at the end of the race you pass the finish line and declare "I am fluent!".

It's more like coloring in a coloring book. Little by little you add color and before you know it you have a completely colored page in your book. The reality is that a good portion of your coloring book has color in it. If fact, you are ALREADY fluent in certain pockets of Japanese.

If you have introduced yourself in Japanese and can do it now without much thought, then you are fluent in Japanese introductions. If you can recall Japanese colors without much effort then you are fluent in Japanese colors. The more subject areas you are able to talk about then the more "pockets" of fluency you add.

When I first did interpreting work for a radiation cancer treatment company I certainly wasn't fluent in that pocket of Japanese. After learning some new words, and learning how the process works I became fluent in radiation treatment and for the last 8 years I have had constant work from this company.

For the rest of your learning carrier you will be adding to your pockets of fluency. The order and timing of each of the pockets you learn will be different for each student. It all boils down to your interests and the opportunities you have in each pocket.

So to directly answer the question "When will I be fluent?", the answer is "You already are."

 ## Different sources of learning

As you study Japanese, you undoubtedly will use many sources to study, from books, to teachers, to internet sources, to people you meet in Japan. Many students are distressed to find inconsistencies between sources.

The reality is that EVERY book and learning material is written by a person or group of people. And as you know, people have different opinions. Much of language learning is concrete, after all in Japanese "a cat" will always be ねこ and "a dog" will always be いぬ. But the way concepts are explained are 100% subjective to the teacher.

The way "Japanese From Zero!" teaches one concept will certainly be different from some other sources. This is normal and to be expected with any source of learning material. I encourage everyone to pick up other books and hop online to see what other Japanese language students are saying about the topic you are learning at the moment. In most cases you will be helped by hearing another opinion on that topic.

 ## How this book works

There are serveral sections to each lesson. Many sections contain numbered grammar points. The numbering will continue from prior sections and lessons regardless of where they are in the book. This will make it easier for you to easily find a grammar point later.

What should I know before this book?

This is the 4th book in a 5 part series, "Japanese From Zero!". We assume that you can read and write hiragana, katakana, and the 80 kanji taught in book 3. If you come across a kanji that you do not know please refer to the cheat sheet provided below.

Kanji	Hiragana = くんよみ; Katakana = おんよみ	Meaning
一	ひと、イチ、イツ	one (1)
二	ふた、ニ	two (2)
三	み、みっ、サン	three (3)
四	よ、よっ、よん、シ	four (4)
五	いつ、ゴ	five (5)
六	む、むっ、むい、ロク	six (6)
七	なな、なの、シチ	seven (7)
八	や、やっ、よう、ハチ	eight (8)
九	ここの、キュウ、ク	nine (9)
十	と、とお、ジッ、ジュウ、ジュッ	ten (10)
百	ヒャク	one hundred (100)
千	ち、セン	one thousand (1,000)
日	か、ひ、ジツ、ニチ	day
月	つき、ガツ、ゲツ	moon, month
火	ひ、（ほ）、カ	fire
水	みず、スイ	water
木	き、こ、ボク、モク	tree, wood
金	かな、かね、キン、コン	gold, metal
土	つち、ト、ド	soil, dirt, earth (not planet)
休	やす、キュウ	break, rest
上	あ、うえ、うわ、かみ、のぼ、ショウ、ジョウ	up, above
下	お、くだ、さ、した、しも、（もと）、カ、ゲ	down, below
左	ひだり、サ	left
右	みぎ、ウ、ユウ	right

大	おお、タイ、ダイ	big
中	なか、チュウ	middle, inside
小	お、こ、ちい、ショウ	small
円	まる、エン	yen, circle
人	ひと、ジン、ニン	people, person
目	ま、め、ボク、モク	eye
耳	みみ、ジ	ear
口	くち、ク、コウ	mouth, opening
手	た、て、シュ	hand
足	あし、た、ソク	foot, feet
力	ちから、リキ、リョク	power
立	た、リツ、リュウ	stand
男	おとこ、ナン、ダン	boy, man
女	おんな、め、ジョ、ニョ、ニョウ	girl, woman
子	こ、シ、ス	child
生	い、う、き、なま、は、ショウ、セイ	life, raw, birth
天	あま、あめ、テン	heaven, sky
空	あ、あき、から、そら、クウ	sky, emptiness
気	キ、ケ	spirit, mood
雨	あま、あめ、ウ	rain
山	やま、サン	mountain
川	かわ、（セン）	river
林	はやし、リン	woods, forest
森	もり、シン	forest
石	いし、シャク、セキ、（コク）	stone
花	はな、カ	flower
犬	いぬ、ケン	dog
虫	むし、チュウ	insect
町	まち、チョウ	town
村	むら、ソン	village

田	た、デン	rice field
夕	ゆう、（セキ）	evening
赤	あか、セキ、（シャク）	red
青	あお、セイ、（ショウ）	blue
白	しら、しろ、ハク、（ビャク）	white
見	み、ケン	see, watch
出	だ、で、シュツ、（スイ）	exit
入	い、はい、ニュウ	enter, go in
先	さき、セン	previous, precedence
早	はや、ソウ、（サッ）	early
本	もと、ホン	book, main
文	（ふみ）、ブン、モン	sentence
名	な、ミョウ、メイ	name
字	（あざ）、ジ	character, hand writing
学	まな、ガク	learn
校	コウ	-school
正	ただ、まさ、ショウ、セイ	correct, regular
年	とし、ネン	year
王	オウ	royal
音	おと、ね、オン、（イン）	sound
糸	いと、シ	thread
車	車、シャ	car, wheel
貝	かい	shell
玉	たま、ギョク	coin, ball, sphere
草	くさ、ソウ	grass
竹	たけ、チク	bamboo

Introduction to Formal Japanese

Before This Lesson

1. Know how to read kanji 1-80 (1st grade educational kanji) from Japanese From Zero! book 3, hiragana and katakana.
2. Have an understanding of basic verb conjugation and Japanese conversation covered in Japanese From Zero! books 1-3.

Lesson Goals

1. Learn some of the common "respectful" form of the verbs.
2. Learn some quick ways to sound more polite in Japanese.

From The Teachers

1. Remember that at a minimum you should be polite and use the ます forms of verbs. Only when you are very familiar with the person you are talking with should you use casual language.

Lesson Highlights

1-1. Using でしょう to be more polite

1-2. The どちら word group

1   When will we speak formal Japanese?

In this series so far, we have avoided teaching formal Japanese, also called 敬語 (けいご).
In everyday Japan there are times where けいご is appropriate and expected. However, as a
がいこくじん (foreigner) or がいじん for short, you are not held to the same expectations.
As long as your Japanese is "polite" with people you don't know or your superiors at work and
school, then you won't be considered rude. By "polite Japanese" I mean using です instead of
だ and ます instead of the informal forms of verbs. It's that simple.

In my 20 years of speaking Japanese I can honestly tell you that I only use けいご when
absolutely neccessary. Everyone will have a different opinion, but it's my firm opinion that けい
ご, while important, is not key to your success in Japanese. This lesson will serve as a crash
course in けいご so you aren't caught off guard when you hear it.

1   New Words あたらしい ことば

Progressive	かんじ	えいご
どちら	どちら	where, which and who (polite)
こちら	こちら	this, here, this person (polite)
そちら	そちら	that, there, that person (polite)
あちら	あちら	that over there, over there, that person over there (polite)
てんない	店内	in the store
じだいげき	時代劇	historical play; period drama
ちゅう文	注文	order; request
ごちゅう文	ご注文	order; request (polite)
ダブルチーズバーガー	ダブルチーズバーガー	double cheesburger
アイスティー	アイスティー	ice tea
もちかえり	持ち帰り	take out, to go
竹中	竹中	last name (in the bamboo)
おたく	お宅	home, residence

ごぞんじ	ご存知	knowing, having knowledge of
さま	様	polite version of さん meaning "Mr., Miss, Mrs."
かた	方	person (polite)
ぜんぶ	全部	all
ぜんいん	全員	everyone
せき	席	seat
ただいま	只今	presently, right now
はりねずみ	針鼠	hedgehog

▮1▮ Grammar ぶんぽう

❑ 1-1. Using でしょう to be more polite

There are few quick ways to be more polite in Japanese without overloading up on new grammar. One way is to use でしょうか instead of ですか when asking questions.

Examples

1. この 車（くるま）は いくら <u>でしょうか</u>。
   How much is this car?

2. このねこは あなたの <u>でしょうか</u>。
   Is this cat yours?

3. 西口（にしくち）は どこ<u>でしょうか</u>。
   Where is the west exit? *or entrance*

4. あのかたは おとうさん<u>でしょうか</u>。
   Is that person your father?

You can also add でしょうか after い adjectives and な adjectives to be more polite.

Examples

1. おたくは こちらから とおいでしょうか。
   Is your home far?

2. すしは たかいでしょうか。
   Is sushi expensive?

3. 犬か ねこか どちらが かわいいでしょうか。
   Which are cuter, dogs or cats?

4. このコップは きれいでしょうか。
   Is this cup clean?

5. このいすに すわっても いいでしょうか。
   Is it alright if I sit in this seat?

You can also add でしょうか after verbs. For informal forms make sure you add の before でしょう。 You do not need の with polite forms such as ます、ません、ました。

Example Q&A

1. この 電車は 大阪まで いくのでしょうか。
   Does this train go to Osaka?

   > いくのでしょうか can also be いきます でしょうか

   はい、大阪まで いきます。
   Yes, it goes to Osaka.

   いいえ、大阪まで いきません。
   No, it doesn't go to Osaka.

2. いつから 日本語を べんきょうしているの でしょうか。
   Since when have you been studying Japanese?

   去年から べんきょうしています。
   I have been studying since last year.

   二年まえからです。
   From 2 years ago.

❏ 1-2. The どちら word group

I like to think the どちら word group is "magical" because it's used as the polite versions for four different word groups learned in prior books. Here are the words this group replaces:

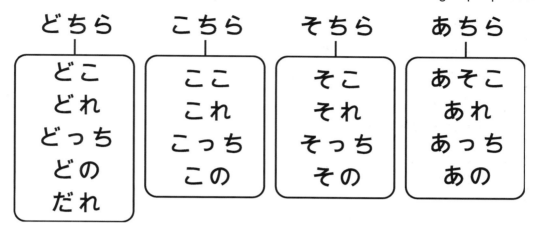

Example Q&A (polite for どっち or どれ word groups)

1. 赤か青か どちらが すきですか。
    Which do you like, red or blue?

    赤のほうが すきです。
    I like red more.

    どちらも すきじゃないです。
    I don't like either.

2. どちらの犬が いちばん かわいいと おもいますか。
    Which dog do you think is the cutest?

    そちらの 白とちゃいろの犬が 一番かわいいです。
    That white and brown dog is the cutest.

    ぜんぶ かわいいと おもう。
    I think they are all cute.

Example Q&A (polite for どこ word group)

1. 竹中さんの 自転車は どちらでしょうか。
   Where is Takenaka's bicycle?

   そちらに あります。
   It's over there.

   あちらの 白いのです。
   It's the white one over there.

2. 田中さんの つくえは どちらですか。
   Where is Tanaka-san's desk.

   こちらです。
   It's this one. / It's here.

   小林さんのつくえの よこに あります。
   It's next to Kobayashi-san's desk.

When using どちら to be polite for the どの word group, you must add の to the どちら word.

Example Q&A (polite for どの word group)

1. どちらの 車が はやいですか。
   Which car is fast?

   トヨタが はやいです。
   Toyota's are fast.

   そちらの 赤いホンダが はやいとおもいます。
   I think that red Honda is fast.

   どちらも はやくないです。
   Both of them, are not fast.

When using どちら to be polite for だれ, it is even more polite if you say どちらさま。

Example Q&A (polite for だれ)

1. どちらさま でしょうか。
   Who are you?

   ジョージです。
   I'm George.

   <ruby>竹中<rt>たけなか</rt></ruby>さんの ともだちです。
   I'm Takenaka-san's friend.

1 **New Phrases あたらしい フレーズ**

1. ただいま、せきを はずしております。
   They are presently away from their desk (seat).
   This is a common phrase used on the phone when calling to talk to a particular person at a company. The ております conjugation is common in formal / polite speech.

You should NEVER use polite verbs when referring to yourself and in many cases you should consider people in your company or school as "yourself" when talking to another company or group.

1 **New Verbs あたらしい どうし**

どうし	えいご	た form	タイプ
いらっしゃる	to come, to go, to be	いらっしゃった	ある
<ruby>召<rt>め</rt></ruby>し<ruby>上<rt>あ</rt></ruby>がる	to eat, to drink	めしあがった	regular
ご<ruby>覧<rt>らん</rt></ruby>になる	to see	ごらんに なった	regular
<ruby>仰<rt>おっしゃ</rt></ruby>る	to say	おっしゃった	ある
なさる	to do, to play	なさった	ある
ござる	to have, to exist	(not used)	ある
はずす	to leave, step out		

1 Verb Usage どうしの つかいかた

In prior books we have introduced 4 types of verbs:

1. Regular
3. いる / える exception

2. いる / える
4. Irregular

In this lesson the ある verb type is introduced. This verb type is a unique type that is only found in the respectful verbs. The good news is there are only a very small amount of this type of verb.

The final る of an ある verb type is changed to い and then the appropriate ending is added.

いらっしゃ⓪ → いらっしゃい + ます etc.
おっしゃ⓪ —→ おっしゃい + ます etc.
なさ⓪ ———→ なさい + ます etc.
ござ⓪ ———→ ござい + ます etc.

As for the informal forms for the ある verb type you simply treat that as any other regular verb. Let's look at how the ある verbs in this lesson are conjugated:

Example Sentences

1. しゃちょうは あした、いらっしゃらない です。(informal future negative)

   The president will not come tomorrow.

2. 日本に いったときは なにを なさいましたか。(polite past positive)

   When you went to Japan what did you do?

3. 先生は きのう、なにを おしゃったの？(informal past positive)

   What did the teacher say yesterday?

❑ 1-3. いらっしゃる (to come, to go, to be)

This is probably the most commonly used formal Japanese, and you will certainly hear it everyday in Japan. いらっしゃる is the けいご version of いく(to go), くる(to come), and いる) to be).

---

1. **Polite conversation between office workers planning a meeting.**

A: つぎの ミーティングは あしたの ８じ です。

B: しゃちょうは いらっしゃいますか。

A: はい、 １０じまで いらっしゃいます。

B: あさっては なんじに いらっしゃいますか。

A: ごぜん １０じに いらっしゃいます。

A: The next meeting will be tomorrow at 8 o'clock.

B: Will the president be there?

A: Yes, (she) will be there until 10 o'clock.

B: What time will she (come in / be in) the day after tomorrow?

A: She will be in at 10 AM.

---

2. **Polite conversation on the phone.**

A: はい、竹中^{たけなか}です。

B: 竹中ゆかりさまは いらっしゃいますか。

A: ただいま、 せきを はずしております。

A: Hello, this is Takenaka.

B: Is this Takenaka Yukari?

A: She is presently not at her desk.

❏ 1-4. めしあがる (to eat, to drink)

めしあがる is the けいご version of たべる (to eat) and のむ (to drink). In Japan when ordering from a fast food place you will most likely be asked:

> てんないで めしあがりますか。
> **Will you be eating in the store?**

Other than this usage you might not hear this often. However, if you watch じだいげき (Japanese historical plays or drama) you will hear much more of formal Japanese

---

Example conversation

1. A: いらっしゃいませ！ごちゅうもんどうぞ。
   B: ダブルチーズバーガー 一つと、エルのアイスティーをおねがいします。
   A: てんないで めしあがりますか。
   B: いいえ、もちかえりです。

   A: Welcome! Your order please.
   B: A double cheeseburger and a large ice tea please.
   A: Will you be eating in the store?
   B: No, it's take out.

❏ 1-5. ご覧に なる (to see)

ごらんに なる is a the けいご verb that replaces みる (to see). Remember you never want to use ごらんに なる when referring to yourself, even if it was asked of you, you should reply with みる.

1. **Polite conversation between a teacher and a student.**
   A: きのう、えいがを ごらんに なりましたか。
   B: いいえ、みません でした。
   A: いつ、ごらんに なりますか。
   B: あした、ともだちと みます。

A: Did you see a movie yesterday?

B: No, I didn't see (one).

A: When will you see it?

B: I will watch (one) tomorrow with a friend.

❑ 1-6. 仰^{おっしゃ}る (to say)

おっしゃる is the けいご version of いう (to say).

> **Example Sentences**
>
> 1. なにを おっしゃいましたか。
>   What did you say?
>
> 2. せんせいは あしたこないと おっしゃいました。
>   The teacher said they weren't coming tomorrow.
>
> 3. しゃちょうは 3じに ミーティングがあると おっしゃいました。
>   The company president said there was a meeting at 3 o'clock.
>
> 4. やまださまは いつ いらっしゃると おっしゃいましたか。
>   When did Mrs. Yamada say that she would be coming?

It's VERY common that you will hear the phrase 「おっしゃるとおり です」 in polite conversation. It simply means "It's exactly as you have stated." It's a polite way to tell someone you agree with them.

たなかさんの いうとおりです。   たなかさんの おっしゃるとおりです。
It's just as Tanaka says.   It's just as Tanaka says.

1. **Conversation on a TV show. Contestants are B and C, the host is A.**

   A: この どうぶつは なんというの でしょうか。

   B: キリン でしょうか。

   A: ちがいます。

   C: ハリネズミ でしょうか。

   A: おっしゃるとおり です！

A: What is this animal called?

B: Is it a giraffe?

A: No, it's not.

C: Is it a hedgehog?

A: It's just as you stated! (exactly)

❑ 1-7. なさる (to do, to play)

なさる is the respectful verb that replaces する. So any verb that is created with する will use なさる instead in the respectful form.

Example Sentences

1. あしたは なにを なさいますか。

   What will you do tomorrow?

2. きのうは どうなさいましたか。

   What did you do yesterday?

Remember that even if someone asks you a question with a respectful verb that you should NEVER use those same respectful verbs when talking about yourself or someone in your group. Look at the following conversations and notice that when responding to questions with respectful verbs the responses are all using the standard forms.

Example conversations
1. **Conversation between: (A) student (B) teacher**

   A: いつから えいごを べんきょう なさっていますか。

   B: しょうがっこうのときから べんきょうしています。

   A: Since when have you been studying English?

   B: I have been studying since when I was in elementary school.

2. **Conversation between: (A) waitress (B) customer**

   A: なにを ちゅうもん なさいますか。

   B: アイスティーを みっつ ください。

   A: What will you be ordering?

   B: Three ice teas please.

3. **Conversation between (A) unknown player (B) pro player**

A: いっしゅうかんに どれぐらいサッカーを なさいますか。

B: 一日に 三じかんぐらい れんしゅう します。

A: In one week about how much soccer do you play?

B: I practice about 3 hours a day.

☐ 1-8. ござる (to have to exist)

ござる is the respectful verb that replaces ある. As with all the other respectful verbs

remember that you shouldn't use any respectful verb when talking about yourself.

> **Example conversations**
> 1. **Conversation between: (A) customer (B) waitress**
>   A: フォークがありますか。
>
>   B: はい、ございます。
>
>   A: Do you have a fork?
>   B: Yes we do (have).
>
> 2. **Conversation between: (A) zoo visitor (B) zoo worker**
>   A: このどうぶつえんに トイレが ありますか。
>
>   B: はい、二つ ございます。
>
>   A: 一番 ちかい トイレは どこですか。
>
>   B: ハリネズミの よこです。
>
>   A: Does this zoo have a restroom?
>   B: Yes, there are 2.
>   A: Where is the closest restroom?
>   B: Next to the hedgehogs.

~でござる is polite for である and both of these mean "it is" and are the same as saying です but have more impact than です and sounds more authoritative and factual. The negative form of である adds in the topic marker は for stress ではない.

Example Sentences

1. これは ハリネズミで ある。

   This is a hedgehog.

2. あれは なにで ございますか。

   What is that over there?

3. これは あなたの 本ではない。

   This is not your book.

---

❶ Culture Clip カルチャー クリップ

Is rude Japanese always rude?

The rules for Japanese are fairly simple. When you don't know someone, then you should be polite. In most cases after you are familiar with someone you can drop the formalities. But even in the case of familiar people there is a certain level of "niceness" that is maintained. The exception to this rule is when you are talking with family and close friends. This is the rare occasion when rude / abrupt Japanese isn't necessarily rude.

---

❶ Mini Conversation ミニ会話

1. **Polite conversation at a restaurant.**

   A: ご注文はお決まりでしょうか？

   B: ダブルチーズバーガーをお願いします。

   A: お飲み物は何を召し上がりますか？

   B: アイスティーをお願いします。

   A: Have you decided on your order?

   B: A double cheeseburger please.

   A: What you will have for your drink?

   B: An ice tea please.

2. Polite conversation between office workers.

A: 社長はいつ新しいお店にいらっしゃいますか？

B: 明日の午後です。店内をご覧になって、東京に帰られます。

A: お忙しいですね。

A: When will the president be coming to the new store?

B: Tomorrow morning. (He) will look inside the store and then return to Tokyo.

A: (He) sure is busy.

Kanji Lesson 1

引雲遠何科夏
kanji 81-86

一 New Kanji あたらしい かんじ

Practice writing each new kanji in the boxes provided. First trace the light gray samples.

Pay attention to stroke order. Practice writing the sample kanji words at least five times each.

引	くんよみ	ひ（く）	number		81
	おんよみ	イン	meaning	pull	

ひ 引く	いんりょく 引力	ひ ぱ 引っ張る	ごういん 強引	ひ ざん 引き算
to pull	gravity	to pull	forceful	subtraction

4 strokes

フ　コ　弓　引

引　引　引　引　引

雲	くんよみ	くも	number		82
	おんよみ	ウン	meaning	cloud	

にゅうどうぐも 入道雲	くも 雲	くも ゆ 雲行き	うんかい 雲海	あまぐも 雨雲
a bank of clouds	cloud	the look of the sky	a sea of clouds	a rain cloud

12 strokes

一　二　テ　干　干　干　雫　雪　雪　雲　雲　雲

雲　雲　雲　雲　雲

| 遠 | くんよみ | とお（い） | number | 83 |
| | おんよみ | エン | meaning | far |

とお 遠い	えんそく 遠足	とおで 遠出	えんきょり 遠距離	えいえん 永遠
far	an excursion	go for an outing	long distance	eternity

13 strokes

一 十 土 吉 声 吉 吉 声 袁 袁 袁 遠 遠

遠 遠 遠 遠 遠

| 何 | くんよみ | なに、なん | number | 84 |
| | おんよみ | カ | meaning | what? |

なに 何か	なんにち 何日	なんばん 何番	なんじ 何時	なに 何も
something	what day?	what number?	what time?	nothing

7 strokes

ノ イ 仁 仁 何 何 何

何 何 何 何 何

| 科 | くんよみ | – | number | 85 |
| | おんよみ | カ | meaning | subject |

かもく 科目	かがく 科学	ないか 内科	じびか 耳鼻科	ひゃっかじてん 百科事典
school subject	science	internal medicine	ear, nose doctor	Encyclopedia

9 strokes

ノ ニ 千 禾 禾 禾 科 科 科

科 科 科 科 科

夏	くんよみ	なつ	number		86
	おんよみ	カ、ゲ	meaning	summer	

げし 夏至	なつやす 夏休み	まなつ 真夏	しょか 初夏	なつふく 夏服
summer solstice	summer vacation	mid-summer	early summer	summer clothing

10 strokes

一 ｢ 厂 丆 百 百 百 頁 夏 夏 夏

夏 夏 夏 夏 夏

一 Kanji Basics かんじの きほん

❏ 1-9. ふりがな

Throughout this book you will see small hiragana characters above kanji words just like it shows below. These are commonly referred to as ふりがな.

(ふりがな) ⟶ かん じ
漢字

ふりがな is commonly used when the reading of the kanji is unusual or difficult. Also you will see ふりがな in まんが (comic books) and books targeted for elementary school students.

❏ 1-10. おくりがな

The hiragana that follows the kanji of a verb is referred to as おくりがな.

(ふりがな) ⟶ た
食べます ⟵ (おくりがな)

━ Kanji Drills かんじ ドリル

❏ **Words you can write**

Write the following words using the kanji that you just learned.

ひ
引く
to pull

| 引 | く | | | | | | | | | |

いんりょく
引力
gravity

| 引 | 力 | | | | | | | | | |

あまぐも
雨雲
a rain cloud

| 雨 | 雲 | | | | | | | | | |

とお
遠い
far

| 遠 | い | | | | | | | | | |

えんそく
遠足
an excursion

| 遠 | 足 | | | | | | | | | |

とお で
遠出
an outing

| 遠 | 出 | | | | | | | | | |

なんがつ
何月
what month?

| 何 | 月 | | | | | | | | | |

なんにち
何日
what day of the month?

| 何 | 日 | | | | | | | | | |

か がく
科学
science

| 科 | 学 | | | | | | | | | |

か もく
科目 | 科 | 目 | | | | | | | | |
subject

なつやす
夏休み | 夏 | 休 | み | | | | | | | |
summer vacation

なつ
ま夏 | ま | 夏 | | | | | | | | |
middle of summer

❑ Fill in the kanji

Fill in the blanks in the following sentences with the appropriate kanji. Then write the English translation on the line below.

なん　がつ　なん　にち
1. きょうは___ ___ ___ ___ですか。

_____

なつ　やす　　　　に　ほん
2. ___ ___ みに ___ ___ に いきました。

_____

か　もく
3. すきな ___ ___ は れきしです。

_____

4. そのドアを ___ いて ___ さい。
<small>ひら　　くだ</small>

_____

5. ___ ___ の ともだちと ___ ___ に いきたいです。
<small>がっ こう　　　　　えん そく</small>

_____

6. あの ___ きい ___ ___ が ___ えますか。
<small>おお　あま ぐも　み</small>

_____

━ Kanji Recognition かんじ にんしき

Kanji is one of the most important parts of your overall Japanese fluency. Learning to write kanji will help you remember the individual kanji, but since you are rarely going to write Japanese in a modern world, it is much more important to be able to read and recognize the kanji. In each lesson, this section will add words that you should learn to recogonize.

❏ Individual words

The following words will no longer have any ふりがな (hiragana on top). Don't worry if you can't write these words. Recognition is the goal for these words.

| <small>かん じ</small>
漢字
kanji | <small>かね</small>
お金
money | <small>くるま</small>
車
car | <small>えん</small>
円
yen |

にほん
日本
Japan

にほんご
日本語
Japanese (language)

にほんじん
日本人
Japanese (person)

くだ
下さい
please

❑ Word groups (months)

Even though it is very common for months to be written using standard numbers, 1 月 2 月

3 月 etc. In order to increase your kanji recognition, we will continue to use the kanji

numbers. From this point forward all months will be written in kanji only.

いちがつ
一月
January

にがつ
二月
February

さんがつ
三月
March

しがつ
四月
April

ごがつ
五月
May

ろくがつ
六月
June

しちがつ
七月
July

はちがつ
八月
August

くがつ
九月
September

じゅうがつ
十月
October

じゅういちがつ
十一月
November

じゅうにがつ
十二月
December

❑ Word groups (generic counter)

The generic counter from this point forward will only be written in kanji.

ひと
一つ
one (things)

ふた
二つ
two (things)

みっ
三つ
three (things)

よっ
四つ
four (things)

いつ
五つ
five (things)

むっ
六つ
six (things)

なな
七つ
seven (things)

やっ
八つ
eight (things)

ここの
九つ
~~five~~ (things)
nine

じっこ
十個
ten (things)

じゅういちこ
十一個
eleven (things)

じゅうにこ
十二個
twelve (things)

❑ Kanji recognition cards

Print and cut out these cards, then write the hiragana and English meaning on the back.
Now you can easily practice your kanji recognition.

漢字	お金	車	円
日本	日本語	日本人	下さい
一月	二月	三月	四月
五月	六月	七月	八月
九月	十月	十一月	十二月
一つ	二つ	三つ	四つ
五つ	六つ	七つ	八つ
九つ	十個	十一個	十二個

☺ COMMENTARY: You want me to what?

I believe UFOs exist and generally can accept a variety of strange government cover-up theories. With that being said, I was really not interested in an interpreting job that came to our company a few years ago.

Our office had taken a call from a woman who wanted an interpreter for a channeling session. A channeler is someone who claims to have contact with angels or other spirits and is able to relay the spirit's thoughts to the living world. Some channelers are purportedly able to let spirits take over their bodies.

I tried to avoid the job by quoting the woman a slightly higher price than normal for interpreting, and also stipulated a three-hour minimum charge, thinking that maybe the price would be too steep for her budget. But the woman agreed to the terms and I was booked for the job.

The next Saturday I met the woman and her male friend – they will be called "Masami" and "Susumu" here. I was hoping that maybe they were reporters writing a story on channeling, but this was not the case. It was Masami's second time visiting this channeler, and Susumu's first.
We arrived at the house where the channeling was to take place, and the channeler invited us in. She seemed normal enough. After we all exchanged names she showed us a painting, explaining, "This is Ashtar," and Masami was happy to see his likeness for the first time. I was thinking, "'Ashtar!?' You've got to be kidding me." Then she pointed to four other paintings on the wall and identified each by names like 'Gabriel.' She said that she was now working with them and was able to channel them in addition to Ashtar.

We were led to a normal room in the house where we were to have the session. The room was unremarkable, with the exception of two lit candles on a bookshelf, which I thought were a nice touch. We sat down, and the channeler explained that Ashtar would pause for me so that I could interpret. The whole time I was wondering why the angel Ashtar didn't just speak Japanese, but I guess English is the standard language in heaven (or wherever Ashtar lived).

(continued in next commentary section)

Having Enough & Making Lists

Before This Lesson

1. Be able to read and write 引雲遠何科夏.

Lesson Goals

1. Learn a common way of saying "only".
2. Learn the small and large machine counters.

From The Teachers

1. If a word uses kanji taught in a prior lesson or book in this series, only the first appearance of the word will have ふりがな.

2. Try not to confuse the two counters introduced in this lesson.

Lesson Highlights

2-7. Owning something

2-12. Machine counter だい

2-13. Machine / airplane counter き

2-14. Saying "only" using しか

2-15. Saying "no" without being rude

2 New Words あたらしい ことば

Progressive	漢字	えいご
じぶん	自分	oneself, myself
くつ下	靴下	socks
いまでも	今でも	even now
よいしょ	よいしょ	umph!, heave ho
なかが いい	仲がいい	get along
アカウント	アカウント	account (internet account)
ウェッブサイト	ウェッブサイト	website
てつや	徹夜	all-nighter, sleepless night
でんしじしょ	電子辞書	electronic dictionary
アイフォン	アイフォン	iPhone
アンドロイド	アンドロイド	Android
スマートフォン	スマートフォン	smart phone

2 Word Usage ことばの つかいかた

❏ **2-1. じぶん (one's self)**

There really isn't an equivalent English word that can replace じぶん, because it can be used to refer to yourself and to other people. Watch how the meaning of じぶん changes depending on the context of the sentence.

> **Example sentences**
>
> 1. じぶんで かんがえて下さい。
>   Please think about it yourself.
>
> 2. じぶんで やります。
>   I will do it by myself.
>
> 3. ともだちは じぶんの へやが ないから、かわいそうです。
>   I feel sorry for my friend because she doesn't have her own room.

❏ 2-2. いまでも (even now)

いまでも is pretty straight forward in its use. You just place it in front of the phrase. Like its English equivalent, it implies that something hasn't changed, "even now".

Example sentences

1. わたしは いまでも 田中_{たなか}さんと なかが いいです。
   I get along well with Mr. Tanaka even now.

2. 竹田_{たけだ}さんは いまでも いちごジュースが すき です。
   Even now, Mrs. Takeda likes strawberry juice.

3. スミスさんは いまでも 漢字の べんきょうを しています。
   Mr. Smith is studying kanji even now.

2　New Adjectives あたらしい けいようし

The following adjectives are true adjectives. True adjectives always end with an い (and are also called い adjectives). The particle の is not necessary to make the word an adjective.

日本語	漢字	えいご	タイプ
くさい	臭い	smelly, bad smelling	い adjective
おもい	重い	heavy	い adjective
かるい	軽い	light (weight)	い adjective

The following words are な adjectives. They require な after them to directly modify something.

日本語	漢字	えいご	タイプ
ひつよう	必要	necessary, needed	な adjective
かわいそう	可哀想	so sad, pitiful	な adjective

2   Culture Clip カルチャー クリップ

The inner and outer circle

As a rule, you always want to be polite to people above you in social status, such as the president of a company, your boss, your teacher, and even a classmate in an upper grade. However, when speaking about someone in your inner circle, such as someone in your company, to someone in another company then you do not have to be polite about them. It is in fact more polite to the person in the outer circle if you are less polite with the people in your group. You can drop the さん from their last name and not use polite verbs.

2   Adjectives Usage けいようしの つかいかた

❑ 2-3. ひつよう (necessary, needed)

Look at some of the examples below to see how ひつよう can be used.

Example Q&A

1. お金は いくら ひつよう ですか。
   How much money is needed?

   お金は ひつようじゃないです。
   Money is not needed.

   せんえん
   千円 ひつようです。
   A 1000 yen is needed.

   > You don't need a が after 千円 because it's an amount. Amounts can use が but it isn't required.

2. あたらしい くつが ひつようですか。
   Do you need need shoes?

   いいえ、 ひつようが ありません。
   No, I don't need them.

   > ひつようじゃない and ひつようが ありません are different ways to say "I don't need. / Isn't neccessary".

   はい、 ひつようです。
   Yes, I need them.

---

3. にんじんと たまごを かいたいです。
I want to buy carrots and eggs.

ひつような ものを かって下さい。
Buy the things you need.

4. あとは 何が ひつようですか。
What else do you need?

かみと えんぴつが ひつようです。
I need paper and a pencil.

なにも いりません。
I don't need anything.

> いりません means "don't need". The verb いる (to need) is taught in Book 5.

❑ 2-4. かわいそう (pitiful, so sad, poor)

You will hear かわいそう quite often when speaking about sad events. It is used as a word of compassion when hearing of an unfortunate event or situation.

Example conversations

1. A: きのう わたしのねこが しにました。   Yesterday my cat died.
   B: かわいそう！   How sad!

2. A: かれには おかあさんが いないです。   He doesn't have a mother.
   B: かわいそうな子です。   Poor child.

3. A: かれを かわいそうに おもいます。   I feel sorry for him.
   B: なんで？   Why?
   A: おなかが いたいからです。   Because his stomach hurts.

---

2   New Verbs あたらしい どうし

どうし	えいご	た form	タイプ
持(も)つ	to hold, have, carry	もった	regular
足(た)りる	to have enough of	たりた	いる/える
作(つく)る	to make, to build	つくった	regular
思(おも)い出(だ)す	to recall, to remember	おもいだした	regular
徹夜(てつや)をする	to pull an all-nighter	てつやをした	する
使(つか)う	to use	つかった	regular

2   Verb Usage どうしの つかいかた

❑ 2-5. もつ (to hold, have, carry, own)

The item that you have, are carrying, or holding is "marked" with the を particle. In the Japanese From Zero! series we say "marked" to mean "attached" or "following" a word. In Japanese grammar you can often move words around in a sentence AS LONG as you keep the particle attached. In examples 1 and 2 below the word order has been changed but notice that the particles are still attached to the their words.

1. ともだち<u>は</u> 一月<u>に</u> とうきょう<u>に</u> いきます。
   My friend is going to Tokyo in January.

2. 一月<u>に</u> ともだち<u>は</u> とうきょう<u>に</u> いきます。
   In January my friend is going to Tokyo.

❑ 2-6. A reminder about using particles with counters and units

In most cases, counters (amounts) are not followed by a particle. もつ is commonly used to say "I have a certain number of items" such as "I have 3 cars." or "He has 9 hats."

For example, let's say you have 5 items such as a bottle or some other cylindrical object. You would say: ５本(ほん) もっています。 You would NEVER say ５本を もっています。 The object marker を should ALWAYS following the item and not the amount.

Example sentences

1. えんぴつを 5本 もっています。
    ほん
    I have 5 pencils.

2. ペンを 5本 もっています。
    I have 5 pens.

3. ハブラシを 5本 もっています。
    I have 5 toothbrushes.

4. 車を 5だい もっています。
    I have 5 cars.

> The "car / machine / electronics" counter だい is covered later in this lesson.

❏ 2-7. Owning something

Did you notice that all of the sentences in the prior examples are in the ています verb form?

This form is used because you are "holding" the items being discussed.

Even if you aren't actually holding something at the moment, if you are saying that you "own" something then you must use the ています form because you "currently" own these items.

For items owned in the past that you no longer own you would say もっていました。

> **(thing) を もつ**
> **to hold, have, own, carry a (thing)**

> **Example sentences**
> 1. お金をもっていますか。   Do you have money?
>   はい、五万ドル もっています。   Yes, I have $50,000.
>
> 2. 車を もっていますか。   Do you own a car?
>   はい、三だい もっています。   Yes, I own three.
>
> (notice that there is no を after ドル and だい since they are units and counters)

Example conversations

1. A: このテレビは おもいですね。

   B: もちましょうか。

   A: おねがいします。

   This TV is heavy!

   Shall I carry it?

   Please.

2. A: これを もって下さい。

   B: なんですか。

   A: わたしの くさい くつしたです。

   B: もちたくないですよ。

   Please hold these.

   What are they?

   They're my smelly socks.

   I don't want to hold them!

3. A: <ruby>アイポッド</ruby>iPodを もっていますか。

   B: はい、<ruby>去年<rt>きょねん</rt></ruby> かいました。あなたは？

   A: 2だい もっています。

   B: すごい！

   Do you have an iPod?

   Yes, I bought it last year. You?

   I have 2.

   Wow!

❏ 2-8. <ruby>足<rt>た</rt></ruby>りる (to have enough, to be enough, to be sufficient)

が marks the item that there is enough of unless は is being used for stress.

> (thing) が 足りる
> to have enough of (thing)

Example Q&A

1. お<ruby>金<rt></ruby>が <ruby>足<rt>た</rt></ruby>りますか。
   Is there enough money?

   いいえ、<ruby>足<rt>た</rt></ruby>りません。
   No, there is not enough.

   はい、<ruby>足<rt>た</rt></ruby>ります。
   Yes, there is enough.

   いいえ、あと ３００円が ひつようです。
   No, I need 300 yen more.

2. どうしたの？
What happened?

あしたは テストだけど、じかんが 足りない です！
There is a test tomorrow, but I don't have enough time!

スタッフが 足りないから、しごとが いそがしいです。
I am busy at work because there aren't enough staff.

3. パーティーのじゅんびは どうですか。
How are the party preparations?

さらが 足りないです。あと、３まい ひつようです。
There aren't enough plates. We need 3 more.

フォークは 足りるけど、スプーンが 足りないです。
There are enough forks, but not enough spoons.

Particle で is used when marking an amount when asking if the amount is "sufficient" or

"enough" to accomplish the task a hand, whatever that might be. In the example Q&A watch

how the new adjective ひつよう is used in combination with たりる。

> **(amount / thing) で 足りる**
> **(amount / thing) is sufficient OR enough**

Example Q&A

1. １０００円で 足りますか。
   Is 1000 yen enough?

   はい、１０００円で 足ります。
   Yes, 1000 yen is enough.

   はい、１０００円で だいじょうぶです。
   Yes, 1000 yen is fine.

   いいえ、１５００円が ひつようです。
   No, you need 1500 yen.

2. いくら ひつようですか。２５０円で 足りますか。
   How much is needed? Is 250 yen enough?

   はい、足ります。
   Yes, it's enough.

   あと、５０円が ひつようです。
   Another 50 yen is needed.

3. 二つで 足りますか。
   Is 2 enough?

   いいえ、二つじゃ 足りません。
   No, 2 isn't enough.

   > Here じゃ is used instead of で to add emphasis. It's more casual than では which also emphasizes.

   はい、二つで 足ります。
   Yes, 2 is enough.

❏ 2-9. つくる (to make, build)

The item that is being made is marked with を.

> **(thing) を つくる**
> **to make a (thing)**

> **Example sentences**
>
> 1. たくさんの ともだちを つくりたいです。
>   I want to make a lot of friends.
>
> 2. きょう、ケーキを つくります。
>   I will make a cake today.
>
> 3. やまださまは 今 FaceBookのアカウントを つくっています。
>   Right now Mr. Yamada is making a FaceBook account.
>
> 4. 去年の七月に 会社が 新しいウェブサイトを つくりました。
>   In July of last year our company made a new website.

❑ 2-10. おもい出す (to recall, to remember)

The item that is being recalled is marked with を. This "remember" is always to "recall" something that has already been remembered. It is NOT used to refer to memorizing or remembering something new.

> **(someone, something) を おもいだす**
> **to remember (someone, something)**

Example sentences

1. よく おじいちゃんを おもい出します。
   I often recall my grandfather.

2. かれの なまえを おもい出して下さい。
   Please remember (recall) his name.

3. きのうの たんじょうパーティーを おもい出したくない です。
   I don't want to recall yesterday's birthday party.

4. あの漢字が おもい出せない！
   I can't recall that kanji!

   > Here が is used instead of を to show emphasis on the kanji that can't be recalled.

❑ 2-11. つかう (to use)

The item that is being used is marked with を.

> **(something) を つかう**
> **to use (something)**

Example sentences

1. ともだちの 車を つかいました。
   I used my friend's car.

2. ミルクをのむときは ストローを つかいますか？
   When you drink milk do you use a straw?

3. ペンか えんぴつ、どっちを つかいますか。
   Which do you use, a pen or a pencil?

4. ステーキに ケチャップを つかわないで 下さい。
   Please don't use ketchup on steak.

5. すしを たべるとき おはしを つかいますか。
   Do you use chopsticks when you eat sushi?

2 New Counters あたらしい カウンター

❑ **2-12. Machine counter だい**

When counting computers, TV's, trucks, automobiles, and most electrical appliances,
the だい counter is used.

How many? なんだい				
1 いちだい 一台	**2** にだい 二台	**3** さんだい 三台	**4** よんだい 四台	**5** ごだい 五台
6 ろくだい 六台	**7** ななだい 七台	**8** はちだい 八台	**9** きゅうだい 九台	**10** じゅうだい 十台

Example sentences

1. 車は なんだい ありますか。
   How many cars do you own?

2. ともだちは テレビを 五だい もっています。
   My friend owns five television sets.

3. 駐車場に 車が 百だい あります。
   There are 100 cars in the parking lot.

4. アイフォンを 三だい もっています。アンドロイドも 三だい もっています。
   I have 3 iPhones. I also have 3 Androids.

❏ 2-13. Large machine / airplane counter ー き

For really big machines, such as airplanes, the き counter is used.

How many? なんき				
1 いっき 一機	2 にき 二機	3 さんき 三機	4 よんき 四機	5 ごき 五機
6 ろっき 六機	7 ななき 七機	8 はっき（はち き） 八機	9 きゅうき 九機	10 じゅっき 十機

Example sentences

1. きょう、大きい ひこうきを 三き 見ました。
   I saw three big airplanes today.

2. アメリカは 五きの スペースシャトルを もっていました。
   America had 5 space shuttles.

2　Grammar ぶんぽう

❏ 2-14. Saying "only" using しか

There is no English equivalent for しか, and using it can be very confusing at first, but it is very common in Japanese. しか can be thought to mean "with the exception of," or "only."

It must always be accompanied with a negative verb. Look at the examples below.

Example sentences

1. 一ドルしか ありません。　　　　　　I only have $1.00.
2. わたしは 円しか もっていません。　　I only have yen.
3. おじいさんは おすししか たべません。　My grandfather will only eat sushi.
4. かれは 日本語しか わからないです。　He only understands Japanese.
5. あと、一つしか なかった。　　　　　There was only one left.
6. この車に 4人しか のれません。　　　Only 4 people can ride in this car.

7. 新^{あたら}しいのを <u>かう</u>しかないです。   The <u>only thing to do is buy</u> a new one.

8. わたしには <u>あなた</u>しか いません。   For me <u>there is only</u> you.

9. あした、しんかんせんで とうきょうに <u>いくしかない</u> です。
    <u>My only option is to go</u> to Tokyo by bullet train tomorrow.

10. ベッドが 足りないから ソファで <u>ねるしかない</u> です。
    Because there aren't enough beds, <u>my only option is to sleep</u> on the sofa.

❑ 2-15. Saying "no" without being rude

If you want to be successful in Japanese society you have to learn how to be tactful. You can't just tell someone "no" to a request. You must learn how to say "no" without actually saying "no". This is accomplished by being vague, dropping hints, misdirecting, using excuses, and of course, actual reasons why something can't be done. Let's run through each method one by one. Once you understand the methods, for certain you will realize that they have been used on you or you have seen them in a Japanese TV Drama etc.

1. Being Vague

The most interesting method of refusal to answer a question or to turn someone's request down is by using the word ちょっと. There is really nothing else required. You must make sure however that ちょっと is said with the correct inflection and look on your face.

It is said in a sort of trailing off way and your face will look slightly troubled. You will know it when you see it. Most Japanese people will understand that this means "no" and will not push any further. If they do push further then you can try other methods.

2. Dropping Hints

If you feel a request coming that you want to avoid, then you can always drop subtle hints such as "I am so tired today" きょうはつかれた prior to the request. Anything that will help you with turning the request down will work. Japanese people most of the time will pick up on this and not even make the request. This of course is taking advantage of Japanese people's good nature. They really look out for other people's interest and don't want to めいわくをかける "to burden" anyone.

3. Using Excuses

This is close to lying. But there just are those times when people won't catch the hints or vagueness of your answers so you will have to give absolute reasons as to why you can't do their request. In America we can just say, "I don't want to do it." but Japanese tend to be less direct so giving a reason like "I have an appointment with a friend" ともだちと やくそくを している will really do the trick. You don't actually have to have a やくそく (promise) with your friend but this will work just about 100% of the time. If this doesn't work then the person you are talking to might not be Japanese!

4. Actual Reasons

Of course you can always tell them real reasons why something can't be done. This is pretty obvious, but if you have work at 4 o'clock and they want to have dinner with you, you can simply tell them よじから しごとです, "I have work at 4."

5. In Conclusion

The bottom line is that you don't want to be direct. You don't want to tell them "no" if you can avoid it. One example of Japanese vagueness and unwillingness to say no is the situation in which someone likes someone and perhaps they ask the person very directly わたしの ことが すきですか, "Do you like me?" A really nice answer to this is きらいじゃないです which means, "I don't dislike you." (NOTE: こと usage is taught in lesson 3) This answer doesn't make the person feel bad, yet indirectly says, "I don't like you".

Now let's look at some sentences that skillfully refuse someone's request.

---

1. **Example conversation between two friends**
    A: おすしを つくりました。どうですか。
    B: きらいじゃないけど、すしは あまり たべません。
    A: そうですか。じゃあ、ピザは どうですか。
    B: はい、ピザは 大<ruby>すきです<rt>だい</rt></ruby>。

    A: I made some sushi. Would you like some?
    B: I don't dislike it, but I don't eat that much sushi.
    A: I see. Well then, how about pizza?
    B: Yes, I love pizza.

2. **Example conversation between two friends**

A: きょう、えいがに いきませんか。

B: きょうは ちょっと・・・

A: じゃあ、こんしゅうまつは どうですか。

B: あしたは だいじょうぶです。

A: Why don't we go to the movie today?

B: Today is a little…

A: Well then, how about this weekend?

B: Tomorrow is fine.

---

2 Mini Conversation ミニかいわ J→E

Read the following Japanese conversations and try to translate them into English. The English translation is provided below each conversation.

1. **Informal conversation between a Japanese and American friend.**

A: いまでも 日本の ホストファミリーを おもい出す。

B: いつ、日本に いったの？

A: 十二年まえ。

B: また 日本に いきたい？

A: うん、たぶん らい年 いくと おもう。

A: Even now, I remember my Japanese host family.

B: When did you go to Japan?

A: 12 years ago.

B: Do you want to go to Japan again?

A: Yes, I think maybe I will go next year.

2. Polite conversation between co-workers.

A: 小学校のとき、よく ねぼうして いました。

B: いまでも しごとに おくれますね。いえは ちかいですか。

A: うちから 車で 十五ふんしか かかりません。

B: じゃ、何で いつも おくれますか。

A: よく 徹夜を するからです。

A: When I was in elementary school, I often overslept.

B: Even now you are sometimes late to work aren't you. Is your house close?

A: It only takes 15 minutes from my house by car.

B: Then, why are you always late?

A: Because I often pull all nighters.

3. Polite conversation between friends.

A: 日本に いったとき、何を しましたか。

B: おみやげを たくさん かいました。

A: いいですね。お金は 足りましたか。

B: お金は あまり もってなかったから、やすいものを かいました。

A: What did you do when you went to Japan?

B: I bought many souvenirs.

A: That's nice. Did you have enough money?

B: I didn't have that much money, so I bought cheap things.

4. Polite conversation between friends.

A: きょうの パーティーには ピザが 3まい ひつようです。いまは 一まいしかないです。

B: じゃ、たりないですね。

A: For today's party I need 3 pizzas. Right now I only have one.

B: Well then, there isn't enough.

2 | Mini Conversation ミニかいわ E→J

Read the following English conversations and try to translate them into Japanese.
The Japanese translation is provided below each conversation.

1. Polite conversation between friends in a Japanese restaurant.

A: Can you use chopticks?

B: I can't really use them.

A: はしが つかえますか。

B: あまり つかえない です。

> を particle can be used, but It's more common to use が particle with the "can do / can't do" form verbs.

2. Polite conversation between friends.

A: I want three cars.

B: Three cars is (too) many.

A: Why?

B: Because you're in Japan, they are not necessary.

A: 車が 三だい ほしいです。

B: 三だいは おおいですよ。

A: 何で？

B: 日本に いるから、ひつようが ないです。

3. Informal conversation between friends.

A: I want one more boyfriend.

B: How many boyfriends do you have now?

A: I only have two. But that is not enough.

B: You are an interesting person.

A: かれが もう一人 ほしい。

B: いま、かれが 何人 いるの？

A: いまは 二人しか いない。でも、足りないよ。

B: おもしろい人だね。

4. Polite conversation between friends.

A: I am going to travel to Japan next month.

B: Really? That is nice.

A: But I don't have enough money.

B: Please work hard.

A: らい月、日本に りょこうします。

B: そうですか。いいですね。

A: でも、お金が 足りません。

B: いっしょうけんめい、はたらいて下さい。

5. Informal conversation between friends.

A: When you go to Japan use this electronic dictionary.

B: Thank you. How many do you have?

A: I only have one.

A: 日本に いくとき、このでんしじしょを つかって下さい。

B: ありがとう。なんだい もってるの？

A: 一だいしか もっていない です。

6. Informal conversation between a mother and son.

A: How much money do you have?

B: I only have 5 dollars.

A: Will that be enough?

B: I need another 20 dollars.

A: お金は いくら もってるの？

B: 5ドルしか もっていない。

A: たりるの？

B: あと20ドルが ひつようです。

2 | Reading Comprehension どっかい

Read the sentences below. If you don't understand them, you should review the grammar in this lesson until you do. After you have understood everything, complete the reading comprehension questions in the *Activities* section of this lesson.

① わたしには、おとうさんと おかあさんと おにいさんが います。

② でも、わたしの うちには、テレビが 一だいしか ありません。

③ わたしは いつも、学校から かえってから テレビを 見ます。

④ わたしが テレビを 見ているとき、おかあさんは いつも ばんごはんを つくっています。

⑤ おにいさんは しゅくだいを しています。

⑥ おとうさんは うちに かえったとき、いつも テレビの チャンネルを かえます。

⑦ わたしは おとうさんに おこりますが、おとうさんは ききません。

⑧ 「もう一だい、テレビを かって！」と おねがいするけど、ぜんぜん だめです。

⑨ わたしの うちには、もう一だい、テレビが ひつようです。

New words and expressions in the dialogue

Progressive	漢字	えいご
おこる	怒る	to get mad, to get upset
かえる	変える	to change (active verb)

2 | Lesson Activities

❏ Reading comprehension questions

Answer the following questions about the reading comprehension and short dialogue in this lesson.

1. かぞくは 何人 いますか。

   _____

2. うちに テレビは 何だい ありますか。

   _____

3. テレビを 見ている とき、 おにいさんは 何を していますか。

   _____

4. なぜ おとうさんに おこりますか。

   _____

5. このかぞくは もう 一だい テレビを かいますか。

   _____

❏ Sentence Patterns

Modify the sentence by adding the parts listed. You can add and remove parts as needed so that the final sentence makes sense.

Ex. すきです。

→ don't like	すき<u>じゃない</u>です。
→ liked	すき<u>でした</u>。
→ homework	<u>しゅくだい</u>が すきです。

1. この本が おもしろいです。

   → necessary   _____

   → heavy   _____

   → smelly   _____

2. お金が 足_たりますか。

   → Do you have   _____

   → necessary   _____

   → 100 dollars   _____

3. むかしの ともだちを よく おもい出します。

   → sometimes   _____

   → can't remember at all   _____

   → grandmother   _____

4. 車が 二だい あります。

   → three TVs   _____

   → two old telephones   _____

   → one ship   _____

   → is only one car   _____

❑ Translation

Translate the following sentences into Japanese.

1. I only have dollars.

    _____

2. I only went to Tokyo and Kyoto.

    _____

3. I only have one car.

    _____

4. I can see only one airplane.

    _____

5. I only have one cat.

    _____

❑ Question and answer

Answer the following questions as if they were directly asked to you using the words and patterns in this lesson.

1. いまでも 小学校の ともだちと なかが いいですか。

    _____

2. じぶんで へやの そうじを しますか。

    _____

3. ばんごはんは 何を つくりますか。

    _____

4. よく だれを おもい出しますか。

_____

5. 車を 何だい もっていますか。

_____

Kanji Lesson
2

家歌画回会海
kanji 87-92

| 二 | **New Kanji** あたらしい漢字 |

Practice writing each new kanji in the boxes provided. First trace the light gray samples.

Pay attention to stroke orders. On a separate piece of paper practice writing the sample kanji words at least five times each.

家	くんよみ	いえ、や、うち	number	87
	おんよみ	カ、ケ	meaning	house

かぞく	さっか	おおや	しゃくや	けらい
家族	作家	大家	借家	家来
family	author	landlord	rental house	servant

10 strokes

丶 丶 宀 宀 宇 宇 家 家 家 家

家 家 家 家 家

歌	くんよみ	うた（う）	number	88
	おんよみ	カ	meaning	song

うた	うたばんぐみ	こっか	うたごえ	かしゅ
歌う	歌番組	国歌	歌声	歌手
to sing	music show	national anthem	singing voice	singer

14 strokes

一 一 一 一 一 一 哥 哥 哥 哥 哥 歌 歌 歌

歌 歌 歌 歌 歌

画	くんよみ	–	number		89
	おんよみ	カク、ガ	meaning		stroke, picture, painting

	えいが 映画	けいかく 計画	がか 画家	がぞう 画像	かっきてき 画期的
8 strokes	movie	plan	painter, artist	image	epoch making

一 厂 厂 两 両 画 画 画

画 画 画 画 画

回	くんよみ	まわ（す）	number		90
	おんよみ	カイ	meaning		turn, go around

	まわ 回る	いっかい 一回	かいてん 回転	かいとう 回答	まわ みち 回り道
6 strokes	to spin	once	rotation	reply	detour

丨 冂 冂 同 回 回

回 回 回 回 回

会	くんよみ	あ（う）、え	number		91
	おんよみ	カイ、エ	meaning		meet

	あ 会う	かいしゃ 会社	しゃかい 社会	かいわ 会話	えしゃく 会釈
6 strokes	to meet	company	society	conversation	bow, nod

ノ 人 今 会 会 会

会 会 会 会 会

海	くんよみ	うみ		number		92
	おんよみ	カイ		meaning	ocean	

かいすい 海水	かいがん 海岸	かいがい 海外	うみべ 海辺	かいぐん 海軍
sea water	coast, coastal area	abroad, overseas	beach side	navy

9 strokes

丶 氵 氵 ゙ 汢 氿 海 海 海

海 海 海 海 海

二　Kanji Drills 漢字ドリル

❑ **Words you can write**

Write the following words in the boxes below. This is a great way to practice the new kanji and review the words at the same time.

おおや
大家
landlord

| 大 | 家 | | | | | | | | | |

うた
歌う
to sing

| 歌 | う | | | | | | | | | |

かしゅ
歌手
singer

| 歌 | 手 | | | | | | | | | |

がか
画家
painter, artist

| 画 | 家 | | | | | | | | | |

まわ
回る
to spin

| 回 | る | | | | | | | | | |

<table>
<tr><td>いっかい
一回
one time</td><td>一 回</td><td></td><td></td><td></td><td></td><td></td><td></td><td></td></tr>
<tr><td>あ
会 う
to meet</td><td>会 う</td><td></td><td></td><td></td><td></td><td></td><td></td><td></td></tr>
</table>

❏ Fill in the kanji

Fill in the blanks in the following sentences with the appropriate kanji.

1. りょこうの計___ がありますか。
<small>けい かく</small>
   Do you have plans for a trip?

2. 去___ 、___ に ___ ___ いきました。
<small>きょ ねん　うみ　さん かい</small>
   Last year, I went to the ocean 3 times.

3. ___ ___ 、___ ___ に ___ ちんを はらいました。
<small>せん げつ　おお や　や</small>
   Last month, I paid the owner the rent.

4. ___ ___ さんの ___ 声は きれいですね。
<small>た なか　うた ごえ</small>
   Tanaka's singing voice is pretty.

5. おととい、___ ___ に ___ いました。
<small>が か　あ</small>
   The day before yesterday, I met an artist.

6. ___ ___ で ___ が かいたいです。
<small>かい がい　いえ</small>
   I want to buy a house abroad.

Kanji Recognition 漢字にんしき

❑ Individual words

The following words will no longer have any ふりがな (hiragana on top).

まい にち
毎日
every day

まい つき
毎月
every month

まい とし
毎年
every year

こ とし
今年
this year

へた
下手
unskilled, bad at

じょうず
上手
skilled, good at

> 下手 and 上手 are taught in the next lesson.

❑ Word groups (years and month spans)

The following word groups, will no longer have any ふりがな (hiragana on top). These spans are originally covered in book 3 of this series.

いち ねん
一年
one year

に ねん
二年
two years

さん ねん
三年
three years

よん ねん
四年
four years

いち か げつ
一ヶ月
one month

に か げつ
二ヶ月
two months

さん か げつ
三ヶ月
three months

よん か げつ
四ヶ月
four month

❑ Kanji recognition notes

All years and months spans will now only be written in kanji. Above is just a sampling. In case you were wondering, the ケ character does look like a small katakana "KE", however it is actually an abbreviation of the kanji 箇 (こ、カ) which is a counter for things.

You will see more about this is book 5, but for now, just learn to recognize it and always read it as か.

❑ Kanji recognition cards

Print and cut out these cards, then write the hiragana and English meaning on the back.
Now you can easily practice your kanji recognition.

毎日	毎月	毎年	今年
下手	上手	一年	二年
三年	四年	一ヶ月	二ヶ月
三ヶ月	四ヶ月		

Using Verbs to Describe

Before This Lesson

1. Be able to read and write 家歌画回会海.

Lesson Goals

1. Learn how to describe a noun using a verb.

From The Teachers

1. Remember that when you use verbs to describe, the verb must be in the informal form.

Lesson Highlights

3-4. Verbs for wearing things.

3-8. Modifying with verbs (verb adjectives)

3-9. It appears to be そう adjective ending

3-10. It DOESN'T appear to be なさそう adjective ending

3-11. な adjectives with そう and なさそう endings

3-12. Making な adjectives with the そう ending

3   New Words あたらしい ことば

Progressive	漢字	えいご
じぶん	自分	oneself, myself
はだし	裸足	barefoot
おほしさま	お星様	stars (child version)
じめん	地面	the ground
ぎんか	銀貨	silver coin
さいきん	最近	recently
しあわせ	幸せ	happiness
くに	国	country

3   New Adjectives あたらしい けいようし

日本語	漢字	えいご	タイプ
あたたかい	暖かい	warm	い adjective
上手 (じょうず)	上手	skillful, good at	な adjective
下手 (へた)	下手	unskillful, poor	な adjective

NOTE: When speaking Japanese most Japanese people will say あたかい instead of あたたかい。

3   New Verbs あたらしい どうし

どうし	えいご	た form	タイプ
歩く (ある)	to walk	あるいた	regular
あげる	to give	あげた	いる/える
落ちる (お)	to fall down, drop	おちた	いる/える
着る (き)	to wear (shirts, jackets)	きた	いる/える
履く (は)	to wear (shoes, pants)	はいた	regular
かぶる	to wear (hats, things on head)	かぶった	regular

3 Verb Usage どうしの つかいかた

❑ 3-1. あるく (to walk)

The place that is being walked to is marked with the final destination marker まで. The place that you are walking is of course marked with the "event location" marker で.

> **(place) まで あるく**
> **to walk to a (place)**

> **(place) で あるく**
> **to walk in a (place)**

Example sentences

1. 学校まで あるきました。
   I walked to school.

   > に and へ can also be used to mark the destination. まで is commonly used to mark a final destination.

2. こうえんまで あるきましょう。
   Let's walk to the park.

3. むすめと よく こうえんで あるきます。
   I often walk in the park with my daughter.

❑ 3-2. あげる (to give)

The item that is being given is marked with を. This verb can NEVER be used when something is given to YOU. It is only used when the item is being given outward, as in "I gave it to Tanaka." When saying, for example, "Tanaka gave it to me," あげる *cannot* be used.

> **(thing) を あげる**
> **to give a (thing)**

> **(someone) に あげる**
> **to give to (someone)**

> **(thing) を (someone) に あげる**
> **to give (thing) to (someone)**

Example Q&A

1. だれに あげましたか。
   Who did you give it to?

   おとうさんに あげました。
   I gave it to my father.

2. 何^{なに}を あげたの？
   What did you give?

   イヤリングをあげた。
   I gave earrings.

3. 旦那^{だんな}さんの たん生^{じょう}日^びに 何を あげましたか。
   What did you give on your husband's birthday?

   くつを あげました。
   I gave him a pair of shoes.

☐ 3-3. おちる (to fall down, drop)

The item that falls down is marked with が. The place from which the item has fallen is marked with から.

> **(thing) が (place) から おちる**
> **(thing) drops from (place)**

Example sentences

1. ケーキが テーブルから おちました。　　　The cake dropped off of the table.

2. おじいさんが かいだんから おちました。　　My grandfather fell from the stairs.

❑ 3-4. COMMON MISTAKE ALERT: Verbs for wearing things.

There are several different verbs all meaning "to wear" or "to put on" in Japanese. The verb used is based on how the item is put on. It is very important to get the following verbs right if you don't want to sound like a foreigner in Japan.

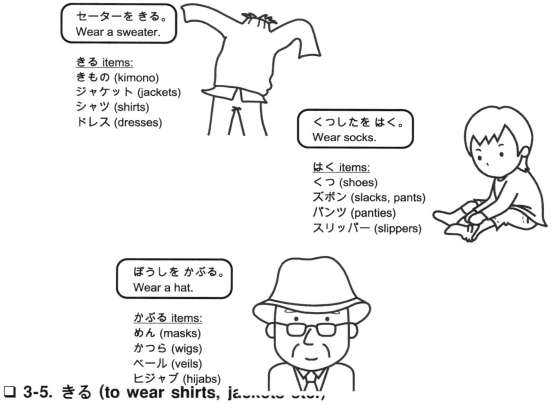

セーターを きる。
Wear a sweater.

きる items:
きもの (kimono)
ジャケット (jackets)
シャツ (shirts)
ドレス (dresses)

くつしたを はく。
Wear socks.

はく items:
くつ (shoes)
ズボン (slacks, pants)
パンツ (panties)
スリッパー (slippers)

ぼうしを かぶる。
Wear a hat.

かぶる items:
めん (masks)
かつら (wigs)
ベール (veils)
ヒジャブ (hijabs)

❑ 3-5. きる (to wear shirts, jackets etc.)

The clothing to be worn is marked with を. Clothing worn above the waist and below the neck will typically use きる.

> ### (clothing) を きる
> **to wear (clothing)**

Example sentences

1. さむいから、ジャケットを きます。
   I will wear a jacket because it is cold.

2. あたたかい ふくを きています。
   I am wearing warm clothes.

3. わたしは ぜんぜん ドレスを きません。
   I don't wear dresses at all.

❑ 3-6. はく (to wear shoes, pants etc.)

The clothing to be worn is marked with を. Clothing below the waist is almost always はく.

> **(clothing) を はく**
> **to wear (clothing)**

Example sentences

1. あたらしい くつを はいていますね。
   You are wearing new shoes, aren't you?

2. わたしは いつも ジーンズを はきます。
   I always wear jeans.

3. きのう、くろい スカートを はきました。
   I wore a black skirt yesterday.

4. あした、スニーカーを はいて 下さい。
   Please wear sneakers tomorrow.

❑ 3-7. かぶる (to wear or put on hats, things on top of head etc.)

かぶる is pretty much only for things on top of your head. Eyeglasses use つける.

> **(item) を かぶる**
> **to wear an (item)**

Example sentences

1. そとは あついから、ぼうしを かぶります。
   It is hot outside, so I will wear a hat.

2. きょう、みゆきちゃんは かわいいぼうしを かぶっています。
   Miyuki is wearing a cute hat today.

3. いえのなかで ぼうしを かぶらないで 下さい。
   Please don't wear a hat inside the house.

3 Grammar ぶんぽう

❏ 3-8. Modifying with verbs (verbs adjectives)

In this lesson we see how the informal version of the verbs can be used to modify nouns. The verb must come directly BEFORE the noun to modify, and it must be in the informal form. There should be no particle in between the modifying verb and the noun it describes.

> **informal form verb + noun**

Prior to this lesson you have learned how to modify a noun using い adjectives.

Examples （い adjectives）

おもしろい ひと	an <u>interesting</u> person
たのしい えいが	an <u>enjoyable</u> movie
つまらない えいが	a <u>boring</u> movie
大きい ビル	a <u>big</u> building
青い ふうせん	a <u>blue</u> balloon

You have also learned how to use nouns to modify other nouns.

Examples （noun adjectives）

にほんの えいが	a Japanese movie
アメリカの ともだち	an American friend
本の タイトル	a book title
むかしの テレビばんぐみ	a TV show from a long time ago

Now let's look at how you can modify a noun using a verb or verb phrase. Look at the examples and see how the verb phrase modifies the noun. Notice how changing the verb tense changes the meaning. Also notice that every verb is in the informal / plain form.

Examples (verb adjectives)

見る えいが	the movie (I) will watch
見た えいが	the movie (I) watched
見ている えいが	the movie (I) am watching
見ていた えいが	the movie (I) was watching
見たい えいが	the movie (I) want to see
見たかった えいが	the movie (I) wanted to see

Once you have modified a noun with a verb or verb phrase you can use it in a sentence just like you would any other.

Example sentences

1. 先週 よんだ本は ながかったです。
   せんしゅう ほん
   The book I read last week was long.

2. いま はいてるくつが かわいいよ！
   The shoes you are wearing now are cute!

3. わたしが いつも のんでいる ジュースは おいしいです。
   The juice I always drink is delicious

4. 明日 あうともだちは だれですか？
   あした
   Who is the friend you are meeting tomorrow?

5. きのう やった しゅくだいは むずかしかったです。
   The homework I did yesterday was difficult.

6. 一ばん いきたいくには にほんです。
   The country I want to go most is Japan.

7. あそこで ねてる人は わたしの おとうさんです。
   The person sleeping over there is my father.

> ねてる is the spoken version of ねている。 い can be removed from other verbs of this form also.

Now let's see how you can integrate this concept into everyday questions.

Example Q&A

1. あなたが いつも のむ ビールは 何ですか。
   What is the beer you always drink?

   さっぽろビールです。
   It's Sapporo beer.

2. 田中さんが すんでいるアパートは 大きいですか。
   Is the apartment that Mr. Tanaka lives in big?

   いいえ、とても 小さいです。
   No, it is very small.

3. 赤いドレスを きている 人は だれですか。
   Who is the person wearing the red dress?

   山田さんだと おもいます。
   I think it is Mrs. Yamada.

❑ 3-9. It appears to be 〜そう adjective ending

The adjective ending そう means "appears (to be)," "looks (to be)," or "seems (to be)."

By dropping the い from any い adjective and replacing it with そう, you can say things like, "you seem to be busy" (いそがしそうです). Look at the following examples:

い adjective minus い + そう
It appears to be + adjective

Example sentences

1. そのピザは おいしそうです。   That pizza <u>looks delicious</u>.
2. あなたの 車は ふるそうですね。   Your car sure <u>looks old</u>.
3. よしひろさんは やさしそうです。   Yoshihiro <u>seems to be kind</u>.
4. このテストは むずかしそうです。   This test <u>looks difficult</u>.
5. それは たかそうです。   That <u>looks expensive</u>.

❑ 3-10. It DOESN'T appear to be ～なさそう adjective ending

If you want to say that something DOESN'T appear hot or cold or some other adjective, then you must first conjugate the adjective into its negative form. In other words あつい becomes あつくない. From the negative conjugation you drop ない and add なさそう.

> **Negative い adjective minus ない + なさそう**
> **It doesn't appear to be (adjective)**

Example sentences

1. きょうは さむくなさそう ですね。
   It doesn't seem cold today.

2. この本は おもしろくなさそう です。
   This book doesn't look interesting.

3. このビールは つめたくなさそう です。
   This beer doesn't seem cold.

❑ 3-11. な adjectives with そう and なさそう endings

な adjectives can also be changed into the そう and なさそう. With な adjectives you can just add そう or じゃなさそう to say "it seems", or "it doesn't seem".

Example sentences

1. あのこうえんは しずかそう です。
   That park looks quiet.

2. ホテルの へやが きれい じゃなさそう です。
   The hotel room doesn't seem clean.

3. この店は とおいから、べんり じゃなさそう です。
   Because this store is far, it doesn't seem convenient.

4. ジョーは ひらがなが 上手<ruby>上手<rt>じょうず</rt></ruby> だから、カタカナも 上手そう です。
   Because Joe is good at hiragana, it seems like he would be good at katakana too.

❏ 3-12. Making な adjectives with the そう ending

You can add な to any そう and さそう conjugated adjectives to make new adjectives.

> い adjective minus い + そうな + (noun)
>
> **a (adjective) looking + (noun)**

Examples

あつそうな ピザ	a hot looking pizza.
たのしそうな パーティー	fun looking party
おもしろくなさそうな 人	a seemingly uninteresting person
つめたそうな のみもの	a cold looking drink
おいしそうな たべもの	delicious looking food
たかくなさそうな 車	an inexpensive looking car
しずかそうな へや	an quiet looking room
べんりじゃなさそうな ばしょ	an inconvenient looking place

Example sentences

1. あなたの おとうさんは やさしそうな ひとです。
   Your father <u>seems</u> to be a <u>kind</u> person.

2. あれは はやそうな 車ですね。
   That sure is a <u>fast looking</u> car.

3. しずかそうな こうえんです。
   It's a <u>quiet looking</u> park.

4. 元気そうな あかちゃんですね。
   What a <u>healthy looking</u> baby.

5. さむそうな てんきだったから ジャケットを かしました。
   Because the weather <u>looked cold</u> I loaned (him) my jacket.

6. きょうは よさそうな てんきだから ぼうしを かぶりません。
   Today since the weather <u>seems good</u> I am not going to wear a hat.

7. おいしくなさそうな スパゲティーは たべたくないです。
   I don't want to eat spaghetti that doesn't look tasty.

3 | Q&A しつもんと こたえ J→E

1. Polite conversation between boyfriend and girlfriend.

A: わたしの つくった りょうりは おいしかったですか。

B: はい、おいしかったですよ。

A: よかった。うれしいです。

A: Did the cooking that I made taste good?

B: Yes, it tasted good.

A: Good. I am happy.

2. Informal conversation between siblings.

A: ぼくが あげた ふくは どこに あるの？

B: いもうとに あげたよ。

A: 何で？

B: もう きられないから。

A: Where are the clothes I gave you?

B: I gave them to my little sister.

A: Why?

B: Because I can't wear them anymore. (They don't fit.)

3. Informal conversation between friends.

A: 何を さがしているの？

B: さいふ。きのうは かばんの 中に あったけど・・・。

A: 車の 中を 見た？

B: ううん、まだ。じゃあ、こんど 車の 中を 見るよ。

A: What are you looking for?

B: My wallet. It was in my bag yesterday, but...

A: Did you look inside your car?

B: Not yet. Well then, I will look in the car next.

3   Q&A しつもんと こたえ E→J

1. Polite conversation between friends.

A: What kind of person is your friend's husband?

B: He seems like a kind person.

A: What type of person do you think the person you will marry be?

B: I don't know. But a kind person would be good.

A: ともだちの ごしゅじんは どんな人でしたか。

B: やさしそうな人でしたよ。

A: じぶんが けっこんする人は どんな人だと おもいますか。

B: わかりません。でも、やさしい人が いいですね。

2. Polite conversation between friends.

A: What happened to you, Mr. Tanaka. You look sleepy.

B: Actually, I worked twelve hours yesterday.

A: I see. Take it easy today.

A: 田中さん、どうしましたか。 ねむそうですね。

B: じつは、きのう 十二じかん はたらきました。

A: そうですか。きょうは ゆっくり 休んで下さい。

3. Casual conversation between friends.

A: Hiroko, you are wearing a cute sweater.

B: Isn't it cute?! I bought this at a department store yesterday.

A: And also you are wearing an expensive looking skirt.

B: This one looks expensive, but it's cheap.

A: ひろこちゃん、かわいいセーターを きてるね。

B: かわいいでしょう！ きのう、デパートで かったの。

A: それに たかそうな スカートも はいてるね。

B: これは たかそうだけど、やすいよ。

3 | Reading Comprehension どっかい

Read the sentences below. If you don't understand them, review the lesson grammar.

① とても さむい日 でした。

② 女の子が 一人、あるいていました。

③ 女の子には おとうさんと おかあさんが もう いません。

④ 家も ない子でした。

⑤ おなかが すいている おじいさんに 会いました。

⑥ 女の子は 一つしかない パンを あげました。

⑦ はだしの子には じぶんの くつを あげました。

⑧ さむそうな おばあさんには スカートを あげました。

⑨ 何も きていない子には じぶんの シャツを あげました。

⑩ はだかに なった 女の子は ほしを 見ました。

⑪ 「ああ おほしさまの ところに いきたい」と おもいました。

⑫ そのとき たくさんの ほしが 空から おちました。

⑬ ほしは 女の子の ドレスに なりました。

⑭ 女の子は とても しあわせに なりました。

3 Lesson Activities

❏ Reading comprehension questions

Answer the following questions about the reading comprehension from the previous page.

1. 女の子は 家^かぞくが いますか。

_____

2. 女の子の 家^{いえ}は どこに ありますか。

_____

3. なぜ おじいさんに パンを あげましたか。

_____

4. なぜ おばあさんに スカートを あげましたか。

_____

5. はだかになった 女の子は どんな 気^きもちだったと おもいますか。

_____

6. ほしが 空^{そら}から おちたとき、女の子は どんな 気もちだったと おもいますか。

_____

❏ Sentence Patterns

Modify the sentence by adding the parts listed. You can add and remove parts as needed so that the final sentence makes sense.

> **Ex.** しごとが すきです。
> → homework   しゅくだいが すきです。
> → don't like homework   しゅくだいが すき<u>じゃない</u>です。

1. わたしは かいだんから おちました。

   → from the escalator _____

   → from the 2nd floor _____

   → my father (fell) _____

   → younger sister (fell)_____

2. ともだちに プレゼントを あげたいです。

   → to my girlfriend _____

   → a wedding ring _____

   → don't want to give _____

   → didn't want to give _____

3. いまの しごとは つまらないです。

   → part-time job _____

   → important _____

   → not difficult _____

   → dangerous _____

4. おもしろそうな 本です。

   → seemingly uninteresting_____

   → person _____

   → movie _____

   → expensive looking _____

5. たかそうな 車です。

   → cheap _____

   → fast _____

   → slow _____

   → not expensive _____

❏ Verb Practice: What are they wearing?

Describe the pictures below using the New Verbs learned in this lesson.

1

She is wearing a jacket.

2

He is wearing a sweater.

3

He is wearing a hat.

4

He is wearing a suit.

5

He is wearing socks.

6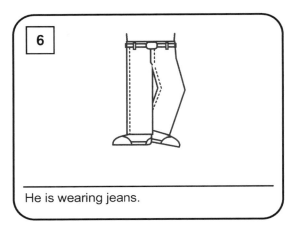

He is wearing jeans.

❏ Modifying with verbs

Look at the pictures below and complete the following conversation with the correct modifying verb phrase.

ジョンさん

ジェニーさん

トムさん

カイルさん

マックスくん

ひろしさん： すみません、トムさんは どの人ですか。

じゅんさん： トムさんは コーヒーを のんでいる 人です。

ひろしさん： じゃあ、ジョンさんは どの人ですか。

じゅんさん： ジョンさんは ① ＿＿＿＿＿＿＿＿＿＿人です。

ひろしさん： そうですか。カイルさんは ② ＿＿＿＿＿＿＿＿＿人ですか。

じゅんさん： はい、そうです。③ ＿＿＿＿＿＿犬は マックスくんですよ。

ひろしさん： かわいいですね。④ ＿＿＿＿＿＿女の人は だれですか。

じゅんさん： あの人は ジェニーさんです。 トムさんの おくさんですよ。

❑ **Practice**

Describe the following pictures by using ～そう.

1

a hot looking coffee

2

a man who looks cold

3

a cold looking beer

4

a warm looking jacket

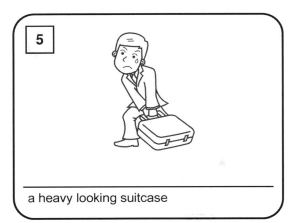

5

a heavy looking suitcase

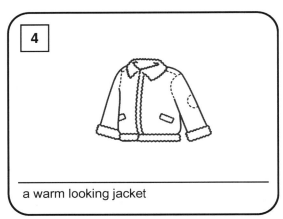

6

a salary man who looks cold

Kanji Lesson 3

絵園外間顔汽
kanji 93-98

三 New Kanji あたらしい漢字

Practice writing each new kanji in the boxes provided. First trace the light gray samples.

Pay attention to stroke orders. Practice writing the sample kanji words at least 5 times each.

絵	くんよみ	–	number	93
	おんよみ	カイ・エ	meaning	picture

えほん 絵本	えにっき 絵日記	え ぐ 絵の具	かいが 絵画	えか 絵描き
picture book	picture diary	paints	picture, painting	artist, painter

12 strokes

く　乡　幺　糸　糸　糸　糸'　糸'　絵　絵　絵

絵　絵　絵　絵　絵

園	くんよみ	その	number	94
	おんよみ	エン	meaning	garden

こうえん 公園	えんげい 園芸	えんじ 園児	はなぞの 花園	でんえん 田園
park	gardening	kindergarten pupil	flower garden	rural districts

13 strokes

｜　门　冂　門　冊　園　園　園　園　園　園　園　園

園　園　園　園　園

外

くんよみ	そと・ほか・はず（す）	number		95
おんよみ	ゲ・ガイ	meaning	outside	

5 strokes

そと 外	はず 外す	がいけん 外見	がい か 外貨	げ か 外科
outside	to remove	outward appearance	foreign money	surgical department

外 外 外 外 外

外 外 外 外 外

間

くんよみ	あいだ・ま	number		96
おんよみ	カン・ケン	meaning	space, interval	

12 strokes

あい ま 合間	じ かん 時間	ひる ま 昼間	にんげん 人間	せ けん 世間
interval	time	during the day	human being	society

丨 冂 冋 冐 冐 門 門 門 門 間 間 間

間 間 間 間 間

顔

くんよみ	かお	number		97
おんよみ	ガン	meaning	face (person)	

18 strokes

かおいろ 顔色	え がお 笑顔	しんがお 新顔	どうがん 童顔	せんがん 洗顔
complexion	smiling face	new face	child-faced	face-washing

丷 亠 产 产 立 产 彦 彦 彦 彦 彦 顔 顔 顔 顔 顔 顔

顔 顔 顔 顔 顔

汽	くんよみ	–		number	98
	おんよみ	キ		meaning	steam, vapor

きしゃ	きせん	きてき	きしゃちん	きすい
汽車	汽船	汽笛	汽車賃	汽水
train (steam)	steamship	steam whistle	train fare	brackish water

7 strokes

丶　丶　氵　汃　汀　汽　汽

汽	汽	汽	汽	汽									

三 Kanji Drills 漢字ドリル

❑ Words you can write

Write the following words in the boxes four times each. This is a great way to practice the new kanji and review the words at the same time.

えほん
絵本
picture book

絵	本								

かいが
絵画
picture, painting

絵	画								

えん
こう園
a park

こ	う	園							

はなぞの
花園
flower garden

花	園								

でんえん
田園
rural districts

田	園								

はず
外す
to remove

外	す								

がいけん
外見
outward appearance

外	見								

にんげん
人間
human being

人	間								

あいだ
間   間
between, gap, interval

かお
顔   顔
face

がお
え顔   え 顔
smiling face

きしゃ
汽車   汽 車
steam train

きすい
汽水   汽 水
brackish water

❏ Fill in the kanji

Fill in the blanks in the following sentences with the appropriate kanji.

こう えん   え ほん
1. 公＿＿＿で＿＿＿ ＿＿＿をよみました。
   I read a picture book at the park.

にん げん   がい けん
2. 人＿＿＿は＿＿＿ ＿＿＿だけでは はんだんが できません。
   You can't decide on a human just by outer appearance.

かお   あか
3. ＿＿＿が ＿＿＿く なりました。
   (My) face got red.

4. ヨーロッパで＿＿ ＿＿が ＿＿たい です。
_{かい が み}

I want to see paintings in Europe.

5. あの＿＿ ＿＿は ＿＿きくて、＿＿いです。
_{き しゃ おお ふる}

That steam train (over there) is big and old.

三 Kanji Recognition 漢字にんしき

❑ Individual words

The following words will no longer have any ふりがな (hiragana on top). Don't worry if you

can't write these words. Recognition is the goal for these words.

きょう 今日 today	きのう 昨日 yesterday	あした 明日 tomorrow	わたし 私 I, me
おお 大きい big	ちい 小さい small	あか 赤い red	あお 青い blue
しろ 白い white	かい がい 海外 overseas, abroad		

❑ Word groups (times)

The following word group, will no longer have any ふりがな (hiragana on top).

いっかい 一回 one time	に かい 二回 two times	さん かい 三回 three times	よん かい 四回 four times

ごかい
五回
five times

ろっかい
六回
six times

しちかい
七回
seven times

はっかい
八回
eight times

きゅうかい
九回
nine times

じっかい
十回
ten times

じゅういちかい
十一回
eleven times

じゅうにかい
十二回
twelve times

❏ Kanji recognition notes

十回 is officially read as じっかい however it is very commonly read as じゅっかい. After this 十一回 and 十二回 respectively are read and said as じゅういっかい and じゅうにかい and never vary from reading.

二十回 and 三十回 etc also are read officially as にじっかい and さんじっかい but also are commonly read as にじゅっかい and さんじゅっかい.

❑ **Kanji recognition cards**

Print and cut out these cards, then write the hiragana and English meaning on the back.
Now you can easily practice your kanji recognition.

今日	昨日	明日	私
大きい	小さい	赤い	青い
白い	海外	一回	二回
三回	四回	五回	六回
七回	八回	九回	十回
十一回	十二回		

Have you ever...?

Before This Lesson

1. Be able to read and write 絵園外間顔汽.

Lesson Goals

1. Learn how to relay experiences that you have or have not had.

From The Teachers

1. Knowing the た form (informal past tense) of the verbs will help you tremendously with this lesson.

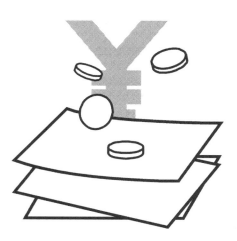

Lesson Highlights

4-5. Talking about things with こと

4-6. Using こと with adjectives

4-7. "Strange" uses of こと

4-8. Have you ever...?

4-9. "I have..." and "I have never..."

4-10. This much, that much – どんなに word group

4-11. Looking forward to something

4 New Words あたらしい ことば

日本語	漢字	えいご
ボーナス	ボーナス	bonus
こんかい 今回	今回	this time
かいがい 海外	海外	abroad, overseas
かいがい 海外りょこう	海外旅行	a trip abroad
せいせき	成績	grades, standing in class
おいわい	お祝い	celebration
あじ	味	flavor
テレビばんぐみ	テレビ番組	a television show
おさけ	お酒	alcohol, liquor, sake (polite)
コーヒーぎゅうにゅう	コーヒー牛乳	coffee milk (popular drink)
わかめ	わかめ	seaweed
スープ	スープ	soup
おみそしる	お味噌汁	miso soup
シェークスピア	シェークスピア	Shakespeare
ホームページ	ホームページ	home page
ウェブサイト	ウェブサイト	web site
ジェットコースター	ジェットコースター	roller coaster
バイク	バイク	motorcycle
あな	穴	a hole
しゅうまつ	週末	the weekend
せんしゅうまつ	先週末	last weekend
こんしゅうまつ	今週末	this weekend
らいしゅうまつ	来週末	next weekend
こんなに	こんなに	this much, so ~
そんなに	そんなに	that much, so ~
あんなに	あんなに	to that extent, to that degree
どんなに	どんなに	(no matter) how much

4 Culture Clip カルチャー クリップ

Many Japanese companies pay a bonus to their full time workers. Under the bonus system, each worker is normally paid two bonuses per year. The amount can range from 1.5 to 3 times the monthly salary of the worker. Usually bonuses are paid in June and December.

The amount of the bonus can change depending on the performance of the individual and also the overall performance of the company. Many Japanese use their bonus money for major purchases, such as buying a car or going on family vacations. Many retailers often defer payment on goods until after bonuses have been paid.

4 New Phrases あたらしい かいわ

1. たのしみに しています。	I am looking forward to it.
2. たのしみです。	I am looking forward to it.

4 New Verbs あたらしい どうし

どうし	えいご	た form	タイプ
出る	to appear, to come out	でた	いる/える
知る	to know	しった	いる/える exception
運転する	to drive	うんてんした	する
乗る	to ride, to get on, to get in	のった	regular

4 Verb Usage どうしの つかいかた

❏ 4-1. でる (to appear, to come out, to leave)

The particle が marks the thing that is appearing or coming out. However, the place that is being left from can be marked with から (from) or を (object marker).

> **(thing) が でる**
> **(thing) appears or comes out**

Example sentences

1. 明日 わたしの きゅうりょうが 出ます。
   My pay comes out tomorrow. (I will get my salary tomorrow.)

2. 私は今日、七じに 家を 出ます。
   I am going to leave my house at seven.

3. せいせきが 出てから、おいわいを しましょう。
   Let's celebrate after I get my grades (my grades come out).

❑ 4-2. しる (to know)

The particle を marks the item that is known. When asking if something is known, the てい ます form of the verb is used since knowledge of something is on going.

It is NOT correct to say 「(something) を しりますか。」or 「(something)を しります。」

> **(thing) を しています**
> **to know a (thing)**

Example conversations

1. A: 中村さんの でんわばんごうを しっていますか。
   B: いいえ、しりません。

   A: Do you know Miss Nakamura's phone number?
   B: No, I don't know it.

2. A: いいレストランを しっていますか。
   B: たぶん、ジョンさんが しっていますよ。

   A: Do you know any good restaurants?
   B: Maybe, John knows.

❏ 4-3. うんてんする (to drive)

The particle を marks the vehicle that is being driven.

> **(vehicle) を うんてんする**
> **to drive a (vehicle)**

Example sentences

1. 明日、おとうさんの車を うんてんします。
   I will drive my father's car tomorrow.

2. おさけを のんだから、うんてんして下さい。
   I had a drink, so please drive.

3. 日本で、何さいから うんてんを しますか。
   In Japan from what age do you drive?

4. フェラリーを うんてんした ことがありますか。
   Have you ever driven a Ferrari?

> This usage is explained in grammar 4-7 of this lesson.

As with any する verb, できる is used to ask "can you do this". When asking if someone is able to drive できる is used with the particle が is used to mark the thing being "driven".

> **(vehicle) が うんてんできる**
> **to be able to drive a (vehicle)**

Example sentences

1. 車が うんてんできますか。
   Are you able to drive a car?

> Just like example #3 車の うんてんが できますか is another way to say "Can you drive a car?"

2. 私の むすこは 車が うんてんできません。
   My son can not drive a car.

3. トラックのうんてんが できますか？
   Can you drive a truck?

❏ 4-4. のる (to ride, to get on, to get in)

The particle に marks the vehicle that is being rode or thing you are getting on or in.

のる can be used with cars, park rides, airplanes, or anything that you get on top of.

```
(vehicle) に のる
to ride a (vehicle)
```

Example sentences

1. こんしゅうまつに ジェット・コースターに のりたいです。
   I want to ride a roller coaster this weekend.

2. いつも しごとまで じてん車に のっています。
   I always ride a bike to work.

3. テーベルの上に のらないで 下さい。
   Please don't get on top of the table.

4. むかしから、しんかんせんに のりたかったです。
   I have wanted to ride the bullet train from long ago.

5. タクシーに のりましょう。
   Let's (take) ride in a taxi.

4 Grammar ぶんぽう

❏ 4-5. Talking about things with こと

こと literally means, thing, matter, fact, circumstances, business, reason, experience. But all of that will never fit in your head. So we will teach you こと little by little. It is a super versatile thing to know so PAY ATTENTION. The most basic usage of こと is when it means "about". For example if you want to say "about cars" you would say, 車のこと, and also if you wanted to say something like "about dogs" you would say 犬のこと.

Examples

1. 学校の こと	about school
2. しごとの こと	about work
3. かの女の こと	about my girlfriend

Now let's look at こと in action in full sentences.

Example sentences

1. 何^{なん}の ことですか。
   What is it about?

2. おかあさんの ことを おもい出しました。
   I remembered (about) my mother.

3. 私は 日本の れきしの ことを べんきょうしています。
   I am studying (about) Japanese history.

❑ 4-6. Using こと with adjectives

こと by itself can mean "about" or "thing". When it is used as taught in the prior grammar point it almost always translates to "about". However when you put こと after an adjective then it is translated as "thing".

Examples

1. たのしいこと	fun things
2. おもしろいこと	interesting things

❑ 4-7. "Strange" uses of こと

You probably learned that, "I like you" is あなたがすきです. But another common way to say you like someone is あなたのことがすきです. It seems strange to say "I like about you" but this is not strange at all in Japanese. こと can also be used after question words.

For example, maybe you are talking with someone and they say, "Remember that terrible food we ate?", and you have forgotten when this was. You can ask, いつのことですか to mean "When are you (talking) about?".

Example sentences

1. だれの<u>こと</u> ですか。

   Who are you (talking) about? / Who do you mean?

2. どのページの<u>こと</u> ですか。

   Which page are you (talking) about? / Which page do you mean?

3. どこの<u>こと</u> ですか。

   Where are you (talking) about? / Where do you mean?

❑ 4-8. Have you ever...?"

When you combine こと with an informal verb and ある, you can ask if someone has had a

certain "experience" or basically if they have ever done the thing being discussed.

> **(た form verb) + こと が ありますか。**
> **Have you ever (verb)?**

NOTE: The た form is the informal past tense verb. Do NOT change the tense of the verb

that is directly before the こと or else the meaning can change drastically.

Example sentences

1. おみそしるを <u>のんだことが ありますか</u>。

   <u>Have you ever drunk</u> miso soup?

2. ロシアに <u>いったこと ありますか</u>。

   <u>Have you ever been</u> to Russia?

   > In spoken Japanese the particle が is sometimes dropped. The meaning of the sentence doesn't change.

3. ジェットコースターに <u>のったことが ありますか</u>。

   <u>Have you ever ridden</u> a roller coaster?

4. シェークスピアーを <u>よんだことが ありますか</u>。

   Have you ever read Shakespeare?

5. さしみを <u>たべたことが ありますか</u>。

   Have you ever eaten sashimi?

> **Example Q&A**
>
> 1. 日本に いったことが ありますか。
>   **Have you ever been to Japan?**
>
>   いったことないけど、らいしゅうまつに いきます。
>   I have never been, but I am going next weekend.
>
>   はい、あります。毎年３月に いきます。
>   Yes, I have. I go every year in March.
>
> 2. さしみを たべたことが ありますか。
>   **Have you ever eaten sashimi?**
>
>   たべたことが ありません。でも、たべたいです。
>   I have never eaten it. But I want to eat it.

❏ 4-9. "I have…" and "I have never…"

The tense of ある can be changed to say that the experience has been had or not.

> **(た form verb) + ことが あります。**
> **I have (verb-ed)**

> **(た form verb) + ことが ありません。**
> **I have never (verb-ed)**

Example sentences

1. 日本の えいがは 見たことが ありません。

   I have never seen a Japanese movie.

2. ともだちから お金を かりたことが ありますか。

   Have you ever borrowed money from a friend?

3. 外国には いったことが ないです。

   I have never been to a foreign country.

   > ないです is a more casual version of ありません.

4. 田中さんは キムチを <u>たべたことが ないと</u> いいました。

Tanaka san said he <u>has never eaten</u> kimchee.

Example Q&A

1. へびを たべたことが ありますか。
   Have you ever eaten a snake?

   いいえ、たべたことが ありません。
   No, I have never eaten one.

   はい、たべたことが あります。
   Yes, I have eaten one.

2. 海外で うんてんしたことが ありますか。
   Have you ever driven overseas?

   はい、二回、あります。
   Yes, I have done it twice.

   うんてんしたことが ありません。いつも バスに のります。
   I have never driven. I always ride the bus.

   日本では 毎日 うんてんしますが、海外では うんてんしたことが ないです。
   I drive everyday in Japan, but I have never driven overseas.

3. きょうとに いったことが ありますか。
   Have you ever been to Kyoto?

   いいえ、ありません。でも、とうきょうには いったことが あります。
   No, I haven't. But I have been to Tokyo.

❏ 4-10. This much, that much 〜どんなに word group

The こそあど pattern was first introduced in book 1 of this series with これ、それ、あれ and どれ. こんなに、そんなに、あんなに and どんなに are demonstrative words.

For example, with your arms stretched out you could say こんなに たべました (I ate this much). Just like with the other こそあど word groups the physical closeness of the of the topic and the subject determine which word you use.

Example sentences

1. なんで そんなに パンを かったの？
   Why did you buy <u>so much</u> bread?

2. きゅうりょうが 出るまで こんなに お金は つかえないです。
   Until my pay comes, I can't use <u>this much</u> money.

3. あんなに 大きい 魚^{さかな} は みたこと ないです。
   I have never seen <u>such a</u> big fish.

4. こんなに すしを たべたことがない。
   I have never eaten <u>this much</u> sushi.

5. あしたの テストは どんなに むずかしいですか。
   <u>How</u> hard is tomorrow's test?

❏ 4-11. Looking forward to something

You can look forward to doing something using the phrase たのしみに しています. The thing you are looking forward to is marked with を.

> **(thing) + を たのしみに しています。**
> **I am looking forward to (thing)**

Example sentences

1. 休^{やす}みを たのしみに しています。

   I am looking forward to <u>a vacation (days off)</u>.

2. 明日を たのしみに しています。

   I am looking forward to <u>tomorrow</u>.

You can also combine a こと verb phrase to say you are looking forward to an event.

> **(う form verb phrase) + ことを たのしみに しています。**
> **I am looking forward to (verb phrase)**

Example sentences

1. <u>日本に いくことを</u> たのしみにしています。

   I am looking forward to <u>going to Japan</u>.

2. <u>ともだちに 会うことを</u> たのしみにしています。

   I am looking forward to <u>meeting my friends</u>.

たのしみに しています, can also be shortened into たのしみ or おたのしみ. When used it means, "ITEM is something to look forward to. / ITEM is anticipated".

Example sentences

1. 明日の 休み<u>は</u> たのしみです。

   I am looking forward to tomorrow's day off.

   > Notice that since たのしみ is a noun and not a verb phrase, instead of を, は or が particle is used.

2. パーティーは たのしみです。

   I am looking forward to the party.

3. 日本は ほんとうに たのしみでした。

   I was really looking forward to Japan.

4 Mini Conversation ミニかいわ J→E

1. Casual conversation between a father and his son.

A: なんで こんなに シャンプーを つかったの？

B: かみが くさかったから です。

A: How come you used this much shampoo?

B: Because my hair smelled bad.

2. Polite conversation between two company workers

A: シカゴに いったことが ありますか。

B: 二ヶ月まえに いきました。何で ですか。

A: らい月 シカゴに てんきんに なります。どんなところですか。

B: さむいところです。

A: Have you ever been to Chicago?

B: I went two months ago. Why?

A: I am being transferred to Chicago next month. What kind of place is it?

B: It's a cold place.

3. Polite conversation taking place after a crime has taken place

A: けいさつです。この人を 見たことが ありますか。

B: たぶん 見たことが あると おもいます。

A: いつ、どこで ですか。

B: 先週の 木よう日に スーパーで 見たと おもいます。

A: ありがとうございます。

A: I am a police officer. Have you ever seen this person?

B: I think I might have seen him before.

A: When and where?

B: I think I saw him last Thursday at the supermarket.

A: Thank you very much.

4. Polite conversation between friends at lunch

A: これは 何ですか。

B: わかめの おみそしるです。

のんだことが ありますか。

A: ありません。どんな あじですか。

B: おいしいですよ。のんで下さい。

> In Japanese, medicines and soups are "drunk" のむ and not "taken" とる or "eaten" たべる.

A: What is this?

B: It is seaweed miso soup. Have you ever drunk it?

A: No, I have not. What kind of flavor is it?

B: It tastes good. Please drink some.

4 Mini Conversation ミニかいわ E→J

1. Informal conversation between friends

A: I think I want to save 1 million yen in a year.

B: You!? I don't think you can do it. (lit: "I think you can't do it.")

A: I can do it. A long time ago, I have saved. (had the experience of saving)

B: Really? How much did you save?

A: About 10,000 yen.

A: 一年で 百まん円、ためたいと おもってる。

B: あなたが？！ できないと おもうよ。

A: できるよ。むかし ためたことが あるから。

B: ほんとう？ いくら ためたの？

A: 一まん円ぐらい。

2. Polite conversation between two students studying Japanese

A: What Japanese TV shows do you like?

B: I don't know. I have never seen any Japanese TV.

A: Well then, how come you know "Kureyon Shinchan"?

B: Because I have seen it once on video.

A: 日本の テレビばんぐみは 何が すきですか。

B: わかりません。わたしは 日本の テレビを 見たことが ありません。

A: じゃ、なんで 「クレヨンしんちゃん」を しっていますか？

B: 一回 ビデオで 見たことが あるからです。

3. Polite conversation between friends

A: What is the drink you always drink?

B: It's coffee milk. Have you ever drunk it?

A: Yes, I also often drink it.

A: いつも のむ のみものは 何ですか。

B: コーヒーぎゅうにゅう です。のんだことが ありますか。

A: はい。わたしも よく のみます。

4. Informal conversation between friends

A: Today was really cold.

B: I don't think today was so cold.

A: I think today was the coldest day this week.

B: I think tomorrow will be colder than today.

A: 今日は とっても さむかった。

B: 今日は そんなに さむくなかったと おもう。

A: こんしゅうの 一番さむい日だと おもう。
<small>いちばん</small>

B: 今日より明日の ほうが さむいと おもう。

---

4 Reading Comprehension どっかい

Read the selection below. If you don't understand them, you should review the grammar in this lesson until you do. After you have understood this reading, answer the comprehension questions in the *Activities* section for this lesson.

---

① 昨日、私の 夏の ボーナスが 出ました。

② 今回の ボーナスは 四十五まん円でした。
<small>こんかい</small>

③ その お金と きょ年から ためていたお金で 海外りょこうが したいです。
<small>ねん</small>

④ たのしみに しています。

⑤ 一ばん いきたいところは スイスです。

⑥ 家ないは ヨーロッパに いったことが あるけど、わたしは いったことが ありません。
<small>か</small>

⑦ 家ないが ヨーロッパに いったとき、わたしは しごとで いそがしかった から、いけませんでした。
<small>か</small>

⑧ 毎年りょこうが したいけど、お金が かかるから できません。

4 | Lesson Activities

❑ Reading comprehension questions

Answer the following questions about the reading comprehension in this lesson.
わしゃ means "a speaker". Use this word as needed to answer the questions.

1. わしゃは いつ ボーナスが 出ましたか。

    _____

2. わしゃは いま、何を たのしみに していますか。

    _____

3. わしゃの おくさんは どこに いったことが ありますか。

    _____

4. なぜ わしゃは ヨーロッパに いけませんでしたか。

    _____

5. わしゃは 何を がまんしていますか。

    _____

6. 日本の 会社では、一年に 何回ぐらい、ボーナスが ありますか。
    　　　かいしゃ

    _____

❑ **Sentence Jumble**

Using ONLY the words and particles provided, create Japanese sentences that match the English translation. You can conjugate adjectives and verbs and reuse items if needed.

1. こと・はじめて・ある・まで・に・と・が・よこしまさん・うま・せんしゅうまつ
    のる・見る・おもう・を・は

    _____

    I saw a horse for the first time last weekend.

    _____

    Yokoshima san hadn't ever ridden a horse until last weekend.

    _____

    Do you think Yokoshima san has ever ridden a horse?

2. こんなに・できる・たべる・ある・しぬ・らいしゅうまつ・きゅうりょう
    わかめ・が・を・に・は・うんてん・こと・車・きょうりゅう・こと

    _____

    I have never eaten such delicious seaweed!

    _____

    I don't get paid until next weekend. (pay doesn't come out)

    _____

    Because the dinosaurs are dead, they can't drive cars.

3. あだちさん・上手・こと・を・が・しる・きく・おんがく・ある・あんなに
    つくる・に・と・の

    _____

    Have you ever heard Adachi san's music?

    _____

    Do you know Adachi san?

    _____

    Did you know that Adachi san could make such skilled music?

❑ Practice

Look at the pictures below and make sentences using ～たことがあります.

1. I have worn a yukata (summer cotton kimono).

_____

2. I have been (appeared) in a movie.

_____

3. I have given a ring to my girlfriend before.

_____

4. I have never skied before.

_____

5. I have never raised a dog.

_____

❏ Short Dialogue

田中さん：　トムさんは テレビ番組（ばんぐみ）に 出（で）たことが あるの？

トムさん：　ううん、ないよ。田中さんは？

田中さん：　あるよ。むかし、クイズ番組に 出た。

トムさん：　ええ！すごいね。どんな 番組だったの？

田中さん：　しつもんに ぜんぶ こたえられたら、
　　　　　　海外りょこうが あたる番組だったよ。

トムさん：　それで、どうなったの？

田中さん：　さいごの こたえが わからなかったから、だめだった…。

トムさん：　ざんねんだったね。また チャレンジするの？

田中さん：　ううん。もう五回、チャレンジしたから、あきらめたよ。

トムさん：　ぼくは テレビ番組に 出たことが ないから、いつか 出たいな。

❏ New Words and Expressions in the Dialogue

Progressive	Kanji +	English
あたる	当たる	to hit, to win
あきらめる	諦める	to give up
こたえられたら	答えられたら	if you can answer

❏ Short Dialogue Activities

1. Practice reading the short dialogue in pairs.

2. Play Tanaka-san's role and talk about your experience on a TV show.

Kanji Lesson 4

記帰牛魚京教

kanji 99-104

四 **New Kanji あたらしい漢字**

Practice writing each new kanji in the boxes provided. First trace the light gray samples.

Pay attention to stroke orders. Practice writing the sample kanji words at least 5 times each.

記	くんよみ	しる（す）	number		99
	おんよみ	キ	meaning	chronicle	

しる 記す	きにゅう 記入	きじ 記事	にっき 日記	あんき 暗記
to note or mark down	form entry	article	diary	memorization

10 strokes

｀ ゛ ゛ ゜ 言 言 言 訂 訂 記

記	記	記	記	記					

帰	くんよみ	かえ（る）	number		100
	おんよみ	キ	meaning	return	

かえ 帰る	かえ　みち 帰り道	きたく 帰宅	ひがえ 日帰り	ふっき 復帰
to return	the way back	returning home	day trip	return, comeback

10 strokes

刂 刂 刂ヨ 刂ヨ 刂ヨ 帰 帰 帰 帰 帰

帰	帰	帰	帰	帰					

牛	くんよみ	うし	number		101
	おんよみ	ギュウ	meaning	cow, cattle	

うしごや	ぎゅうにく	ぎゅうかわ	ぎゅうにゅう	こうし
牛小屋	牛肉	牛革	牛乳	子牛
cow shed	beef	cowhide	milk	calf

4 strokes

ノ ┌ 仁 牛

牛	牛	牛	牛	牛					

魚	くんよみ	さかな・うお	number		102
	おんよみ	ギョ	meaning	fish	

さかなや	きんぎょ	ぎょかい	にんぎょ	さかなつ
魚屋	金魚	魚介	人魚	魚釣り
fish store	goldfish	seafood	mermaid	fishing

11 strokes

ノ ク ク 色 角 角 魚 魚 魚 魚 魚

魚	魚	魚	魚	魚					

京	くんよみ	–	number		103
	おんよみ	キョウ・ケイ	meaning	capital, ten quadrillion	

とうきょう	じょうきょう	きょうと	きょうふう	けいはん
東京	上京	京都	京風	京阪
Tokyo	proceeding to the capital	Kyoto	Kyoto style	Keihan area (Kyoto-Osaka area)

8 strokes

ゝ 一 宀 宁 市 京 京 京

京	京	京	京	京					

教	くんよみ	おし (える) ・ おそ (わる)	number		104
	おんよみ	キョウ	meaning		teach, instruction

おし 教える	おそ 教わる	きょうしつ 教室	きょういく 教育	しゅうきょう 宗教
to teach	to be taught	classroom	education	religion

11 strokes

二　十　土　耂　耂　孝　孝　孝　教　教　教

教	教	教	教	教								

四 Kanji Drills 漢字ドリル

❑ Words you can write

Write the following words in the boxes. This is a great way to practice the new kanji, review the words, and learn new words at the same time. For unknown kanji write in hiragana.

しる
記す
to mark

記	す								

にっき
日記
diary, journal

日	記								

き にゅう
記入
form entry

記	入								

かえ
帰る
to return

帰	る								

き こく
帰国
return to one's country

帰	こ	く							

うし
牛
cow

牛									

こ うし
子牛
calf

子	牛								

きんぎょ
金魚
goldfish

金	魚								

さかなや
魚屋
fish store

| 魚 | 屋 | | | | | | | | | | |

にんぎょ
人魚
mermaid

| 人 | 魚 | | | | | | | | | | |

とうきょう
東京
Tokyo

| と | う | 京 | | | | | | | |

きょうと
京都
Kyoto

| 京 | と | | | | | | | | |

きょうか
教科
subject, curriculum

| 教 | 科 | | | | | | | | |

おし
教える
to teach

| 教 | え | る | | | | | | |

ぎゅうにく
牛肉
beef

| 牛 | に | く | | | | | | |

ひがえ
日帰り
day trip

| 日 | 帰 | り | | | | | | |

❑ **Fill in the kanji**

Fill in the blanks in the following sentences with the appropriate kanji.

1. 私は 毎＿＿、＿＿ ＿＿を かきます。
   まい にち　　にっ き
   I write in my diary everyday.

2. 東＿＿に ＿＿ ＿＿り 旅 行 しましょう。
   とうきょう　　ひ　がえ　　りょこう
   Let's take a day trip to Tokyo.

3. ＿＿屋で まぐろを＿＿匹 買って＿＿さい。
   さかな や　　　　　よんひき か　　　くだ
   Please buy 4 tuna at the fish shop.

4. ＿＿ ＿＿はどんな＿＿＿＿を＿＿えていますか。
   せん せい　　　　　きょう か　　おし
   What kind of subjects do you teach, teacher?

5. ＿＿で＿＿肉を食べてから、＿＿ ＿＿に いきます。
   うち　ぎゅうにく　　た　　　　　が　っこう
   After I eat some beef at my house, I will go to school.

6. ここに＿＿前を＿＿＿＿して＿＿さい。
   な　　き にゅう　　くだ
   Please input your name here.

7. ＿＿く＿＿ ＿＿に＿＿りたいです。
   はや　に ほん　　かえ
   I want to return home to Japan soon.

8. ＿＿ ＿＿は ＿＿きいのと＿＿さいのが います。
   きん ぎょ　　おお　　　ち い
   There are small and big goldfish.

四 Kanji Recognition 漢字にんしき

❏ Individual words

The following words will no longer have any ふりがな (hiragana on top). Don't worry if you can't write these words. Recognition is the goal for these words.

せんせい 先生 teacher	みぎ 右 right	ひだり 左 left	うえ 上 up, above
あ 上がる to go up	なかむら 中村 Nakamura (last name)	たなか 田中 Tanaka (last name)	した 下 down, below
て 手 hand	ひと 人 person, people	おおさか 大阪 Osaka	とうきょう 東京 Tokyo
でぐち 出口 exit	いぐち 入り口 entrance		

> 出口 and 入り口 are taught in the next lesson, but you have already learned the kanji in book 3.

❏ Word groups (counter rank)

The following word groups, will no longer have any ふりがな (hiragana on top). The rank counter (taught in book 3) is created by added the kanji 目 after any counter. Here are some example counter ranks that will no longer have ふりがな.

ひと　　め 一つ目 the first one	ふた　　め 二つ目 the second one	いっかいめ 一回目 the first time	に　かいめ 二回目 the second time
いっかげつめ 一ヶ月目 the first month	に　か　げつめ 二ヶ月目 the second month	いちねんめ 一年目 the first year	に　ねんめ 二年目 the second year

❑ Kanji recognition cards

Print and cut out these cards, then write the hiragana and English meaning on the back.
Now you can easily practice your kanji recognition.

先生	右	左	上
上がる	中村	田中	下
手	人	大阪	東京
出口	入り口	一つ目	二つ目
一回目	二回目	一ヶ月目	二ヶ月目
一年目	二年目		

How something is done

Before This Lesson

1. Be able to read and write 記帰牛魚京教.

Lesson Goals

1. Learn how to tell directions in Japanese and to ask how something is done.

From The Teachers

1. You should start to notice the benefit of knowing kanji. Look for the kanji in this lesson. The kanji you know will become part of a quick reference guide in your head.

5

Lesson Highlights

5-5. Particles with
まっすぐ

5-6. Asking how something is done with
どうやって

5-7. Demonstrating how an action was done

5-8. Counting floors

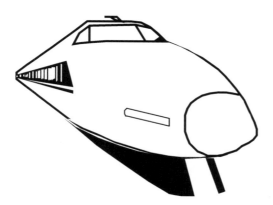

5 | New Words あたらしい ことば

日本語	漢字	えいご
どうやって	どうやって	how is it done, in what way
しゅっちょう	出張	business trip
ししゃ	支社	branch office
ほんしゃ	本社	headquaters, home office
かいぎ	会議	meeting
出口 <small>でぐち</small>	出口	exit
入り口 <small>いくち</small>	入口	entrance
かど	角	corner
こうさてん	交差点	intersection
こうそくどうろ	高速道路	freeway, highway
みち	道	road
まっすぐ	真っ直ぐ	straight ahead
つきあたり	突き当たり	end (of street or hallway etc.)
いきどまり	行き止まり	dead end (of street)
フロント	フロント	front desk (hotel)
それから	それから	then, and then, after that

5 | New Verbs あたらしい どうし

どうし	えいご	た form	タイプ
曲がる <small>ま</small>	to turn	まがった	regular
上がる <small>あ</small>	to go or come up	あがった	regular
下りる <small>お</small>	to go down, get off of	おりた	いる/える
出張する <small>しゅっちょう</small>	to take a business trip	しゅっちょうした	する
歩く <small>ある</small>	to walk	あるいた	regular

5 Verb Usage どうしの つかいかた

❏ 5-1. まがる (to turn)

It can be a bit tricky trying to figure out which particle to use with まがる.

A) Use で when you are turning at a designated spot (stoplight, red house etc).

B) Use に when you are turning into a direction (left, right, east etc).

C) Use を when you are following a certain path (turning a curve etc)

Example sentences

1. 右に まがって下さい。
   Turn right please.

2. まだ まがらないで下さい。
   Don't turn yet.

3. つぎの かどを まがります。
   I will turn the next corner.

4. しんごうで まがりました。
   I turned at the stoplight.

5. ここで まがって下さい。
   Please turn here.

6. 左に まがって下さい。
   Turn left please.

❏ 5-2. あがる (to go or come up)

When going up something such as a mountain, then を is used. When you go up to a location then the location marker に is used. NOTE: See the "Counting Floors" section in this lesson.

(something) を あがる
to go up (something)

(location) に あがる
to go up to a (location)

Example sentences

1. かいだんを 上がりましょう。
   Let's go up the stairs.

2. おくじょうに 上がって下さい。
   Please go up to the rooftop.

3. 二かいに 上がったとき、田中さんに 会いました。
When I went up to the second floor, I met Mr. Tanaka.

4. 三がいに 上がって しゃちょうと はなして 下さい。
Please go up to the 3rd floor and speak with the company president.

❑ 5-3. おりる (to go down, get off of, climb down)

おりる is used to come down off of something like a mountain or something that you might have been standing on. It is also used for getting out of a car, airplane and other transportation.

> (something) から おりる
> **to get off from (something)**

> (something) を おりる
> **to get off of (something)**

Example sentences

1. エレベーターで おります。
I will go down by elevator.

2. ここからは おりられません。
You can't get down from here.

3. 車から おりました。
I got out of a car.

4. こうそくどうろから おりて下さい。
Please get off of the freeway.

5. いっしょに 一かいに おりましょう。
Let's go down to the first floor together.

6. エレベーターがないから かいだんで おりるしか ないです。
Since there isn't an elevator we can only go down by the stairs.

❏ 5-4. しゅっちょうする (to take a business trip)

The location you are going for the business trip is marked with the location marker に.

> (place) に しゅっちょうする
> **to take a business trip to (place)**

Example sentences

1. 東京に しゅっちょうします。
   I will take a business trip to Tokyo.

2. 一年に 三回、しゅっちょうします。
   I take three business trips a year.

3. むかしは よく しゅっちょうしました。
   I used to take business trips often.

4. かんこくに しゅっちょうするから かんこくごを べんきょうしています。
   Because I am taking a business trip to Korea, I'm studying Korean.

5. あんまり、しゅっちょうしたくないです。
   I don't really want to take business trips.

5 Grammar ぶんぽう

❏ 5-5. Particles with まっすぐ

Although the に particle is used with 右 (right) and 左 (left) to denote direction, it is NOT used with まっすぐ (straight ahead). If you think about it, this makes sense because in English we say, "turn to the right" and "turn to the left", but you don't say "go to straight". It is the same in Japanese.

Example sentence

まっすぐ いって下さい。   Please go straight ahead.

まっすぐ いかないで下さい。   Please don't go straight ahead.

❑ 5-6. Asking how something is done with どうやって

When asking how something is done どうやって + verb can be used.

The verb can be in a variety of forms depending on what you want to say.

> どうやって+ (verb phrase)?
>
> **How do you (verb phrase)?**

Example Q&A

1. これを どうやって たべますか。
   How do you eat this?

   フォークで たべます。
   You eat it with a fork.

   手で たべます。
   You eat it with your hands.

   おはしで たべます。
   You eat it with chopsticks.

2. どうやって いくの？
   How do you go?

   まっすぐ いってから、右に まがります。
   Go straight and then you turn right.

3. あした どうやって きますか。
   How will you come tomorrow?

   ひめじえきまで でん車に のってから、あるいて いきます。
   I will take a train to Himeji station and then I will go by foot.

4. どうやって ここに きましたか。
   How did you get here?

   車で きました。
   I came here by car.

5. どうやって 日本語を べんきょうしましたか。
    How did you study Japanese?

    日本語学校で べんきょうしました。
    I studied at a Japanese language school.

❏ 5-7. Demonstrating how an action was done

When a question is asked using どうやって you can respond with こうやって, そうやって, ああやって and point to how the task was done or even demonstrate.

For example, if someone asks how to write your name, 名まえを どうやって かきますか, then you can write it on a piece of paper hold it up and say, こうやってかきます, "You write it like this." You can also act out how something was done and say, こうやって しました, "I did it like this."

こうやって is used when you are actually doing the demonstration, or holding the representation of the action in question. If you are referring to an action not done by yourself or something that is farther away from you then そうやって or ああやって is used.

Example Q&A

1. すしを どうやって たべますか。
    How do you eat sushi?

    こうやって たべます。
    I eat it like this.

2. きっぷを どうやって かいますか。
    How do you buy train tickets?

    ああやって かいます。
    You buy them like that.

Example sentences

1. そうやって あるくときは おもしろいよ！
    It's interesting when you walk that way!

2. こうやって わたしの なまえの 漢字を かきます。
    You write the kanji for my name this way.

3. どうやって 日本語を じょうずに なりましたか？
    How did you get skilled at Japanese?

❑ 5-8. Counting floors

Look at the following chart to see the pattern of the first 10 floors. After the first 10 floors the same pattern is repeated. Pay attention to the 3rd floor since it is special.

1st floor	2nd floor	3rd floor	4th floor	5th floor
いっかい	にかい	さんがい	よんかい	ごかい
一階	二階	三階	四階	五階
6th floor	7th floor	8th floor	9th floor	10th floor
ろっかい	ななかい	はちかい	きゅうかい	じゅっかい
六階	七階	八階	九階	十階
What floor? なんかい				

Example sentences

1. 二かいに 上がって 下さい。
   Please go up to the second floor.

2. 会しゃは 三がいに あります。
   The company is on the third floor.

3. 日本の ビルには ときどき 4かいが ないです。
   Sometimes, Japanese buildings don't have a 4th floor.

5 Mini Conversation ミニかいわ J→E

1. Polite conversation between a newcomer to Japan and a Japanese person

A: おすしを どうやって たべますか。

B: 東京の人は 手で たべます。

A: おはしで たべませんか。

B: おはしで たべる人は 大阪の人が おおいと おもいます。

A: How do you eat sushi?

B: People in Tokyo eat with their hands.

A: Don't they eat with chopsticks?

B: I think Osaka has many people that eat with chopsticks.

2. Polite conversation at a department store

A: お手あらいは どこに ありますか。

B: 三がいに あります。

A: 三がいの どこに ありますか。

B: エレベーターを おりてから、左に まっすぐ いって下さい。

A: Where is the bathroom?

B: There is one on the third floor.

A: Where is it on the third floor?

B: After you get off of the elevator, please go straight to the left.

3. Polite conversation between strangers

A: ショッピングセンターは どこに ありますか。

B: ダウンタウンに あります。

A: ここから ダウンタウンまで 車で どうやって いきますか。

B: まっすぐ きたに いってから、三つ目の しんごうを 右に まがります。

それから、まっすぐ 十五ふんぐらい いって下さい。すぐに わかりますよ。

A: Where is the shopping center?

B: It is downtown.

A: How do you go downtown by car from here?

B: Go straight north, then at the 3rd stoplight, you turn right.
Then please go straight about 15 minutes. You will find it soon.

5 | Mini Conversation ミニかいわ E→J

1. Polite conversation between co-workers

A: Tomorrow I have a business trip to New York.

B: That sure is far.

A: How do you go to the airport?

B: You go north on the freeway. Then get off at the airport exit.

A: 明日、ニューヨークに しゅっちょうします。

B: とおいですね。

A: くうこうまで どうやって いきますか。

B: こうそくどうろを きたに いって下さい。

それから、くうこうの 出口で おりて下さい。

2. Polite conversation between neighbors

A: How do I get to Mr. Nakamura's house?

B: Go straight here and there is a dead end. Please turn left there.

end of street

A: Thank you very much.

B: You are welcome.

A: 中村さんの うちに どうやって いきますか。

B: ここを まっすぐ いきます。 そして、 つきあたりを 左に まがって下さい。

A: ありがとうございます。

B: どういたしまして。

3. Polite conversation between strangers

A: Excuse me. Where is the bookstore?

B: Please go up to the 4th floor by elevator.

A: Ok. And then?

B: Please go straight to the left. It is a big bookstore, so you will find it.

A: すみません、本やは どこに ありますか。

B: エレベーターで 四かいまで あがって下さい。

A: わかりました。 それから？

B: 左に まっすぐ いって下さい。 大きい本や だから、 わかりますよ。

5 | Reading Comprehension どっかい

Read the sentences below. If you don't understand them, you should review the grammar in this lesson until you do. After you have understood this reading, answer the questions in the *Activities* section in this lesson.

① 明日スコットさんは 大阪に はじめて 出張(しゅっちょう)します。

② 明日 大阪支社(おおさかししゃ)で ごご 一時(じ)に かいぎが あります。

③ スコットさんは しんじゅくの 本社(ほんしゃ)に いってから 大阪に いきます。

④ スコットさんは 会社(かいしゃ)で 一番(いちばん) やさしそうな 中村さんに いろいろな ことを ききました。

❏ Dialogue: Scott and Mr. Satou

スコットさん:	大阪支社(ししゃ)は どこに ありますか。
中村さん:	梅田(うめだ)えきの 前(まえ)の ビルに ありますよ。
スコットさん:	ここから どうやって いきますか。
中村さん:	しんじゅくえきから 電車(でんしゃ)で 東京えきに いってから、 しんかんせんで 新大阪(しんおおさか)えきまで いきます。
スコットさん:	新大阪(しんおおさか)えきから 梅田(うめだ)えきまで どうやって いきますか。
中村さん:	電車(でんしゃ)で いきます。梅田(うめだ)えきの 出口を 左に まがってから、 まっすぐ いきます。つきあたりの かいだんを 二かいまで あがります。支社(ししゃ)は そこに ありますよ。
スコットさん:	どれぐらい かかりますか。
中村さん:	会社(かいしゃ)から 四時間(よじかん)はんぐらい かかると おもいます。
スコットさん:	わかりました。ありがとうございます。 じゃあ、 いってきます。
中村さん:	いってらっしゃい。

5 Lesson Activities

❑ Reading comprehension questions

Answer the following questions about the reading comprehension from the previous page.

1. スコットさんは なぜ 中村さんに いろいろ きいたと おもいますか。

_____

2. 大阪の ししゃに 何と何で いきますか。

_____

3. スコットさんは 大阪に いったことが ありますか。

_____

4. 大阪の ししゃまで どれぐらい かかりますか。

_____

5. 梅田えきから 大阪の ししゃまで 電車で いきますか。
   _{うめ だ}   _{でんしゃ}

_____

❑ Sentence Jumble

Using ONLY the words and particles provided, create Japanese sentences that match the English translation. You can conjugate adjectives and verbs and reuse items if needed.

1. かいだん・上がる・あるく・まで・から・どうやって・ここ・エレベーター
   で・四かい・四じ・に・おりる

_____

How did you walk here?

_____

Come up to the 4th floor by the elevator by 4 o'clock.

_____

Because I couldn't go down to the 4th floor by elevator, I went down by the stairs.

2. まっすぐ・入り口・に・で・の・おりる・まがる・左・右・つきあたり
それから・こうそくどうろ・こうさてん・三つ目・フロント・みち・まで・つぎ
下さい・さがす

_____

Turn left at the 3rd intersection, then go straight until the end of the street.

_____

After you get off the freeway, turn right at the next intersection.

_____

Go to the front desk, then please look for the hotel's entrance.

3. しゅっちょうする・しゅっちょう・2013年・に・この・フランス
いっしゅうかん・いく・かえる・いえ・まっすぐ・おわる・とき

_____

I took a business trip in 2013 for one week.

_____

After my business trip ended, I went straight to my house.

_____

When I return home from this business trip, I want to go to France.

❑ Question and Answer

Answer the following questions as if they were asked to you using the words and patterns in this lesson.

1. どうやって 日本語を べんきょうしますか。

_____

2. どうやって 会社 / 学校に いきますか。
　　　　　 かいしゃ

_____

3.　どうやって 三がいまで あがりますか。

_____

4.　よく しゅっちょうに いきますか。

_____

5.　あなたに 一番 <ruby>いちばん</ruby> ちかい 出口は どこですか。

_____

6.　あなたの いえから どこまで あるけますか。

_____

7.　日本に いった ことが ありますか。

_____

❑ Short Dialogue

Look at the picture below and translate the English portions of the following conversation.

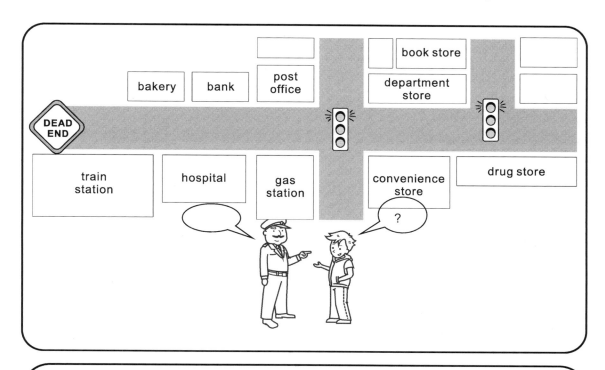

ジョンくん: すみません。びょういんは どこに ありますか。
けいさつかん: あそこに こうさんてんが ありますね。
けいさつかん: ① Please turn left at the intersection.

_____

② The hospital is on the left.

_____

ジョンくん: じゃあ、デパートは どこに ありますか。
けいさつかん: ③ Please go straight ahead. It's on the right.

_____

ジョンくん: ありがとうございます。

Kanji Lesson 5

強角近形計元

kanji 105-110

五 New Kanji あたらしい漢字

Practice writing each new kanji in the boxes provided. First trace the light gray samples while paying attention to stroke order. Then on a separate piece of paper practice writing the sample kanji words at least five times each.

強	くんよみ	つよ（い）・し	number		105
	おんよみ	キョウ・ゴウ	meaning	strong, strengthen	

つよ 強い	べんきょう 勉強	し 強いる	ごういん 強引	きょうふう 強風
strong	study	to impose	to force, overbearing	strong wind

11 strokes

フ　コ　弓　弓ノ　弓ツ　弘　弘　弘　強　強　強

強　強　強　強　強

角	くんよみ	かど・つの	number		106
	おんよみ	カク	meaning	angle, corner	

かど 角	さんかく 三角	まちかど 街角	ちょっかく 直角	かくど 角度
corner	triangle	street corner	right angle	angle

7 strokes

ノ　ノ｀　广　角　角　角　角

角　角　角　角　角

近	くんよみ	ちか（い）	number	107
	おんよみ	キン	meaning	near, approach, recent

7 strokes

ちか 近い	ちかみち 近道	さいきん 最近	きんじょ 近所	きんきょう 近況
close, near	short cut	most recent	neighborhood	recent state

﹁ 厂 戶 斤 斤 近 近

近 近 近 近 近

形	くんよみ	かた・かたち	number	108
	おんよみ	ケイ・ギョウ	meaning	form,shape,type,figure

7 strokes

かたち 形	にんぎょう 人形	ずけい 図形	かたみ 形見	てがた 手形
shape	doll	figure	memento	promissory note

一 二 テ 开 开 形 形

形 形 形 形 形

計	くんよみ	はか（る）	number	109
	おんよみ	ケイ	meaning	Measure, plan, count

9 strokes

はか 計る	けいさん 計算	けいかく 計画	ごうけい 合計	とけい 時計
to measure	calculation	plan	total amount	clock, watch

ヽ 亠 亖 言 言 言 言 計 計

計 計 計 計 計

元	くんよみ	もと	number		110
	おんよみ	ゲン・ガン	meaning		the origin, cause

ひ もと	じ もと	がんじつ	がん そ	げん き
火の元	地元	元日	元祖	元気
origin of fire	local	New Year's Day	originator	energetic, vigor

4 strokes

⇉ 元 元 元

元	元	元	元	元									

五 Kanji Drills 漢字ドリル

❑ **Words you can write**

Write the following words in the boxes. This is a great way to practice the new kanji and review the words at the same time. For the kanji that hasn't been taught yet, use hiragana.

つよ
強い
strong

| 強 | い | | | | | | | | | |

ごういん
強引
forceful

| 強 | 引 | | | | | | | | | |

つよ き
強気
self assured

| 強 | 気 | | | | | | | | | |

かど
角
corner

| 角 | | | | | | | | | | |

さんかく
三角
triangle

| 三 | 角 | | | | | | | | | |

ちか
近い
close

| 近 | い | | | | | | | | | |

きんじょ
近所
neighborhood

| 近 | じ | よ | | | | | | | | |

かたち
形
shape

| 形 | | | | | | | | | | |

にんぎょう
人形
doll

| 人 | 形 | | | | | | | | | |

はか
計る
to measure

| 計 る | | | | | | | | |

けいかく
計画
a plan

| 計 画 | | | | | | | | |

と けい
時計
a clock, watch

| 時 計 | | | | | | | | |

がんじつ
元日
New Year's Day

| 元 日 | | | | | | | | |

げん き
元気
energetic, vigor, healthy

| 元 気 | | | | | | | | |

ひ もと
火の元
the origin of a fire

| 火 の 元 | | | | | | | |

❑ Fill in the kanji

Fill in the blanks in the following sentences with the appropriate kanji.

かど　みぎ　　　　　くだ
1. あの＿＿＿を＿＿＿に まがって＿＿＿さい。
Please turn right at that corner over there.

た　なか　　　　　　つよ　き
2. ＿＿＿＿＿さんは いつも＿＿＿＿＿ですね。
Tanaka-san is always self assured.

と　けい
3. おばあさんの＿＿＿＿＿は とても ふるいです。
My grandmother's watch is very old.

らい げつ　　えん そく　　けい かく
4. 来＿＿、＿＿ ＿＿の＿＿ ＿＿が あります。
Next month I have a plan for an excursion.

さいきん　　べんきょう　　じ かん
5. 最＿＿、勉＿＿ する時＿＿が ありません。
Recently I don't have time to study.

は や　　げん き　　　　　　く だ
6. ＿＿く＿＿ ＿＿に なって＿＿さい。
Please get healthy soon.

はやし　　　　　ごう いん
7. ＿＿さんは＿＿ ＿＿なときが あります。
There are times when Hayashi-san is forceful.

五　漢字にんしき

❑ **Individual words**

The following words will no longer have any ふりがな (hiragana on top). Don't worry if you can't write these words. Recognition is the goal for these words.

き
気
spirit, mind

いえ
家
house, home

やす
休み
a break, day off

やす
休む
to take a break

みず
水
water

いぬ
犬
dog

きょう と
京都
Kyoto

べん きょう
勉強
study

あし
足
foot, leg

かえ
帰る
to return

❑ Word groups (days of the week)

The following word group will no longer have any ふりがな (hiragana on top).

げつ よう び
月曜日
Monday

か よう び
火曜日
Tuesday

すい よう び
水曜日
Wednesday

もく よう び
木曜日
Thursday

きん よう び
金曜日
Friday

ど よう び
土曜日
Saturday

にち よう び
日曜日
Sunday

なん よう び
何曜日
What day?

❑ Kanji recognition cards

Print and cut out these cards, then write the hiragana and English meaning on the back.
Now you can easily practice your kanji recognition.

気	家	休み	休む
水	犬	京都	勉強
足	帰る	月曜日	火曜日
水曜日	木曜日	金曜日	土曜日
日曜日	何曜日		

Is it okay if I...?

6

Before This Lesson

1. Be able to read and write 強角近形計元.

Lesson Goals

1. Learn how to ask permission to do things and how to respond to such requests.
2. Learn how to connect sentences with が.

From The Teachers

1. Knowing how to make the て form of the verbs is important for this lesson and coming lessons. If you don't know how to easily make them we recommend you review now.

Lesson Highlights

6-1. Asking permission with てもいいですか

6-2. Giving permission with ても いいです

6-3. Denying permission with ては いけません

6-4. Informal versions of ては いけません and てもいいですか

6-6. A review of けど and でも

6 New Words あたらしい ことば

日本語	漢字	えいご
おかんじょう	お勘定	bill (at a restaurant/store)
レジ	レジ	register
チップ	チップ	tip
きっさてん	喫茶店	café, coffee shop
ふどうさんや	不動産屋	real estate office
えきまえ	駅前	in front of the train station

6 New Phrases あたらしい かいわ

1. そうでもないです。   That's not the case.
2. 気をつけて（下さい）。   Be careful (please)
3. 気をつけます。   I will be careful.
4. かしこまりました。   Certainly. (store staff to customer)

6 Culture Clip カルチャー クリップ

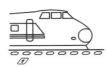

In the large cities of Japan, it is almost impossible to live without using the extensive train and subway system. The trains are clean, regular, safe and almost never late. If the train comes late, the first thing you should check is to make sure that your clock isn't wrong!

When you visit Japan make sure you get a Suica or Pasmo card at the train station. This card will make it very easy for you to enter and leave train stations. Normally you would need a ticket for each trip, but not with Suica and Pasmo cards, since they are prepaid. You simply tap your card on the turnstyle and it will open for you. You can also use both cards at convenience stores and many vending machines to pay for things with just a tap.

6 Grammar ぶんぽう

☐ **6-1. ～ても いいですか (Is it okay to ～, Is it okay to ～, May I ～)**

When asking if it is all right to do something, all you need to do is add もいいですか to the
て form of any verb.

> **て form verb + も いいですか。**
> **Is it all right if I [verb]?**

Example sentences

1. これを たべても いいですか。
   Is it all right if I eat this?

2. 中村さんの 家に いっても いいですか。
   Is it all right if I go to your house, Mr. Nakamura?

3. このジュースを のんでも いいですか。
   Is it okay if I drink this juice?

4. えいがを 見ても いいですか。
   Is it okay if I watch a movie?

5. 4じに かえっても いいですか。
   Is it okay if I return home at 4 o'clock?

☐ **6-2. ～ても いいです (It's all right to～, It's okay to～, You may ～)**

Use the pattern below when answering the question ～てもいいですか, and when simply
saying, "I can do this or that."

> **て form verb + も いいです。**
> **It is okay if you [verb].**

You might hear slight variations in the responses. For example, よ might be added at the
end. And it isn't even necessary to answer with the verb. You can simply say いいです
or いいですよ.

Example conversation 1:

A: 今日は びょうきだから、休んでも いいですか。

B: いいですよ。 ゆっくり、ねて下さい。

A: ありがとうございます。 明日は だいじょうぶだと おもいます。

B: わかりました。 じゃあ、また 明日。

A: I am sick today, so may I take the day off?

B: Okay. Please have a good rest.

A: Thank you. I think I will be fine tomorrow.

B: All right. See you tomorrow then.

Example conversation 2:

A: あのケーキは おいしそう ですね。 一つ、かっても いいですか。

B: いいよ。 ぼくも ちょっと たべても いいですか。

A: もちろん、だいじょうぶです。

A: Those cakes sure look delicious. Is it okay if I buy one?

B: It's okay. Is it okay if I eat a little?

A: Of course it's okay.

❏ 6-3. ～ては いけません It's not all right to ～ / You can't～

You would think that when someone asks [*verb*] ～ても いいですか, "Is it okay if I (do something)" you could just simply respond with [*verb*] ～ても よくないです, but this is not normal, nor is it grammatically or culturally correct.

It's important to remember that Japanese people don't like to be so direct when saying "no" to a request. Even a grammatically correct response like だめです (no) sounds very direct. You will normally respond with だめ only when you are speaking to young children.

Even then it can be so direct that you would only say it to your own children, as it would be strange to be so direct with someone else's children.

The official, grammatically correct and polite way to answer "no" to ~ても いいですか is as follows:

> て form verb + は いけません。(は pronounced わ)
> **It is not all right if you [verb].**

Example Q&A

1. この水を のんでも いいですか。
   Is it all right if I drink this water?

   いいえ、のん<u>では</u> いけません。
   No, it's not all right if you drink it.

   いいえ、それは わたしのです。
   No, that is mine.

2. あなたの車に のっても いいですか。
   Is it all right if I ride in your car?

   いいえ、のっ<u>ては</u> いけません。
   No, it's not all right if you ride.

   いいけど、せまいですよ。
   It's okay, but it's cramped.

❑ **6-4. Informal versions of ～ては いけません and ～てもいいですか**

Despite what your teachers might have taught you, informal speaking is very common in Japan. Even in business settings, once you know the people you are doing business with, the level of formality can be lower. Also, as a foreigner speaking Japanese, Japanese people will give you a lot of flexibility when speaking Japanese.

You can experiment with formality and find out what you feel more comfortable with.

The following informal version is commonly used when talking to children and even pets.

> ちゃ form verb + だめ。
> **You aren't allowed to [verb].**

The ちゃ form is made by replacing て with ちゃ or で with じゃ in the て form of any verb.

Examples

1. いって ⇒ いっちゃ (go)
2. たべて ⇒ たべちゃ (eat)
3. 見て ⇒ 見ちゃ (see, look)
4. よんで ⇒ よんじゃ (read)
5. して ⇒ しちゃ (do)
6. のんで ⇒ のんじゃ (drink)

You can also drop the も from the しても いいですか phrase and just ask して いい？ or して いいですか。して いい is informal but can be used by any age range.

> **て form verb + いい？**
> **Can I [verb]?**

Example Q&A

1. ママ 、 キャンディーを たべて いいの？
   Mama, can I eat some candy?

   たべちゃ だめ！
   No you can't eat!

2. おばあさん、 ゲームを しても いいですか。
   Grandma, can I play a game.

   べんきょうが おわるまでは しちゃだめよ。
   You can't play until you're done with your studies.

   > Verb + まで (until verb) is convered in Lesson 12

3. パパ 、 犬と あそんで いい？
   Papa can I play with the dog?

   あそんで いいよ。
   Yes you can play.

   > You can't say あそんじゃ いいよ. The じゃ version can only be used with だめ.

   しゅくだいが おわるまで あそんじゃ だめ！
   Until you're done with homework you can't play!

4. プールで およいで いい？
   Can I swim in the pool?

   今日は さむいから およいじゃ だめだよ。
   You can't swim because it's cold today.

   ５じに おじいさんの 家に いくけど、 ４じまで およいで いいよ。
   We are going to grandfather's house at 5 o'clock, but you can swim until 4 o'clock.

❏ 6-5. Let's not be rude (politely telling someone "no")

If someone asks you a しても いいですか question, in most cases you will NOT want to answer with しては いけません. Instead you should answer with the positive answer いいですよ or a softened negative answer, as we learned in Lesson 2.

Example Q&A

1. 明日、車を かりても いいですか。
   Can I borrow your car tomorrow?

   明日は つかうので ちょっと できないです。(ちょっと is a softener)
   Since I am going to use it tomorrow I can't do it.

2. ケイタイを つかっても いいですか。
   Can you use your cell phone?

   でんちが あんまりないので、すみません。
   Since there isn't much battery, sorry.
   (maybe this isn't true but it's better than just saying "NO")

3. さいごの りんごを たべても いいですか。
   Can I eat the last apple?

   わたしの りんごじゃないので、わからないです。
   It's not my apple so I don't know.
   (Don't use this one if you are the only one living in the house!)

❏ 6-6. A review of けど and でも

Before we introduce the next sentence connector, が (but), it's important that you recall how the other "but" words we have learned are used. In prior courses we have learned けど and でも. でも is not a connector, but is used at the beginning of a sentence.

Example sentences（でも）

1. お金が ないです。<u>でも</u>、じかんは たくさんあります。

   I don't have money. But I have a lot of time.

2. いもうとに このドレスを あげたくないです。<u>でも</u>、このくつは あげても いいです。

   I don't want to give this dress to my younger sister. But it's okay to give these shoes.

けど is used to combine two sentences into one. In the sentence 日本に いきたいけど、 フランスには いきたくないです, you will notice that フランスに has a は after it to stress the fact that you do not want to go to France. It is *very* common for "but" sentences to follow this pattern. You generally begin by saying a supporting fact that enhances the main point of your statement.

If, for instance, you like rap music but hate rock music, the most important thing you want to convey is stated in the second half.

Example sentences （けど）

1. お金が ないけど、 じかんは たくさんあります。
   I don't have money but I have a lot of time.

2. いもうとに このドレスを あげたくないけど、 このくつは あげても いいです。
   I don't want to give this dress to my younger sister, but it's okay to give these shoes.

It really doesn't matter if you use けど or でも in your speaking but you will hear けど a lot more in everyday Japanese conversations since it flows better.

❑ 6-7. Connecting sentences with が

Sentences can also be connected using a が. The が used to connect the sentences means "but" or "however." This way of connecting sentences is most commonly used with polite sentences. For informal conversations けど will be used instead of が。

Example sentences

1. ラップが すきですが、ロックは きらいです。
   I like rap music, but I hate rock music.

2. 東京に いきますが、京都には いきません。
   I will go to Tokyo, but I will not go to Kyoto.

3. 学校で 勉強しますが、家では 勉強しません。
   I study at school, but I don't study at home.

Usage wise, が is similar to けど, however notice in the prior example sentences that the sentence that comes before が is always in the polite form, whereas the sentence that comes before けど sounds more natural with an informal sentence.

6 Mini Conversation ミニかいわ J→E

1. Polite conversation between friends at a party.

A: これは おいしそうですね。 たべても いいですか。

B: いいですよ。何だと おもいますか。

A: とりにく ですか。

B: いいえ、ちがいます。かえるの足ですよ！

A: This sure looks delicious. Is it okay if I eat it?

B: Yes, it's okay. What do you think it is?

A: Is it chicken?

B: No, it's not. It's a frog's leg!

2. Polite but direct conversation between a woman and a man who dislikes her.

A: いまから 田中さんの家に いっても いいですか。

B: いいえ、こないで 下さい。いまから しゅくだいを しますから。

A: じゃ、明日は どうですか。

B: 明日は ともだちと サッカーをします。 ごめんなさい。

A: Is it all right if I go to your house, Mr. Tanaka?

B: No, please don't come because I am going to start doing homework now.

A: Well then, how about tomorrow?

B: I am going to play soccer with my friends. Sorry.

3. Casual conversation between a mother and her son.

A: ひるごはんと ケーキが れいぞうこの 中に あるよ。

B: わかった。学校から 帰ってから たべるよ。

A: ごはんの まえに ケーキを たべちゃだめだよ。

B: わかった。わかった。

A: There is lunch and some cake in the refrigerator.

B: Okay, I will eat after I return from school.

A: Don't eat the cake before the meal!

B: I know. I know.

4. Polite conversation between a waitress and a customer.

A: クレジットカードで はらっても いいですか。

B: いいえ、小切手か 現金で おねがいします。

A: そうですか。じゃあ、現金で はらいます。

B: はい。六千四百円です。

A: Is it all right if I pay by credit card?

B: No, check or cash please.

A: I see. Well then, I will pay with cash.

B: Okay. It is 6,400 yen.

6 | Mini Conversation ミニかいわ E→J

In the conversation below it might seem weird for A: to ask "Is it alright if I ask them on the phone?" but Japanese people have a culture of asking for permission.

1. Polite conversation between friends

A: Since it is close to the train station, this apartment appears to be expensive.

B: That is not the case. This place is cheap.

A: How did you find the apartment?

B: I went to the real estate broker in front of the train station. They are nice over there.

A: I am also looking for a cheap apartment. Is it alright if I ask them on the phone?

B: Of course. The phone number is 88-6549

A: えきに ちかいから、このアパートは たかそうですね。

B: そうでもないですよ。 ここは やすいです。

A: どうやって このアパートを さがしましたか。

B: えきまえの ふどうさんやに いきました。あそこは しんせつですよ。

A: わたしも やすいアパートを さがしています。でんわで きいても いいですか。

B: もちろん。でんわばんごうは 八八の 六五四九です。

> Hypens in numbers are often said as の

2. Polite conversation between friends

A: I bought some new clothes.

B: That's nice. What kind of clothes?

A: A red one piece dress. I am going to wear it at a party.

B: Would it be okay if I saw it? (Can I see it?)

A: Of course.

A: あたらしい ふくを かいました。

B: いいですね。どんな ふくですか。

A: 赤の ワンピースです。 パーティで きます。

B: 見ても いいですか。

A: もちろん。

3. Polite conversation between a car salesman and a customer.

A: What kind of car would you like?

B: I would like a small, new car, but I only have $10,000.00.

A: This car is $9,500.00.

B: It's nice. Is it all right if I take a ride in it?

A: Yes. Go ahead and take a ride.

A: どんな 車が いいですか。

B: 小さくて、あたらしい 車が ほしいですが、一まんドルしか ありません。

A: この車は 九千五百ドルですよ。

B: いいですね。のっても いいですか。

A: はい、どうぞ のって下さい。

4. Polite conversation between a yoga instructor and a woman

A: From what time until what time is the yoga class.

B: It's Mondays and Wednesdays, from ten to eleven.

A: That sounds good. Can I join the class?

B: Sure. Please don't be late.

A: ヨガの クラスは 何じから 何じまで ですか。

B: 月曜日と 水曜日の 十じから 十一じまで です。

A: いいですね。クラスに 入っても いいですか。

B: いいですよ。 おくれないで 下さいね。

6 | Reading Comprehension どっかい

Read the sentences below. If you don't understand them, you should review the grammar in this lesson until you do. After you have understood everything, complete the reading comprehension questions in the *Activities* section of this lesson.

① スミスさんは はじめて 東京に いきました。

② 日本には ともだちが ぜんぜん いないから、一人で りょこうしました。

③ 一日目は かいものを してから、きっさてんに 入りました。

きっさてんで。

スミスさん:	すみません。コーヒーを 下さい。
ウェイトレス:	ホットですか、アイスですか。
スミスさん:	ホットで おねがいします。
ウェイトレス:	はい、かしこまりました。

三十分ご。

スミスさん:	すみません、コーヒーだいは ここで はらっても いいですか。
ウェイトレス:	おかんじょうは あそこの レジで はらって 下さい。
スミスさん:	ああ、そうですか。わかりました。

レジで。

ウェイトレス:	三百五十円です。
スミスさん:	チップも ここで はらっても いいですか。
ウェイトレス:	いいえ、ここは 日本ですから、チップは はらわなくても いいですよ。

6 | Lesson Activities

❑ Reading comprehension questions

Answer the following questions about the reading comprehension from the previous page.

1. スミスさんは むかし、日本に いったことが ありますか。

   _____

2. 一日目に 何を しましたか。

   _____

3. 日本の きっさてんでは テーブルで お金を はらいますか。

   _____

4. あなたの国<small>くに</small>では、何パーセント、チップを はらっていますか。

   _____

❑ Sentence Patterns

Modify the sentence by adding the parts listed. You can add and remove parts as needed so that the final sentence makes sense.

> **Ex.** ミルクを かって下さい。
> → to drink   ミルクを のんで下さい。
> → don't buy   ミルクを かわないで下さい。

1. やちんを はらって下さい。

   → bill (at a restaurant) _____

   → Did you pay? _____

   → I didn't pay _____

   → tip _____

2. うんてんしても いいですか。

→ look   _____

→ eat   _____

→ turn right   _____

→ make dinner   _____

3. 家を 出ます。

→ Is it ok if I leave?   _____

→ It is not ok if you leave   _____

→ want to leave   _____

→ at 10 o'clock   _____

❏ Translation

Translate the following sentences into Japanese.

1. It's ok if you go by the elevator, but it's not ok if you go up by the escalator.

   _____

2. I want to drink coffee, but I won't because I can't sleep.

   _____

3. There is only one cake (left), but is it ok if I eat it?

   _____

4. I always drive, but I will go to school on foot today.

   _____

5. You can turn right here, but please be careful.

   _____

❏ **Short Dialogue**

Ken is going to have lunch with his spoiled girlfriend.

けん:　　　　ゆみこちゃん。お腹が空いたね。何を食べる？

ゆみこ:　　　あのフレンチのレストランで 食べてもいい？

けん:　　　　えっ、あの高級なところで？

ゆみこ:　　　もうすぐ 私の誕生日でしょう。

　　　　　　　おいしい物を食べようよ。

けん:　　　　分かったよ。じゃあ、行こう。

レストランの中で

ゆみこ:　　　すみません。ワインリストを見せて下さい。

ウェイター:　はい、かしこまりました。

けん:　　　　えっ、昼間からワインを飲むの？

ゆみこ:　　　当たり前でしょう？ 赤ワインを飲んでもいい？

けん:　　　　いいよ...

ゆみこ:　　　それと、前菜にキャビアを食べてもいい？

けん:　　　　ワインは いいけど、キャビアは ちょっと...

ゆみこ:　　　けっち！

けん:　　　　...

❑ New Words and Expressions in the dialogue

Progressive	Kanji +	English
こうきゅう（な）	高級（な）	high end, high class
たべよう	食べよう	Let's eat (informal)
いこう	行こう	Let's go (informal)
見せる	見せる	to show
ひる間	昼間	daytime, during the day
ぜんさい	前菜	appetizer
もうすぐ	もうすぐ	almost, very shortly
けっち	けっち	stingy
あたりまえでしょう？	当たり前でしょう？	Do you even need to ask? Of course!

❑ Short Dialogue Activities

Practice reading the short dialogue in pairs.

Play the girlfriend role and tell your partner what you want to eat and drink.

❑ Practice

Give some advice to the following people using any of the following:

〜てはいけません、 〜て下さい、 〜ないで下さい.

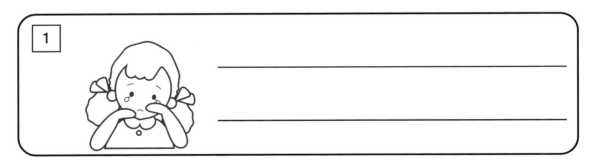

2

_____

_____

3

_____

_____

Kanji Lesson
6

原戸古午後語

kanji 111-116

六 New Kanji あたらしい漢字

Practice writing each new kanji in the boxes provided. First trace the light gray samples while paying attention to stroke order. Then on a separate piece of paper practice writing the sample kanji words at least five times each.

原	くんよみ	はら	number		111
	おんよみ	ゲン	meaning	field, source, origin	

のはら 野原	げんいん 原因	げんざいりょう 原材料	げんさん 原産	げんこく 原告
field	cause, reason	raw materials	country of origin	plaintiff, prosecutor

10 strokes

一 厂 厂 厂 盾 盾 盾 原 原 原

原 原 原 原 原

戸	くんよみ	と	number		112
	おんよみ	コ	meaning	door	

とぐち 戸口	とだな 戸棚	とまど 戸惑う	こせき 戸籍	ひ　ど 引き戸
door	cupboard	to be bewildered	official family registry	sliding door

4 strokes

一 ラ ヨ 戸

戸 戸 戸 戸 戸

古	くんよみ	ふる（い）	number	113
	おんよみ	コ	meaning	old

ふる 古い	ふるほん 古本	ふる ぎ 古着	ちゅうこしゃ 中古車	ふる お古
old	secondhand books	secondhand clothing	used car	used article

5 strokes

一 十 古 古 古

古 古 古 古 古

午	くんよみ	–	number	114
	おんよみ	ゴ	meaning	noon

ごぜん 午前	ご ご 午後	しょうご 正午	うまどし 午年	ごぜんさま 午前様
morning, A.M.	afternoon, P.M.	noon	Year of the horse	person who stays out all night

4 strokes

ノ ⌐ 午 午

午 午 午 午 午

後	くんよみ	のち、うし、あと、おく（れる）	number	115
	おんよみ	ゴ、コウ	meaning	after, behind, later

こうはん 後半	あとまわ 後回し	のちほど 後程	さいご 最後	あとかたづ 後片付け
second half	to postpone	momentarily	last	tidying up

9 strokes

ノ ク ク イ 彳 彳 径 後 後 後

後 後 後 後 後

語	くんよみ	かた		number		116
	おんよみ	ゴ		meaning		speak, word, language

かた 語る	ごがく 語学	けいご 敬語	ものがたり 物語	えいご 英語
to talk, speak	language study	honorific language	story	English

14 strokes

ヽ ⸗ ⸗ 言 言 言 言 訓 訓 語 語 語 語 語

語	語	語	語	語									

六　Kanji Drills 漢字ドリル

❑ **Words you can write**

Write the following words in the boxes. This is a great way to practice the new kanji and review the words at the same time. For the kanji that hasn't been taught yet, use hiragana.

そうげん
草原
grasslands, meadow

草	原									

のはら
野原
field

野	原									

とぐち
戸口
door, doorway

戸	口									

ひ　ど
引き戸
sliding door

引	き	戸							

ふる
古い
old

古い

ふるほん
古本
used book

古本

ちゅう こ しゃ
中古車
used car

中古車

しょう ご
正午
noon

正午

ご ご
午後
afternoon, PM

午後

うし
後ろ
behind, back

後ろ

かた
語る
to talk, to recite

語る

ご がく
語学
language study

語学

❑ Fill in the kanji

Fill in the blanks in the following sentences with the appropriate kanji.

いぬ　　そう　げん　　　　　　まわ
1. ___は___ ___を はしり___りました。

The dog ran around the meadow.

2. この___<ruby>き<rt>ひ</rt></ruby>___<ruby>ど<rt></rt></ruby>は___<ruby>ふる<rt></rt></ruby>いですか。
Is this sliding door old?

3. きょう___<ruby>ご<rt></rt></ruby> ___<ruby>ご<rt></rt></ruby>に___<ruby>あ<rt></rt></ruby>いましょう。
Let's meet today in the afternoon.

4. ___<ruby>に<rt></rt></ruby> ___<ruby>ほん<rt></rt></ruby> ___<ruby>ご<rt></rt></ruby>で___<ruby>うた<rt></rt></ruby>を ___<ruby>うた<rt></rt></ruby>いました。
I sang a song in Japanese.

5. わたしは ___<ruby>ちゅう<rt></rt></ruby> ___<ruby>こ<rt></rt></ruby> ___<ruby>しゃ<rt></rt></ruby>を うっています。
I sell used cars.

6. ___<ruby>うし<rt></rt></ruby>ろに___<ruby>せん<rt></rt></ruby> ___<ruby>せい<rt></rt></ruby>が いますよ。
The teacher is behind you.

六　Kanji Recognition 漢字にんしき

❏ Individual words

The following words will no longer have any ふりがな (hiragana on top). You might already know some of these words, but don't worry if you can't write them as recognition is the goal.

生きる	金魚	早く	早い
to be alive	goldfish	early, soon, quickly	early (adj)

天気	木	名前	大学
weather	tree	name	college

おし
教える

あめ
雨

to teach　　　　rain

❏ Word groups (years old)

The following word group will no longer have any ふりがな (hiragana on top). There are two ways to write "years old" in kanji, 才 and 歳. 歳 is complicated as it has many strokes, so many Japanese people write the simpler 才. Both should be recognized to mean "years old".

いっさい
一歳
one year old

いっさい
一才
one year old

じっさい
十歳
10 years old

じっさい
十才
10 years old

じゅうごさい
十五歳
15 years old

さい
15才
15 years old

ひゃくさい
100歳
100 years old

なんさい
何歳
How old?

❏ Kanji recognition notes

Similarly to 十回 being read as じっかい, 十歳 and 十才 are read officially as じっさい however are commonly read and said as じゅっさい.

Also keep in mind that numbers in Japanese are many times written in the arabic numbers, 1,2,3 etc. In order to allow for more practice with the kanji numbers we will keep using kanji numbers for the majority of numbers in this book.

❑ **Kanji recognition cards**

Print and cut out these cards, then write the hiragana and English meaning on the back.

Now you can easily practice your kanji recognition.

生きる	金魚	早く	早い
天気	木	名前	大学
教える	雨	一歳	一才
十歳	十才	十五歳	15才
100歳	何歳	何才	

Making decisions

Before This Lesson

1. Be able to read and write 原戸古午後語.

Lesson Goals

1. Learn how to tell something you have decided or something that has been decided by somebody else.
2. Learn to distinguish between an active and a passive decision.
3. Learn how to connect sentences with ので.

From The Teachers

1. Pay attention to how the verbs きめる and きまる work in this lesson since this pattern type will show up again.

Lesson Highlights

7-8. Using する to choose things

7-9. ことにする (to decide on, choose to do something)

7-10. Rules of behavior ことにしています

7-11. ことになる (it has been decided, it has come to be)

7-12. Connecting sentences with ので

7-13. Using かどうか to say "or not"

7 | New Words あたらしい ことば

日本語	漢字	えいご
そつぎょう	卒業	graduation
そつぎょう りょこう	卒業旅行	graduation trip
しゃいん りょこう	社員旅行	company trip (for fun)
しんこん りょこう	新婚旅行	honeymoon
しんろ	進路	course, route, way
オーストラリア	オーストラリア	Australia
イギリス	イギリス	England
とこ	所	place (same as ところ)
すごく	凄く	very
もっと	もっと	more
ので	ので	since, because
しゃくり	しゃくり	the hiccups
うんどう	運動	excercise, motion
ちょうれい	朝礼	morning assembly (meeting)
てき	敵	enemy

7 | New Adjectives あたらしい けいようし

日本語	漢字	えいご	タイプ
たいへん	大変	hard, awful, terrible	な adjective
さいこう	最高	awesome, great	な adjective

7 | Adjectives Usage けいようしの つかいかた

❑ 7-1. さいこう (awesome, great, amazing)

Even though さいこう is a な adjective you will hear it used with both な and の when it's modifying a word. If you search the web for both versions, 最高の and 最高な, you will find plenty of examples for both being used.

Example sentences

1. ゴジラは さいこう<u>の</u> えいがです。
   Godzilla is an amazing movie.

2. あなたは さいこう<u>の</u> ともだちです。
   You are a great friend.

3. 今日は さいこう<u>の</u> 日でした。
   Today was an awesome day.

4. 昨日 さいこう<u>の</u>本を よみました。
   Yesterday I read an amazing book.

5. この本は さいこうです。
   This book is amazing.

7　Culture Clip カルチャー・クリップ

The largest travel agency in Japan and one of the largest in the world is a company called JTB (Japan Travel Bureau). Many Japanese companies offer their employees domestic or foreign trips every year or two. When Japanese college and some high school students graduate, many take a trip to celebrate. Also, many newlyweds travel abroad for their honeymoon.

7　New Verbs あたらしい どうし

どうし	えいご	た form	タイプ
辞める	to quit one's job or responsibility	やめた	いる/える
止める	to stop, to quit	やめた	いる/える
決める	to decide	きめた	いる/える
決まる	to be decided, be settled	きまった	regular
生きる	to be alive	いきた	いる/える
死ぬ	to die	しんだ	regular

7 | Verb Usage どうしの つかいかた

❏ 7-2. 辞める (to quit one's job, to resign)

The thing you are quitting is marked with を. 辞める is used to quit jobs and activities such as club, playing an instrument etc.

Example sentences

1. 今日、しごとを 辞めました。
   I quit my job today.

2. いそがしいから、テニスクラブを 辞めます。
   I am busy, so I am going to leave the tennis club.

3. 勉強を 辞めては いけません。
   You shouldn't stop studying.

❏ 7-3. 止める (to stop, to quit)

The thing you are ending is marked with を. 止める is used to stop a plan, quit smoking or other habits etc.

Example sentences

1. タバコを 止めました。
   I quit smoking.

2. どうやって しゃくりを 止めますか。
   How do you stop the hiccups?

3. おもしろくないから、このゲームを 止めます。
   I am going to stop this game because it's not interesting.

❑ 7-4. きめる (to decide, to choose) active verb

きめる and the following verb きまる are the first 'active' and 'passive' verb sets that you will learn in this series. きめる is used when YOU or someone is actively deciding something. The item you are deciding is marked with を. The item you have selected is marked with に.

Example sentences

1. これに きめました。
   I decided <u>on</u> this.

2. 一つ、きめて下さい。
   Please choose one.

3. りょこうの日を きめましたか?
   Have you decided your trip date?

4. ドレスを きめたいです。
   I want to choose a dress.

5. 五月三日に きめました。
   I decided <u>on</u> May 3rd.

6. まだ きめていません。
   I haven't decided yet.

7. らいしゅう がっこうを きめます。
   I will decide the school next week.

8. どの車に きめましたか。
   Which car did you decide <u>on</u>?

❑ 7-5. きまる (to be decided, to be settled, determined) passive

きまる is very different from きめる. When きまる is used it means the decision was not decided by any one person actively. It is normally used to describe something that was decided by a committee or group where the speaker didn't have any direct involvement. Also you will notice that the particle marking the item decided is now が and not を.

Example sentences

1. しゃいんりょこうの日が きまりました。
   The date of our company's trip has been decided.

2. むすめの そつぎょうが きまりました。
   My daughter's graduation has been decided.

3. つぎの しごとが きまっていません。
   My next job has not been decided.

4. ことしの なつの アルバイトが きまりました。
   My summer part time job has been determined.

❑ 7-6. いきる (to be alive)

The most common form of this verb is 生きています to say "I am alive" or to ask a friend if

someone is alive or not, 生きていますか.

> **Example sentences**
>
> 1. あなたの おとうさんは まだ生きていますか。
>   Is your father still alive?
>
> 2. 100 歳まで生きることが むずかしいです。
>   Living until 100 years old is difficult.
>
>   > VERB + こと is taught in lesson 8.
>
> 3. 100 歳までは 生きたくないです。
>   I don't want to live until 100 years old.
>
> 4. エインスタインは もう 生きていません。
>   Einstein is no longer living.

❑ 7-7. しぬ (to die)

There are more polite ways to say someone is dead besides しぬ such as なくなる but し

ぬ is a very commonly used verb. It can be used to talk about death for people and for even

electronics and cars.

> **Example sentences**
>
> 1. 私の金魚が 死にました。
>   My goldfish died.
>
> 2. ともだちが かっていたうまが 死にました。
>   The horse my friend was raising died.
>
> 3. 200 年まえの ひとたちは みんな 死んでいます。
>   All people from 200 years ago are dead.
>
>   > ています form is used because death is an ongoing state.
>
> 4. 早く死にたくないから毎日エクササイズをしています。
>   Since I don't want to die early, I exercise every day.

7 Grammar ぶんぽう

❑ 7-8. Using する to choose things

You just learned きめる to say "I decide". Now we will learn another way to say you choose something. The verb する combined with the particle に can be used to say that something will be chosen over another item. する can only be used as a decision word when combined with に. With any other particle its usage changes. Also you can NOT use する to just say "I decided." For that you must use きめる。

> [thing] に する
> to choose [thing]

Example Q&A

1. のみものは 何が いいですか。
   What would you like to drink?

   オレンジジュースに します。
   I'll have orange juice.

   日本ちゃに します。
   I'll have Japanese tea.

3. どのねこに しますか。
   What cat are you choosing?

   ちゃいろのに します。
   I choose the brown one.

   りょうほうに します。
   I choose both.

5. のみものは 何に したの？
   What drink did you choose?

   コーラに した。
   I chose coke.

2. 明日、何を きますか。
   What are you going to wear tomorrow?

   赤いドレスに します。
   (I choose) a red dress.

   スーツに します。
   (I choose) a suit.

4. りょこうは どこに しますか？
   Where are you taking your trip?

   ハワイに しました。
   I chose Hawaii.

   まだ、きめていない。
   I haven't decided yet.

6. 何の 車を かったの？
   What car did you buy?

   トヨタ カムリーに しました。
   I went with (chose) a Toyota Camry.

❏ 7-9. ことにする (to decide on, choose to do something)

You can add to the prior grammar by adding ことにする to any informal verb to say things like たべる ことに しました (I've decided to eat). Although there is the verb きめる (to decide), you can use ことにする to say they will, have decided, or chose to do something.

> **informal verb + ことにする**
> **I will decide to (verb).**

Example sentences

1. あなたと いくことに しました。
   I have decided to go with you.

2. 帰ることに しました。
   I decided to go home.

3. ４じに おきることに した。
   I have decided to wake up at 4 o'clock.

4. いかないことに しました。
   I decided not to go.

❏ 7-10. ことにしています (I make it a rule to-)

When you use ことに しています now you are saying something equivalent to "I make it a rule to do this" or "It's my policy to do this". The actual English translation can vary as long as the point is made.

> **informal verb + ことにしています**
> **I make it a rule (verb).**

Example sentences

1. にくを たべないことに しています。
   I have decided not to eat meat. / I don't eat meat. / It's my policy to not eat meat.

2. おさけを のまないことに しています。
   I have decided not to drink alcohol. / I don't drink alcohol.

3. まいあさ ６じに おきることに しています。
   I have made it a rule to wake up every morning at 6 o'clock.

4. しゅうに ３かい うんどうを することに しています。
   I have made it a rule to exercize 3 times a week.

5. ヘルシーな たべものを たべることに しています。

I have made it a rule to eat healthy foods.

6. 毎日 30 ぷん 日本語を勉強することに しています。

I have made it a rule to study Japanese 30 minutes everyday.

❑ 7-11. ことになる (it has been decided, it has come to be, it's a rule)

This is used when something has been decided or something has come about without the direct control of the speaker or person being talked about.

> **informal form verb + ことになる**
> **It has been decided [*verb*].**

Example sentences

1. 東京に てんきんする ことに なりました。

   It was decided that I would transfer to Tokyo.

2. 会社を やめる ことに なりました。

   It was decided that I would quit my company.

3. 明日、学校に いく ことに なっています。

   I am supposed to go to school tomorrow.

   > ことに なっています is used to show a rule, decision, or policy that is current and ongoing.

4. 学校の パーティでは、おさけを のまない ことに なっています。

   It has been decided not to drink alcohol at school parties.

5. この会社では あさ 7 じに ちょうれいが はじまることに なっています。

   At this company there is a rule that the morning assembly starts at 7 o'clock.

6. 来年 けっこんすることに なりました。

   It's been decided I am getting married next year.

7. 来月からは ドイツで はたらくことに なりました。

   I will be working in Germany from next month.

Look at the example Q&A below. The first question uses ことになる, and the second one uses ことにする. Notice the difference.

Example Q&A

1. 来月、京都に てんきんする ことに なりました。
   <ruby>来月<rt>らいげつ</rt></ruby>
   It was decided that I will transfer to Kyoto next month.

   それは たいへん ですね。
   That sure is hard?

   はい、ききました。がんばって下さいね。
   Yes, I heard that. Please do your best.

2. 今日、田中さんと たべる ことに しました。トムさんも どうですか。
   Today I decided to eat with Mr. Tanaka. Would you like to join us, Tom?

   はい、いきたいです。
   Yes, I would like to go.

   今日は ちょっと・・・
   Today is a little...

3. 林さんは 何に しますか。
   What are you going to have, Mrs. Hayashi?

   ビールに します。
   I will have a beer.

   まだ きめていません。
   I haven't decided yet.

❑ 7-12. Connecting sentences with ので

ので means the same thing as から and is also used when connecting sentences. The difference is that it has a more formal sound.

Example sentences
1. <ruby>子供<rt>こども</rt></ruby>が いる<u>ので</u> 毎日、たのしいです。
   I am happy every day because I have children.

2. お金が ない<u>ので</u> レストランに いけません。
   I can't go to a restaurant because I have no money.

3. シアトルは 雨の日が おおい<u>ので</u>、いつも かさを もっています。
   There are a lots of rainy days in Seattle, so I always bring my umbrella.

4. もう おそい<u>ので</u>、帰りましょうか。
   It is late already, so shall we go home?

If you are connecting a sentence that would end in です, such as with nouns and な adjectives, then you must use なので.

> **Example sentences**
> 1. 明日は 月曜日<u>なので</u> 学校に いきます。
>   Because tomorrow is Monday, I will go to school.
>
> 2. おもしろい本<u>なので</u> よんだほうが いいです。
>   It's an interesting book so you should read it.

❑ 7-13. Using かどうか to say "to do or not"

When you don't know something, you often say phrases like "I don't know if I am going or not." This is easy to say by combining かどうか after an う form verb.

> **Example sentences**
> 1. 東京に <u>すむかどうか</u>まだ きめていません。
>   I haven't decided if <u>I will live</u> in Tokyo <u>or not</u> yet.
>
> 2. ともだちが <u>くるかどうか</u>わかりません。
>   I don't know if my friend <u>will come or not</u>.
>
> 3. 明日、<u>いくかどうか</u>は わかりません。
>   I don't know <u>if I am going</u> tomorrow <u>or not</u>.
>
> 4. お金が <u>たりるか</u>は わかりません。
>   I don't know <u>if I have enough</u> money.
>
> 5. かれは 日本語が <u>わかるか</u>は わかりません。
>   I don't know <u>if he understands</u> Japanese.

> You can also say just
> <u>う form VERB + か</u> to make
> sentences without "or not".

The following example sentences are made using い and な adjectives, nouns, and a variety of verb forms in combination with かどうか. The final verb can be a variety of verbs as you will see in the following examples.

Example sentences

1. 明日、<u>休むかどうか</u>は まだ きめていません。
   I haven't decided yet <u>if I will take time off or not</u> tomorrow.

2. このえいがは <u>おもしろいかどうか</u>を おしえて下さい。
   Please tell me if this movie <u>is interesting or not</u>.

3. 明日の 天気は <u>あついか</u> わかりません。
   I don't know if tomorrow's weather <u>will be hot</u>.

4. そのこうえんは <u>しずかかどうか</u>が わかりません。
   I don't know if that park <u>is quiet or not</u>.

Once you know how to use かどうか you can replace the どう with other verbs and adjectives to create more advanced sentences.

Example sentences

1. 明日は <u>あついか さむいか</u>が わかりません。
   I don't know whether tomorrow will be <u>hot or cold</u>.

2. かれは <u>ともだちなのか てきなのか</u> わからない！
   I don't know whether he is a friend or an enemy!

   > Like many Japanese sentences は or が may be dropped when speaking.

3. この木は <u>生きてるか しんでるか</u>が わかりません。
   I don't know if this tree <u>is alive or dead</u>.

4. いま <u>たべたいか のみたいか</u> わかりません。
   I don't know <u>whether I want to eat or want to drink</u> now.

7 Mini Conversation ミニかいわ J→E

1. Polite conversation between co-workers

A: 田中さんは いつも 何時に 会社に いきますか。

B: あさの 七時に いくことに しています。

A: 早いですね。 どうしてですか。

B: ゆっくり コーヒーを のんでから、しごとを するので。

A: What time do you go to work, Mr. Tanaka?
B: I make it a rule to get there at seven o'clock in the morning.
A: That is early. Why is that?
B: Because I start working after I drink coffee and relax.

2. Polite conversation between friends

A: 来年、日本語学校に いくことに なりました。

B: そうですか。よかったですね。

A: たくさん 勉強しないと いけないので、大変です。

B: がんばって下さい。

A: It was decided that I will go to a Japanese language school next year.
B: I see. That is good.
A: I have to study a lot, so it is going to be hard.
B: Please do your best.

3. Polite conversation between neighbors

A: らいしゅうから ジムに いくことに しました。

B: すごいですね。 どうして ですか。

A: さいきん、うんどうを していないので。

B: じつは、私も かんがえています。

A: I am going to the gym starting next week.
B: That is great. Why?
A: Because I haven't been working out recently.
B: Actually I am thinking about (doing that) too.

4. Polite conversation between friends

A: 車を かいたいけど、まよっています。

B: 何に まよっていますか。

A: ニッサンか トヨタを かいたいですが、きめられません。

A: I want to buy a car, but I am perplexed [unable to decide].

B: What are you perplexed about?

A: I want to buy either a Nissan or a Toyota, but I can't decide.

---

7 Mini Conversation ミニかいわ E→J

1. Polite conversation between a stranger and a person who got lost

A: Excuse me, I am lost. Where is Ueno station?

B: You go straight down this road and turn left at the second stoplight.

A: Thank you very much.

B: You are welcome.

A: すみません。みちに まよいました。上野えきは どこに ありますか。

B: このみちを まっすぐ いってから、二番目の しんごうで 左に まがります。

A: ありがとう ございました。

B: どういたしまして。

2. Polite conversation between students

A: My Japanese class is very hard.

B: How long have you been studying Japanese?

A: Let's see... about half a year.

B: That's still a short time.

A: Yes. I will do my best a little more. [I will decide to do my best a little more]

A: 日本語の じゅぎょうは とても むずかしいです。

B: どのぐらい 日本語を 勉強していますか。

A: そうですね。半年ぐらいです。

B: まだ みじかいですよ。

A: はい。もうちょっと、がんばることに します。

3. Polite conversation between friends

A: What are you going to do tomorrow?

B: I decided to play soccer with my friends.

A: Can I join you guys too?

B: Of course.

A: 明日 何を しますか。
<small>あした</small>

B: ともだちと サッカーを することに しました。

A: 私も 入っても いいですか。

B: もちろん。

---

7 | Reading Comprehension どっかい

Read the sentences below. If you don't understand them, you should review the grammar in this lesson until you do. Then answer the comprehension questions in the *Activities* section.

① 私の 名前は まりなです。

② 来年、大学を そつぎょうするので、すごく たのしみに しています。
<small>らいねん</small>

③ ともだちと そつぎょうりょこうに いくことに しました。

④ いく ところは まだ きめていません。

⑤ オーストラリアに いきたいという ともだちが います。

⑥ また、イギリスに いきたいという 人も います。

⑦ 私は オーストラリアと イギリスに いったことが あるので、
ニューヨークに いきたいと おもっています。

一年ご

⑧ そつぎょうりょこうは すごく たのしかったです。

⑨ みんなは いくばしょに まよいましたが、けっきょく、ニューヨークに
いくことにしました。

⑩ ニューヨークは あぶないとこだと ききましたが、だいじょうぶでした。

⑪ また いきたいと おもっています。

7 Lesson Activities

❏ Reading comprehension questions

Answer the following questions about the reading comprehension from the previous page.

1. まりなさんは 今、高校生ですか。
   _{こうこうせい}

   _____

2. まりなさんは オーストラリアに いきたいですか。

   _____

3. けっきょく、どこに いきましたか。

   _____

4. そこは あぶなかったですか。

   _____

5. あなたは そつぎょうりょこうを します。どこに いきたいですか。

   _____

❏ Sentence Patterns

Modify the sentence by adding the parts listed. You can add and remove parts as needed so that the final sentence makes sense.

> Ex. みなこさんは 日本に すんでいます。
>
> → America   みなこさんは アメリカに すんでいます。
>
> → Where?   みなこさんは どこに すんでいますか。

1. ともだちの家に いきます。

   → honeymoon   _____

   → company trip   _____

   → Is it ok if I ~?   _____

   → It is not good if you~ _____

2. 昨日、しごとを しました。

    → I quit   _____

    → I decided (chose)   _____

    → I decided not to go   _____

    → I decided to take a day off   _____

3. おちゃが のみたいです。

    → I will have…please (polite)   _____

    → Is it ok if I drink…?   _____

    → It is not ok if you have…   _____

    → I decided to drink   _____

    → I have drunk before   _____

❑ Practice

A) Make sentences using ~ ことにする and the pictures below.

1. I have decided to play golf.

_____

_____

2. I have decided to go on a business trip by airplane.

_____

_____

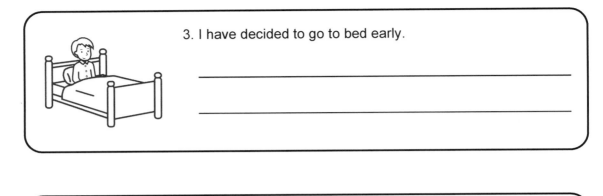

3. I have decided to go to bed early.

_____

_____

4. I have decided to quit smoking.

_____

_____

B) Make sentences using ～ことになる and the pictures below.

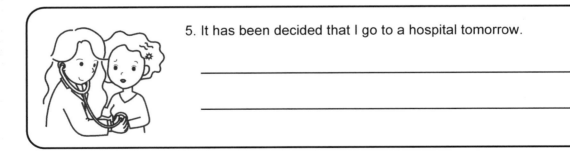

5. It has been decided that I go to a hospital tomorrow.

_____

_____

6. It has been decided that I graduate college next month.

_____

_____

7. It has been decided that I take medicine once a day.

_____

_____

❏ Short Dialogue

Mr. Tanaka is having a job interview at a trading company.

面接官（めんせつかん）:　田中さんは 営業（えいぎょう）をしたことがありますか。

田中さん:　はい、あります。 ガス会社（がいしゃ）で 五年間、していました。

面接官:　営業（えいぎょう）の仕事（しごと）に むいていると 思（おも）いますか。

田中さん:　はい、思（おも）います。 私は外交的（がいこうてき）ですので、事務（じむ）より 営業のほうが
合（あ）っています。

面接官:　そうですか。じゃあ、あなたのセールスポイントを もっと教えて
下さい。

田中さん:　はい。 私は 積極的（せっきょくてき）で 人との会話（かいわ）が得意（とくい）です。

そして、時間（じかん）に正確（せいかく）ですので、締（し）め切（き）りに 遅（おく）れません。

面接官:　では、プレッシャーにも 強いですか。 この業界（ぎょうかい）は 厳（きび）しいですよ。

田中さん:　はい、大丈夫（だいじょうぶ）です。 おねがいします。

❏ New Words and Expressions in the dialogue

Progressive	Kanji +	English
えいぎょう	営業	sales and marketing
じむ	事務	office work
～に むく	～に向く	to be suited for
がいこうてき	外交的	out going, diplomatic
あう	合う	to fit, match
セールスポイント	セールスポイント	selling point (reason for being good)
せっきょくてき	積極的	aggressive, positive
とくい	得意	good at
せいかく	正確	accurate
しめきり	締め切り	deadline
ぎょうかい	業界	business field / world
きびしい	厳しい	strict, tough

❏ Short dialogue activities

1. Practice reading the preceding short dialogue in pairs.
2. Play Tanaka san's role and sell yourself to the interviewer.

You can use the following adjectives to describe your character.

まえむき 前向き positive, forward-looking	まじめ 真面目 serious, earnest	れいせい 冷静 calm, collected
しゃこうてき 社交的 sociable	き じょうず 聞き上手 good listener	はな じょうず 話し上手 good speaker
おお 大らか easygoing	しょうじき 正直 honest, sincere	

❑ Question and Answer

Answer the following questions using the words and patterns in this lesson.

1. しんこんりょこうに どこに いきたいですか / いきましたか。

_____

2. <ruby>高校<rt>こうこう</rt></ruby>を そつぎょうしてから、何を しましたか / しますか。

_____

3. いま、しんろに まよっていますか。

_____

4. 休みの日が きまっていますか。

_____

5. 毎日、何を することに していますか。

_____

Kanji Lesson 7

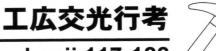

工広交光行考

kanji 117-122

七 **New Kanji あたらしい漢字**

Practice writing each new kanji in the boxes provided. Then on a separate piece of paper, practice writing the sample kanji words at least five times each.

工	くんよみ	–	number		117
	おんよみ	コウ、ク	meaning		artisan, work, craft

こうさく 工作	こうじょう 工場	く ふう 工夫	こうじ 工事	だい く 大工
handicraft	factory	scheme, device	construction work	carpenter

3 strokes

一 丁 工

工	工	工	工	工								

広	くんよみ	ひろ	number		118
	おんよみ	コウ	meaning		wide, broad, spread

ひろ 広い	こうこく 広告	せ びろ 背広	ひろ ま 広間	ひろ ば 広場
spacious	advertisement	business suit	hall	plaza

5 strokes

亠 广 広 広 広

広	広	広	広	広								

交	くんよみ	まじ・ま・か（わす）	number	119
	おんよみ	コウ	meaning	intercourse, exchange

か 交わす	こうつう 交通	こうさてん 交差点	こうばん 交番	こうりゅう 交流
to exchange (messages)	traffic	intersection; crossing	police box	to mix; alternating current

6 strokes

ᵃ 一 亠 六 六 亥 交

交 交 交 交 交

光	くんよみ	ひか（る）・ひかり	number	120
	おんよみ	コウ	meaning	light, shine, brilliance

かんこう 観光	げっこう 月光	こうねつひ 光熱費	こうえい 光栄	けいこうとう 蛍光灯
sight-seeing	moonlight	cost of fuel and heating	honor	fluorescent light

6 strokes

丨 丷 丷 当 屵 光

光 光 光 光 光

行	くんよみ	い・ゆ・おこな（う）	number	121
	おんよみ	コウ・ギョウ	meaning	go, do, conduct, stroke

い 行く	おこな 行う	ぎんこう 銀行	ぎょうれつ 行列	りょこう 旅行
to go	to perform	bank	line up, line	trip, travel

6 strokes

丿 彳 彳 彳 行 行

行 行 行 行 行

	くんよみ	かんが		number		122
考	おんよみ	コウ		meaning		think, consider

かんが 考え	かんが　ごと 考え事	び こう 備考	こうあん 考案	さんこう 参考
idea	(deep) thinking	note	plan	reference

6 strokes

一　十　土　耂　考　考

考	考	考	考	考									

七 Kanji Drills 漢字ドリル

❑ **Words you can write**

Write the following words in the boxes. This is a great way to practice the new kanji and review the words at the same time. For the kanji that hasn't been taught yet, use hiragana.

だい く
大工
carpenter

大	工									

こうさく
工作
handicraft

工	さ	く								

ひろ
広い
spacious, wide

広	い								

ひろ ま
広間
hall, spacious room

広	間									

交_まぜる
to mix, to blend

| 交 | ぜ | る | | | | | | | | | |

交通_{こうつう}
traffic

| 交 | つ | う | | | | | | | | | |

月光_{げっこう}
moonlight

| 月 | 光 | | | | | | | | | | |

光_{ひか}る
to shine

| 光 | る | | | | | | | | | | |

行_いく
to go

| 行 | く | | | | | | | | | | |

旅行_{りょこう}
trip, travel

| 旅 | 行 | | | | | | | | | | |

考_{かんが}える
to consider, to think

| 考 | え | る | | | | | | | | | |

参考_{さんこう}
reference

| さ | ん | 考 | | | | | | | | | |

❏ Fill in the kanji

Fill in the blanks in the following sentences with the appropriate kanji.

だい　く　　あめ　ひ

1. ___ ___は___の___に しごとが できません。

Carpenters can't work on rainy days.

2. あの___い___ ___で___ いましょう。
<small>ひろ　こう えん　　あ</small>

Let's meet in that spacious park.

3. つぎの___差点を___に まがって___さい。
<small>こう さてん　みぎ　　　　　くだ</small>

Please turn right at the next intersection.

4. 銀___に___ってから、___に ___ります。
<small>ぎん こう　　い　　　　　うち　かえ</small>

After I go to the bank I will return home.

5. ___えるとき へんな___をします。
<small>かんが　　　　　　　　　かお</small>

When I think I make a strange face.

6. ___ ___には たくさんの ___が___りますね。
<small>ひろ ま　　　　　　　　　　ひかり　はい</small>

A lot of light comes into the hall.

七 Kanji Recognition 漢字にんしき

❑ **Individual words**

The following words will no longer have any ふりがな (hiragana on top). You might already

know some of these words, but don't worry if you can't write them as recognition is the goal.

<small>えい ご</small> 英語 English language	<small>ご</small> 〜語 ~language	<small>ふる</small> 古い old	<small>じん せい</small> 人生 life
<small>こ ばやし</small> 小 林 last name	<small>しょう がっ こう</small> 小学校 elementary school	<small>ほん とう</small> 本当 real, truth	<small>い</small> 行く to go

❑ Word groups (hours and minutes)

The following word groups will no longer have any ふりがな (hiragana on top). You will learn 時 (じ) in this book in lesson 11, and 分 (ぶん) in book 5. That however won't stop you from being able to recognize them now.

いちじ 一時 1 o'clock	にじ 二時 2 o'clock	さんじ 三時 3 o'clock	よんじ 四時 4 o'clock
ごじ 五時 5 o'clock	ろくじ 六時 6 o'clock	しちじ 七時 7 o'clock	はちじ 八時 8 o'clock
くじ 九時 9 o'clock	じゅうじ 十時 10 o'clock	じゅういちじ 十一時 11 o'clock	じゅうにじ 十二時 12 o'clock
いっぷん 一分 1 minute	にふん 二分 2 minutes	さんぷん 三分 3 minutes	よんぷん 四分 4 minutes
ごふん 五分 5 minutes	ろっぷん 六分 6 minutes	ななふん 七分 7 minutes	はっぷん 八分 8 minutes
きゅうふん 九分 9 minutes	じっぷん 十分 10 minutes	じゅうごふん 十五分 15 minutes	さんじっぷん 三十分 30 minutes

❑ **Kanji recognition cards**

Print and cut out these cards, then write the hiragana and English meaning on the back.
Now you can easily practice your kanji recognition.

英語	〜語	古い	人生
小林	小学校	本当	行く
一時	二時	三時	四時
五時	六時	七時	八時
九時	十時	十一時	十二時
一分	二分	三分	四分
五分	六分	七分	八分
九分	十分	十五分	三十分

How do you do that?

Before This Lesson

1. Be able to read and write 工広交光行考.

Lesson Goals

1. Learn to say how something is done by conjugating the associated verb.
2. Learn how to say you are good or bad at something.

From The Teachers

1. There is an important grammar point hidden in the Verb Usage section under the verb びっくりする. Make sure you don't miss it!

Lesson Highlights

8-6. How to do something

8-7. Using 上手 and 下手 correctly

8-8. The difference between うまい and 上手

8-9. Making a verb phrases into a noun with の and こと

8-10. Different grammar same meaning

8 New Words あたらしい ことば

日本語	漢字	えいご
さいしょ	最初	first (at first, in the beginning)
パチンコ	パチンコ	Japanese pinball game
ぜったいに	絶対に	definitely, absolutely, positively
今度 <small>こんど</small>	今度	this time, next time
夜中 <small>よなか</small>	夜中	in the middle of the night
どうぐ	道具	tool
おべんとう	お弁当	lunch box
やきゅうじょう	野球場	baseball stadium
ソフト	ソフト	computer software

8 New Adjectives あたらしい けいようし

日本語	漢字	えいご	タイプ
むしあつい	蒸し暑い	muggy, hot and humid	い adjective
うまい	旨い、美味い	skillful, delicious, tasty	い adjective
とくい	得意	good at	な adjective

8 New Verbs あたらしい どうし

どうし	えいご	た form	タイプ
勝つ <small>か</small>	to win, to beat	かった	regular
当たる <small>あ</small>	to win, to strike, to hit	あたった	regular
負ける <small>ま</small>	to lose (opposite "to win")	まけた	いる/える
びっくりする	to be surprised	びっくりした	する verb
教える <small>おし</small>	to teach	おしえた	いる/える
捨てる <small>す</small>	to throw away	すてた	いる/える
迷う <small>まよ</small>	to get lost, be perplexed be uncertain, to hesitate	まよった	regular

8 Verb Usage どうしの つかいかた

❏ 8-1. かつ (to win, to beat) and まける (to lose)

No particle is necessary for counters such as money.

> 1. 四百ドル かちました。
> I won $400.00.
>
> 2. 四百ドル まけました。
> I lost $400.00.

The object particle に marks the thing that has been won or lost.

> 3. このレースに かちました。
> I won this race.
>
> 4. しあいに まけました。
> I lost the match.

The で particle is used to show the means by which something is won or lost.

> 5. パチンコで 千円 かちました。
> I won 1000 yen at pachinko
>
> 6. カジノで 千ドル まけました。
> I lost 1000 dollars at the casino.

The に particle is used to show who someone beat or whom someone lost to.

> 7. バスケットボールの しあいで、Aチームに かちました。
> We beat team A at the basketball game.
>
> 8. 漢字の しけんで スミスさんに まけました。
> I lost to Mr. Smith on the Kanji test.

❏ 8-2. びっくりする (to be surprised)

NOTE: The following examples for びっくりする are NOT just limited to this verb but can be used with an number of verbs and verb phrases.

The particle で is just one way to mark the reason for being surprised. It is used only after な adjectives and nouns.

Example sentences #1 (using で with な adjectives)

1. 英語が 上手<u>で</u>、びっくりしました。
   I was surprised that your English was good.

2. 田中さんの おくさんが きれい<u>で</u>、びっくりしました。
   I was surprised that Mr. Tanaka's wife was so beautiful.

3. 日本が べんり<u>で</u>、びっくりしました。
   I was surprised that Japan was so convenient.

4. まさひろくんは テニスが 上手<u>で</u>、びっくりしています。
   I am surprised Masahiro is so good at tennis.

When the reason for being surprised is an い adjective, the adjective can be conjugated to the くて form. When using the くて form of the adjective, the tense of the adjective is decided by the tense of the verb that follows.

Example sentences #2 （くて with い adjectives)

1. たか<u>くて</u>、びっくりしました。
   I was surprised it was expensive.

2. とても やす<u>くて</u>、びっくりしました。
   I was surprised that is was very cheap.

3. フロリダは むしあつ<u>くて</u>、びっくりしました。
   I was surprised Florida was so muggy.

With い adjectives, you can just add から after the adjective to say "because it's [adjective]. However, if you are using a な adjective or a noun, you must add だ (です) before から.

Example sentences #3 (な adjectives + から)

1. えい語が 上手<u>だから</u> びっくりしました。
   I was surprised that your English was good.

2. 田中さんの おくさんが きれい<u>だから</u>、びっくりしました。
   I was surprised that Mr. Tanaka's wife was so beautiful.

3. 日本が べんり<u>だから</u>、びっくりしました。
   I was surprised that Japan was convenient.

When using から with い adjectives, the tense of the adjective must be changed accordingly.

Note that the following examples are saying the same thing as 'Example sentences #2' in this section but using different grammar.

Example sentences #4 （い adjectives + から）

1. たかかった<u>から</u> びっくりしました。
   I was surprised because it was expensive.

2. とても やすかった<u>から</u> びっくりしました。
   I was surprised because it was very cheap.

NOTE: The grammar discussed for びっくりする for showing the reason for the surprise can also be used with other verbs.

❑ 8-3. おしえる (to teach)

The verb おしえる means "to teach." It is also very often used to mean "to tell." It is common for Japanese people to say 名前を おしえて下さい, "Tell me what your name is," or literally "teach me your name." The item being taught or told is marked with particle を.

Example sentences

1. 漢字を 教えて下さい。
   Please teach me kanji.

2. いもうとに フランス語を 教えました。
   I taught French to my younger sister.

3. 私は 学校で れきしを 教えています。
   I am teaching history at school.

4. 日本に いたときは 英語を 教えていました。
   When I was in Japan I was teaching English.

❏ 8-4. すてる (to throw away)

The verb すてる means "to throw away". The item being thrown away is marked with the object marker を.

Example sentences

1. ごみを すてて下さい。
   Please throw away the trash.

2. このくつは 古いから、すてます。
   These shoes are old, so I am going to throw them away.

3. このコンピューターも すてることに しました。
   I have decided to throw away this computer also.

❏ 8-5. まよう (to get lost, to be perplexed, to be uncertain, to hesitate)

The thing that you are perplexed, or hesitating about, is marked with the particle に.

まよう is a good verb to use when you are undecided. For example, if you are trying to decide between a blue car and a white car and your friend asks which one you are going to buy you could respond with まよっている.

Examples

1. みちに まよう。   To be lost.
2. 人生に まよう。   To be uncertain in life.

Example sentences

1. みちに まよっています。
   I am lost. (I have lost my way)

2. まよわないで。
   Don't be wishy-washy.

3. けっこんの ことを まよっています。
   I am undecided about marriage.

> This can also be:
> けっこんに まよっています。

8   Grammar ぶんぽう

❑ 8-6. How to do something

When explaining things like "how to eat something" or "the way to go someplace", the かた
suffix is added to a verb. It is applied differently, depending on the verb type.

> **(regular verb い form) + かた**
> **(いる/える verb) minus る + かた**
> **How to [verb] / the way to [verb]**

Examples (regular verbs)

1. いく ⇨ いきかた   how to go
2. かえり ⇨ かえりかた   the way home / the way back
3. およぐ ⇨ およぎかた   how to swim

Examples (いる/える verbs)

1. たべる ⇨ たべかた   how to eat
2. みる ⇨ みかた   how to watch

Examples (irregular verbs)

1. する ⇨ しかた   how to do
2. くる ⇨ きかた   how to come

Example sentences

1. トムさんは おすしの たべかたが わかりません。

    Tom does not know how to eat sushi.

2. 漢字の かきかたを 勉強 しています。

    I am studying how to write kanji.

3. ケーキの つくりかたを 教えて下さい

    Please teach me how to make a cake.

4. この どうぐの <u>つかいかた</u>が わかりません。

I don't know <u>how to use</u> this tool.

5. 行^いきかたを おしえて 下さい。

Please tell me how to get there.

6. このゲームの <u>かちかた</u>を 教えて 下さい。

Please teach me <u>how to win</u> this game.

❑ 8-7. Using 上手 and 下手 correctly

上手 is only used for other people, not for yourself. If you talk about yourself being good at something, then you should use とくい.

> **[thing] + が + 上手 or とくい or へた**
> **good / not good at + [thing]**

Example sentences

1. あの人は スポーツが 上手です。
   That person is good at sports.

2. おかあさんは りょうりが 上手です。
   My mother is good at cooking.

3. 私は やきゅうが とくいです。
   I am good at baseball. / Baseball is my speciality.

4. 私の十六歳の むすこは うんてんが 下手です。
   My sixteen-year-old son is not good at driving.

5. 私は しらない人との 会話^{かいわ}が 下手です。
   I am not good at having a conversation with someone I don't know.

❑ 8-8. The difference between うまい and 上手

うまい is used like 上手 except that it can also be used to say that something tastes good, just like おいしい. Also since うまい is an い adjective, its tense can be changed like other い adjectives.

Example sentences

1. このピザは うまい！
   This pizza tastes good!

   > うまい for "delicious" in kanji is 美味い and 旨い to mean "skilled".

2. 昨日の さしみは うまかった です。
   Yesterday's sashimi was good.

❑ 8-9. Making a verb phrases into a noun with の and こと

In technical terms, we are now going to learn how to "nominalize" a verb. What this means is we are going to take a VERB phrase and turn it into a NOUN phrase. Once you make a verb phrase into a noun phrase you can advance your speaking skill quite a bit.

This grammar will allow you to say things like "I like shopping at 5 in the morning." and "Eating pizza everyday is not good." In this section we will learn two ways to "nominalize" a verb phrase. The first one is こと. You simply add こと after the verb and presto you have a noun phrase.

> (う form verb) + ことは...
> doing (verb) is...

Example sentences

1. 毎日ピザを たべることは よくないです。
   <u>Eating pizza</u> everyday is not good.

2. あさの ５じに かいものすることが すきです。
   I like <u>shopping</u> at 5 in the morning.

3. 日本のドラマを見ることは しゅうみです。
   <u>Watching Japanese dramas</u> is my hobby.

The other way to nominalize verbs is to add の to it. This is most commonly used and heard in conversation. You will hear this much more than the こと way in conversation.

> **(verb) + のは...**
> **doing (verb) is...**

Example sentences

1. 毎日ピザを たべるのは よくないです。
   Eating pizza everyday is not good.

2. あさの ５じに かいものするのが すきです。
   I like shopping at 5 in the morning.

3. 日本のドラマを見るのは しゅうみです。
   Watching Japanese dramas is my hobby.

4. 漢字を かくのが むずかしいです。
   Writing kanji is difficult.

5. ひらがなを かくのが かんたんです。
   Writing hiragana is easy.

❏ 8-10. Different grammar same meaning

Every language has multiple ways to say the exact same thing. Normally you don't notice these multiple ways in your own language. For this reason you might not get satisfactory answers from a Japanese person when asking about Japanese. Just try asking your friends, "What is the difference between は and が?"

Using verb noun phrases you can make new ways to say things you learned in prior lessons. In Course 3 we learned the "potential form" to ask someone if they "can do" something.

> **Example sentences (using the potential verb form)**
> 1. 漢字が かけますか。
>   Can you write kanji?
>
> 2. すしが たべられますか？
>   Can you eat sushi?

You can say the exact same things using the new grammar learned in this lesson.

> **Example sentences (using nominalized verbs)**
> 1. 漢字を かくことが できますか。
>   Can you write kanji?
>
> 2. すしを たべることが できますか？
>   Can you eat sushi?

8 Mini Conversation ミニかいわ J→E

1. Polite conversation between a boy and a girl.

A: 今日、公園（こうえん）に 行きませんか。

B: 公園（こうえん）で 何を しますか。

A: ピクニックを しましょう。 きれいな けしきを 見せたいから。

B: いいですね。じゃあ、行きましょう。

A: 私が おべんとうを つくります。

B: おねがいします。ジョンさんは りょうりが 上手ですからね。

A: Why don't we go to the park today?
B: What are we going to do at the park?
A: Let's have a picnic! Because I want to show you the beautiful scenery.
B: That sounds good. Let's go then.
A: I will make a box lunch.
B: Please do. Since you are a good cook, John.

2. Casual conversation between friends.

A: 先週、イギリスに 行ったよ。

B: いいなぁ。しゃしんを 見せて。

A: ここは タワーブリッジ。大きくて、びっくりしたよ。

B: イギリスの りょうりは どうだった？

A: フィッシュ・アンド・チップスしか たべなかった。

A: I went to England last week.

B: I envy you. Show me the pictures.

A: Here is Tower Bridge. I was surprised it was so big.

A: How was the English cooking?

B: I only ate fish and chips.

3. Polite conversation between neighbors.

A: 昨日 主人と ギャンブルを しました。

B: かちましたか？

A: 私は ちょっと かちましたが、主人は 二百ドルぐらい まけました。

B: だから、私は ギャンブルは よくないと おもいます。

A: Yesterday I gambled with my husband.

B: Did you win?

A: I won a little, but my husband lost about two hundred dollars.

B: That's why I think gambling is not good.

4. Panicked conversation between neighbors.

A: あああああああああ！びっくりした！

B: どうしたの、としこちゃん？

A: くもが いた。こわかった!

B: こわくないよ。としこちゃんの ほうが こわいよ。

A: Aaaaaaaaaaaaaah! That surprised me!

B: What's the matter, Toshiko?

A: There was a spider. I was scared!

B: They aren't scary. You are scarier, Toshiko.

8 Mini Conversation ミニかいわ E→J

1. Casual conversation between friends

A: Why don't we play tennis tomorrow?

B: Tennis is a little… You are good at it Ms. Kobayashi, but I am not.

A: I am not good at it yet.

B: Hmm… How about golf instead of tennis?

A: 明日、テニスを しない？

B: テニスは ちょっと・・・。小林さんは うまいけど、わたしは 下手だから・・・。

A: まだ うまくないよ。

B: うーん・・・。テニスより、ゴルフは どう？

2. Polite conversation between friends.

A: I have pictures of my mother from when she was in elementary school.

B: Really? How old was she then?

A: She was eight years old. Shall I show them to you?

B: Instead of that, show me pictures of you a long time ago.

A: おかあさんが 小学校に いたときの しゃしんが あります。

B: 本当ですか。そのときは 何歳でしたか。

A: 八歳でした。見せましょうか。

B: それより あなたの むかしの しゃしんを 見せて下さい。

3. Polite conversation between friends.

A: Tanaka (teacher) is skilled a teaching math.

B: Is that so? Nakamura (teacher) is unskilled at teaching.

A: 田中先生は すうがくを おしえるのが 上手です。

B: そうですか。中村先生は おしえるのが 下手です。

4. Polite conversation between gamblers.

A: I won 21,000 yen at pachinko.

B: I also won, but I only won 7,000 yen.

A: Did Mr. Shimada win?

B: No. He lost 4,000 yen.

A: パチンコで 二まん一千円、かちました。

B: 私も かちましたが、七千円しか かちませんでした。

A: しまださんは かちましたか。

B: いいえ、四千円、まけました。

5. Polite conversation between neighbors

A: Have you ever made a cake?

B: No, because I am not good at cooking. Why?

A: Tomorrow is my son's birthday, so I want to make a cake. But I don't know how to make one.

A: ケーキを つくった ことが ありますか。

B: いいえ。りょうりが 下手ですから。 なぜですか。

A: 明日は 私の むすこの 誕生日だから、ケーキを つくりたいです。

でも、つくりかたが わかりません。

6. Polite conversation between a new worker at a company and their trainer.

A: Are you able to use this software?

B: No, it's my first time using it. Is that not good?

A: It's okay. I will teach you how to use it.

A: このソフトが つかえますか。

B: いいえ、つかうのは はじめてです。だめですか。

A: だいじょうぶです。つかいかたを おしえます。

8 | Reading Comprehension どっかい

Read the sentences below. If you don't understand them, you should review the grammar in this lesson until you do.

① ベスさんは 先月、日本に きました。

② かいがいに いくのが はじめて でした。

③ わたしの 家に 一週間、ホームステイを しました。
<small>いっしゅうかん</small>

④ 日本語が とても上手で、びっくりしました。

⑤ ベスさんが やきゅうの しあいが 見たいと いったので、いっしょに
　やきゅうじょうに行きました。

⑥ ベスさんは やきゅうが 大好きなので、
<small>だい ず</small>
　とても たのしみに していました。

⑦ ベスさんは シアトルで 一年まえに イチローという 日本のゆうめいな
　せんしゅを 見たと いいました。

⑧ そのとき、シアトル・マリナーズが ニューヨーク・ヤンキーズに
　かちました。

⑨ イチローは とても 足が はやかったので、びっくりしたと いいました。

⑩ ベスさんは 日本で みんなが やきゅうじょうで あまり ピーナツを
　たべないと いいました。

⑪ わたしは ベスさんに 日本と アメリカの やきゅうじょうでは
　たべるものが ちょっと ちがうと 教えました。

  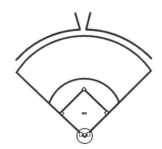

8 Lesson Activities

❑ Reading comprehension questions

Answer the following questions about the reading comprehension from the previous page.

1. ベスさんは どれぐらい 日本に いましたか。

_____

2. ベスさんは 日本で 何がしたかったですか。

_____

3. ベスさんは イチローのことを どう おもいましたか。

_____

4. アメリカの やきゅうじょうでは、どんなものを たべますか。

_____

5. 日本の やきゅうじょうでは どんなものを たべると おもいますか。

_____

6. ベスさんは海外に行くのが何回目ですか。

_____

❏ Sentence Jumble

Using ONLY the words and particles provided, create Japanese sentences that match the English translation. You can conjugate adjectives and verbs and reuse items if needed.

1. かちました・を・が・500円・に・ともだち・しあい・よみました・じゃない・
    したい・は・まけました・すてる

    _____

    I won 500 yen.

    _____

    We lost the game.

    _____

    I lost 500 yen to my friend.

2. です・びっくりしました・きれい・上手・下手・うまい・が・に・を・で
    だから・たべかた・のみかた・むしあつい・あんなに・あなた・は・の

    _____

    I was surprised you were that good (skilled at)

    _____

    I was surprised it was so humid.

    _____

    The way you eat is unskilled.

3. すてかた・の・ごみ・つかいかた・教える・か・を・ほしい・に・で・も・ごみ
    いつから・つくりかた・ピザ・下さい・なんで・わかる・はし・アパート

    _____

    Please teach me how to make pizza.

    _____

    I don't know how to throw it away.

    _____

    Since when do you know how to use chopsticks?

❏ Practice

Circle the appropriate word and complete each conversation.

1. A: 田口さんは テニスが 上手ですね。
   <small>たぐち</small>

   B: はい、じつは わたしも (上手 ・ とくい) ですよ。

2. A: 先生、おくさんの りょうりは (おいしい ・ うまい) ですね。

   B: ありがとう。 わたしも そう おもいます。

3. A: トム、あした テニスを するけど、トムも くる？

   B: うん、行くよ。 あとは だれが くるの？

   A: あとは ジョンと ケリー。 ジョンは テニスが (うまい ・ とくい) から、
   びっくりするよ。

   B: そう。 ぼくは あまり (うまい ・ とくい) じゃないよ。 どうしよう・・・。

❏ Question and Answer

Answer the following questions using the words and patterns in this lesson.

1. すしの つくりかたを しっていますか。

   _____

2. 東京から 大阪への 行きかたが わかりますか。

   _____

3. だれが いつも ごみを すてますか。

   _____

4. どんなスポーツが とくいですか。

   _____

5. おかあさんは 何が 上手ですか。

   _____

6. 日本人の どんなところに びっくりしますか。

   _____

❑ **Short Dialogue**

Ken's girlfriend made him dinner and he must eat no matter what it is.

かの女:　　けん。晩ご飯が できたよ。

けん:　　　すごい！ おいしそうだね。 スパゲティーは ぼくの大好物だよ。

かの女:　　よかった。 私、料理が 得意なのよ。

けん:　　　へえ～。 じゃあ、いただきます。

かの女:　　どうぞ。 いっぱい 食べてね。

けん:　　　・・・。

かの女:　　味は どう？ おいしいでしょう？

けん:　　　あのう・・・、これは 何？

かの女:　　それは メロン。 その茶色いのは 納豆だよ。

けん:　　　えっ？！ スパゲティーに そんなものを 入れるの？

かの女:　　うん、私は いつも 個性的な 料理を作るの。
　　　　　　作り方を 教えてもいいよ。

けん:　　　それは いいよ・・・。 うーん、ごめん。
　　　　　　お腹が いっぱいに なった。

かの女:　　まだ 食べてないでしょう？ もったいないよ！

けん:　　　はい・・・ わかりました。 いただきます。

❑ **New Words and Expressions in the dialogue**

Progressive	Kanji +	English
大こうぶつ	大好物	favorite food
なっとう	納豆	fermented soybeans
こせいてき	個性的	unique, one of a kind
もったいない	もったいない	what a waste

❑ Short dialogue activities

1. Practice reading the preceding short dialogue in pairs.

2. Play the girlfriend role and change the underlined words into something else.

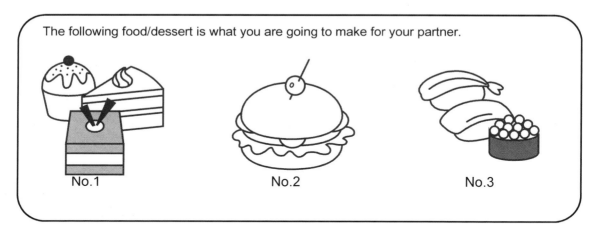

The following food/dessert is what you are going to make for your partner.

No.1   No.2   No.3

Kanji Lesson

8

高黄合谷国黒
kanji 123-128

八 New Kanji あたらしい漢字

Practice writing each new kanji in the boxes provided. First trace the light gray samples while paying attention to stroke order. Then on a separate piece of paper practice writing the sample kanji words at least five times each.

高	くんよみ	たか（い）	number		123
	おんよみ	コウ	meaning	high	

えんだか 円高	こうそく 高速	こうこう 高校	さいこう 最高	こうおん 高温
high-valued yen	high speed	high school	awesome, best	high temperature

10 strokes

〃　亠　广　卞　亩　古　高　高　高　高

高　高　高　高　高

黄	くんよみ	き・こ	number		124
	おんよみ	コウ・オウ	meaning	yellow	

きいろ 黄色	おうごん 黄金	こうが 黄河	きみ 黄身	おうとう 黄桃
yellow	gold	Yellow River	yolk	yellow peach

11 strokes

一　十　艹　共　芖　昔　帯　莆　黄　黄

黄　黄　黄　黄　黄

合 — 125

	くんよみ	あ（う）・あい	number	125
	おんよみ	ゴウ・ガッ・カッ	meaning	combine, join, union, fit

6 strokes

あ 合う	あいず 合図	がっしゅうこく 合衆国	しあい 試合	ごうけい 合計
to fit, to agree, to match	signal, sign	United States	match (sports)	total (amount)

ノ 人 合 合 合 合

合 合 合 合 合

谷 — 126

	くんよみ	たに	number	126
	おんよみ	コク	meaning	valley

7 strokes

たにそこ 谷底	けいこく 渓谷	たにま 谷間	たにがわ 谷川	きょうこく 峡谷
bottom of the valley	canyon	ravine	valley river	ravine, gorge

ノ ハ グ グ グ 谷 谷

谷 谷 谷 谷 谷

国 — 127

	くんよみ	くに	number	127
	おんよみ	コク	meaning	country, nation

8 strokes

こくさい 国際	きこく 帰国	こっき 国旗	ゆきぐに 雪国	こくさん 国産
international	return to country	national flag	snow country	domestic products

丨 冂 冂 冂 国 国 国 国

国 国 国 国 国

黒	くんよみ	くろ (い)		number		128
	おんよみ	コク		meaning		black

くろ	こくばん	くろかみ	ま　くろ	しろくろてれび
黒い	黒板	黒髪	真っ黒	白黒テレビ
black	blackboard	black hair	pitch black	black and white TV

11 strokes

丨 冂 冃 冃 甲 里 黒 黒 黒 黒 黒

黒	黒	黒	黒	黒							

八 Kanji Drills 漢字ドリル

❑ Words you can write

Write the following words in the boxes. This is a great way to practice the new kanji and review the words at the same time. For the kanji that hasn't been taught yet, use hiragana.

たか
高い
expensive, tall

高	い									

こうこう
高校
high school

高	校									

えんだか
円高
high-valued yen currency

円	高									

き　み
黄身
egg yolk

黄	み									

くに
国   country

しろ くろ
白黒   black and white

き こく
帰国   to return to one's own country

くろ
黒い   black

あ
合う   to fit, to match

ごう けい
合計   total (amount)

たに
谷   valley

たに がわ
谷川   valley river

❏ Fill in the kanji

Fill in the blanks in the following sentences with the appropriate kanji.

きょ う　　き おん　　た か
1. ___ ___は___温が___い です ね。

The temperature sure is hot today.

2. ＿＿がすきだけど、＿＿色は すきじゃないです。
<ruby>く<rt></rt></ruby><ruby>ろ<rt></rt></ruby> <ruby>き<rt></rt></ruby><ruby>いろ<rt></rt></ruby>
I like black, but I don't like yellow.

3. 昨日＿＿ ＿＿に ＿＿ ＿＿しました。
<ruby>に<rt></rt></ruby><ruby>ほん<rt></rt></ruby> <ruby>き<rt></rt></ruby><ruby>こく<rt></rt></ruby>
Yesterday, I returned to Japan.

4. アメリカ＿＿ 衆 ＿＿は＿＿い ですね。
<ruby>がっしゅうこく<rt></rt></ruby> <ruby>ひろ<rt></rt></ruby>
The United States of America is spacious.

5. ＿＿ ＿＿ ＿＿のとき、よく＿＿でやきゅうを しました。
<ruby>こう こう せい<rt></rt></ruby> <ruby>たに<rt></rt></ruby>
When I was a high school student I often played baseball in a valley.

八 Kanji Recognition 漢字にんしき

❏ Individual words

The following words will no longer have any ふりがな (hiragana on top). You might already

know some of these words, but don't worry if you can't write them as recognition is the goal.

たくさん	やまだ	むらた	たか
沢山	山田	村田	高い
a lot, many	last name	last name	tall, expensive

あか	あと
赤ちゃん	後
baby	after

❏ **Word groups (people and days of the month)**

The following word groups will no longer have any ふりがな (hiragana on top). The days of

the month

ひとり
一人
one person

ふたり
二人
two people

さんにん
三人
three people

よにん
四人
four people

なんにん
何人
how many people

ついたち
一日
the 1st

ふつか
二日
the 2nd

みっか
三日
the 3rd

よっか
四日
the 4th

いつか
五日
the 5th

むいか
六日
the 6th

なのか
七日
the 7th

ようか
八日
the 8th

ここのか
九日
the 9th

とおか
十日
the 10th

じゅういちにち
十一日
the 11th

じゅうににち
十二日
the 12th

じゅうさんにち
十三日
the 13th

じゅうよっか
十四日
the 14th

じゅうごにち
十五日
the 15th

じゅうはちにち
十八日
the 18th

はつか
二十日
the 20th

なんにち
何日
what day of the month?

❑ Kanji recognition cards

Print and cut out these cards, then write the hiragana and English meaning on the back.
Now you can easily practice your kanji recognition.

沢山	山田	村田	高い
赤ちゃん	後	一人	二人
三人	四人	何人	一日
二日	三日	四日	五日
六日	七日	八日	九日
十日	十一日	十二日	十三日
十四日	十五日	十八日	二十日
何日			

COMMENTARY: You want me to what? (pt 2)

The Session (continued from prior commentary section)

The channeler, Jerry, began by explaining that Ashtar would take over her body, and that we should not be concerned for her safety as she would be sent to a safe place. Masami was concerned that this session would not be taped properly since the B-side of all of the cassettes from her previous session were mysteriously blank. Jerry explained that perhaps the tape machine was malfunctioning, but this was just a minor detail.

The session began when Jerry let Ashtar come into her body. Her voice took on a slight Spanish accent, and Ashtar very poetically greeted the people in the room. Masami had a three-page list of questions, and proceeded to ask them in Japanese while I translated. The questions ranged from "who is my soulmate?" to "at what point does the soul enter a baby?" I must admit that I was impressed at the speed with which Ashtar provided replies. But there were several things that remained unclear in my mind.

First of all, Masami, according to Ashtar, was in a past life a princess at the Emperor's palace in China around the time of the end of the Mao dynasty. Apparently she had fallen in love with a commoner from outside the castle walls and was caught with him by a royal guard. The commoner was beheaded and the princess lived a secluded life in the palace until her death. The entire time I was interpreting this I was thinking, "How come people are always royalty or figures of great importance in their past lives? Where are all of the normal people?" Not wanting to ruin the session, I kept these thoughts to myself and interpreted with the same professionalism I would provide to any customer.

(continued in next commentary section)

Doing things like X, Y and Z

Before This Lesson

1. Be able to read and write 高黄合谷国黒.

Lesson Goals

1. Learn how to use いく and くる in combination with other verbs.
2. Learn how to use the positive たり verb form.
3. Learn how to say "I wonder if..."

From The Teachers

1. The たり verb form is a very commonly used verb type. You will sound native if you use it properly.

Lesson Highlights

9-6. Using いく and くる with other verbs

9-7. Different verb forms and tenses of (verb)に いく / くる

9-8. The たり verb form

9-9. Sentence structure of a たり verb list

9-10. Using the same verb but different form with たり

9-11. Using かな (to wonder if)

9 | New Words あたらしい ことば

Progressive	漢字	えいご
だれか	誰か	somebody
シャワー	シャワー	shower
おゆ	お湯	hot water
おおい！	おおい！	Hey!
そのあと	そのあと	after that
なみだ	涙	tears
せいかく	性格	character; personality
グランド・キャニオン	グランド・キャニオン	The Grand Canyon
しゅうまつ	週末	the weekend
～かな	～かな	wonder [see Grammar section]
きたくち 北口	北口	north entrance/exit
みなみくち 南口	南口	south entrance/exit
ひがしくち 東口	東口	east entrance/exit
にしくち 西口	西口	west entrance/exit

9 | New Adjectives あたらしい けいようし

日本語	漢字	えいご	タイプ
へん	変	strange	な adjective
くやしい	悔しい	regrettable	い adjective
きたない	汚い	dirty, disgusting	い adjective
おかしい	おかしい	funny, strange	い adjective

9 | New Verbs あたらしい どうし

どうし	えいご	た form	タイプ
わら 笑う	to laugh	わらった	regular
おこ 怒る	to be mad or angry	おこった	regular

泣く	to cry	ないた	regular
シャワーを あびる	to take a shower	シャワーを あびた	いる/える
トイレを 流す	to flush the toilet	トイレを ながした	regular
首になる	to be fired	くびに なった	regular

9   Verb Usage どうしの つかいかた

❏ 9-1. わらう (to laugh) and なく (to cry)

There isn't anything special to say about these verbs. Using grammar discussed in prior lessons you can show why you are laughing and crying using で、くて、から etc.

> **Example sentences (using から)**
> 1. おかしい<u>から</u> わらいました。
>   I laughed because it was funny.
> 2. かなしい<u>から</u> なきました。
>   I cried because I was sad.

Here are some examples using the くて form of the い adjectives.

> **Example sentences (using くて form of い adjectives)**
> 1. おかし<u>くて</u> わらいました。
>   I laughed because it was funny.
> 2. かなし<u>くて</u> なきました。
>   I cried because I was sad.

❏ 9-2. おこる (to be mad or angry)

The particle に is used to mark the person someone is mad at. It is important to note that when you are mad at someone, you need to use the ています form because you are in an ongoing state of being mad.

> **(person) に おこる**
> **to be mad at (person)**

Example sentences

1. 私は トムに おこっています。
   I am mad at Tom.

2. 父は 私に おこっています。
   My father is mad at me.

3. 母は 私の せいせきが わるかったので、おこりました。
   My mother was mad because my grades were bad.

4. かれは がんばったから あまり おこらないで 下さい。
   Because he did his best, please don't be mad.

❏ 9-3. シャワーをあびる (to take a shower)

This verb あびる is not limited to showers. You can use it to "bathe" in sunlight and you

might hear it used in other cases where your body is showered with something.

Example sentences

1. いま、シャワーを あびています。

   I am taking a shower now.

2. シャワーを あびてから ねます。

   I will go to bed after taking a shower.

3. あさは シャワーを あびることに しています。

   I make it a rule to take a shower in the morning.

❏ 9-4. ながす (to flush, shed, wash off)

The item that is being flushed or washed off is marked with を.

(thing) を ながす
to flush or wash off (thing)

Example sentences
1. けんちゃん、トイレを ながして下さい。
    Please flush the toilet, Ken-chan.

2. トイレを ながしました。
    I flushed the toilet.

3. くさいから トイレを ながしてよ！
    It smells so flush the toilet!

ながす is also used somewhat poetically to mean "shed tears" and it can also be used to "shed blood".

Example sentences
1. さみしくて、なみだを ながしました。
    I shed tears because I was sad.

2. うれしくて、なみだを ながしました。
    I shed tears because I was happy.

3. 戦争 中 は 沢山の 人が 血を ながします。
    せんそうちゅう　　　　　　　　　 ち
    During war, the blood of many people is shed.

❑ 9-5. くびになる (to be fired)

This is kind of funny if you directly translate it to "become a neck".

Example sentences
1. 今日、くびに なりました。
    Today I got fired.

2. 山田さんが くびに なったと ききました。
    I heard that Mr. Yamada got fired.

9 Grammar ぶんぽう

❑ 9-6. Using いく and くる with other verbs

いく and くる can be used in combination with other verbs to say things like, "I will go to see," and, "go to eat." You can also think of this as a way to state the purpose of your "going" or "coming" somewhere.

For regular verbs the following pattern is used:

> **（い form verb）+ に いく or に くる**
> **will go or come to (verb)**

For いる/える verbs the る must be dropped.

> **（いる/える minus る）+ に いく or に くる**

Examples

会いに 行く	to go and meet (to go visit)
見に 行く	to go and see (to go see)
のみに 行く	to go drinking
しに 行く	to go and do
会いに くる	to come and meet (to come visit)
見に くる	to come and see (to come see)
ききに くる	to come and listen (to come listen)

❑ 9-7. Different verb forms and tenses of (verb)に いく／くる

The verb form and tense of いく and くる can be changed to create other expressions.

Look at the examples below to see the type of powerful sentences that can be made.

Example sentences

1. 明日 家に ばんごはんを たべに きて下さい。
   Please come to my house to have dinner tomorrow.

2. いまから、きってを かいに 行きます。
   I am going to buy some stamps now.

3. 今日、田中くんが あそびに きます。
   Mr. Tanaka is coming to play (hang out) today.

4. 昨日、としょかんに 勉強しに 行きました。
   Yesterday I went to the library to study.

5. ハワイに サーフィンを しに 行きたいです。
   I want to go surfing in Hawaii.

6. ホテルに シャワーをあびに いきました。
   I went to the hotel to take a shower.

❑ **9-8. The たり verb form**

The たり verb form is commonly used to state a series of actions. In English we might say, "I do things like watch TV, eat pizza, and play games." Using the たり verb form you can achieve the same effect; rather than listing everything, you only give a representative list. It's easy to create this verb. Just add り to the informal past form. This pattern works with both the positive and the negative past forms.

> ### informal past <u>positive</u> verb + り

Examples

本を よんだり	like reading books
映画を 見たり	like watching movies
かいものを したり	like shopping

> ### informal past <u>negative</u> verb + り

Examples

本を よまなかったり	like not reading books
勉強を しなかったり	like not studying
シャワーを あびなかったり	like not taking a shower

❑ 9-9. Sentence structure of a たり verb list

You can have as many verbs and verb phrases strung in a row in your たり verb list.

All verbs in the list are changed into the たり form and then する (any form) is added to the end of the list. You can have three or more verbs in a row, or even just one.

Number of たり verbs	Example	Meaning
1	本を よんだりします。	I do things like reading books.
2	本を よんだり、テレビを 見たりします。	I do things like reading books and watching TV.
3	本を よんだり、テレビを 見たり、かいものを したりします。	I do things like reading books, watching TV, and shopping.

Important: The tense of the entire たり sentence is determined by the tense and form of the する verb at the end of the statement. Look at the following three sentences. The only difference in the statements is the する verb at the end.

Example sentences

1. 土曜日に テレビを 見たり、ピザを たべたり、ゲームを したりします。
   On Saturday I <u>do</u> things like watch TV, eat pizza and play video games.

2. 土曜日に テレビを 見たり、ピザを たべたり、ゲームを したりしました。
   On Saturday I <u>did</u> things like watch TV, eat pizza and play video games.

3. 土曜日に テレビを 見たり、ピザを たべたり、ゲームを したりしたいです。
   On Saturday I <u>want to do</u> things like watch TV, eat pizza and play video games.

Example Q&A

1. しごとで どんなこと を していますか。
   What type of things do you do at work?

   レポートを かいたり、かいぎをしたり します。
   I do things like writing reports and doing meetings.

   ウェブサイトを つくったり、プログラミングを したり します。
   I do things like making websites and programming.

2. ラスベガスに 何を しに いきますか。
   What are you going to do in Las Vegas?

   かいものを したり、グランド・キャニオンに 行ったりします。
   I am going to do things like shopping and going to the Grand Canyon.

3. しゅうまつに いつも なにを しますか。
   What do you always do on the weekend?

   ボートに のったり、およいだり します。
   I do things like ride boats and swim.

   じてんしゃに のったり、ランニングしたり します。
   I do things like ride a bicycle and running.

4. どうして かのじょは おこってるの?
   Why is your girlfriend (or "she") mad at you?

   トイレを ながさなかったりするから。
   Because I do things like not flush the toilet.

❏ 9-10. Using the same verb but different form with たり

In the grammar section above, all of the たり expressions used different verbs. In this section we will use the same verb. When the same verb is used in the たり statement you will notice that in English "sometimes" is in the sentences. This is the nuance that is created by using the same verb twice. The final する tense determines the entire tense.

Example sentences
1. 山田さんは しごとを したり、しなかったりします。
   Sometimes Mr. Yamada works and sometimes he doesn't.

2. 九時に おきたり、おきなかったりします。
   Sometimes I wake up at nine and sometimes I don't.

3. 私の 赤ちゃんは ないたり、なかなかったりします。
   Sometimes my baby cries and sometimes she doesn't.

4. わかかったときは お金が あったり、なかったりしました。
   When I was young, sometimes I had money, and sometimes I didn't.

❑ 9-11. Using かな (to wonder if)

かな is added to the end of a sentence to change the sentence into a "I wonder if....." sentence. In the past かな was mostly used only by men and women used かしら which served the same purpose. In modern Japan, most young women say かな as the men do.

Be careful using this when speaking to someone you are not familiar with. Remember that かな is an informal expression and could be considered rude when using it where it is not normally expected. With people you do not know it will be better not to "wonder" but to ask the question to the person directly.

The verb used with かな must be in the informal form.

> **(informal verb / verb phrase) + かな**
> **I wonder if + (verb / verb phrase)**

Example sentences

1. 来年、東京に 行けるかな。
   <u>I wonder if</u> I can go to Tokyo next year.

2. 明日は 雨が ふるかな。
   <u>I wonder if</u> it is going to rain or not tomorrow.

かな can be used with question words, nouns, and adjectives. です should always be removed when using かな. You can also add the informal question marker の in the sentence.

Example sentences

1. 日本は さむいかな。
   <u>I wonder if</u> it is cold in Japan.

2. あのレストランは 高いかな。
   <u>I wonder if</u> that restaurant is expensive.

3. 何でかな。
   <u>I wonder</u> why.

4. どこかな。
   <u>I wonder</u> where (it is).

5. あれは 村田さんかな。
   <u>I wonder if</u> that is Mr. Murata.

6. トムさんは まだ 日本語を勉強しているのかな。 (The の is optional here.)
   <u>I wonder if</u> Tom is still studying Japanese.

9 Mini Conversation ミニかいわ J→E

1. Polite conversation between co-workers.

A: しごとの後、わたしと のみに 行きませんか。
B: 今日は 日本語の じゅぎょうが あるから、明日に しましょう。
A: いいですよ。 じゃあ、あしたの 五時はんに えきの 東口^{ひがしくち}で 会いましょう。
B: わかりました。

A: Won't you go drinking with me after work?
B: I have a Japanese class, so let's make it tomorrow.
A: All right. Then let's meet at the east exit of the train station tomorrow at five thirty.
B: Okay.

2. Polite conversation between a man and a woman.

A: 明日、イタリア りょうりを つくるから、たべに きませんか。
B: うれしい。何を つくりますか。
A: たぶん スパゲッティーを つくると おもいます。
B: ごめんなさい。私は パスタが たべられないです。
A: じゃあ、ピザに しましょう。

A: I am going to cook Italian food tomorrow, so won't you come and eat?
B: I am happy. What are you going to make?
A: I think maybe I will make spaghetti.
B: Sorry. I can't eat pasta.
A: Well then, let's have pizza.

3. Polite conversation between classmates

A: いつも しゅうまつに 何を しますか。

B: 本を よんだり、ビデオ・ゲームを したりします。

A: What do you always do on weekends?

B: I do things like reading books and playing video games.

4. Polite conversation between friends

A: スミスさんは すぐ おこったりするね。

B: そうだね。 なんでかな。

A: せいかく じゃないかな。

B: たぶんね。

A: Mr. Smith gets mad easily, doesn't he?

B: That's true. I wonder why.

A: I wonder if it is his personality.

B: Maybe.

9 | Mini Conversation ミニかいわ E→J

1. Polite conversation between friends

A: That person is strange, huh?

B: Why?

A: He is laughing and talking by himself.

A: あの人は へんですね。

B: 何で ですか。

A: 一人で わらったり、はなしたりしていますよ。

2. Casual conversation between friends

A: We haven't seen Toshiko recently, have we? I wonder what she is doing.

B: I heard she goes to several schools, such as an English language school and a cooking school.

A: She sure is busy.

A: さいきん、年子さんを 見ないね。何を してるのかな。

B: 英会話学校や りょうり学校に 行ったりしていると ききましたよ。

A: いそがしいですね。

3. Polite conversation between classmates.

A: What did you do on the weekend?

B: I read books, watched movies and shopped.

A: I took a trip to Kyoto.

B: That's nice. Weren't there a lot of people?

A: Since it was raining, there weren't that many people.

A: しゅうまつは 何を しましたか。

B: 本を よんだり、えいがを 見たり、かいものを したりしました。

A: 私は 京都に 旅行に 行きました。

B: いいですね。人が たくさん いませんでしたか。

A: 雨だったので あまり いませんでした。

4. Polite conversation between friends.

A: Tomorrow Akiko is coming to hang out at my house.

B: Really!? Can I go too?

A: Sure. We are going to watch a Japanese video.

B: Sounds good (That's nice). I am looking forward to it.

A: 明日、あき子さんが 家に あそびに きます。

B: 本当ですか。 私も 行っても いいですか。

A: いいですよ。 日本の ビデオを 見ます。

B: いいですね。 たのしみに しています。

9 | Reading Comprehension どっかい

Read the sentences below. If you don't understand them, you should review the grammar in this lesson until you do. After you have understood everything, complete the reading comprehension questions in the *Activities* section of this lesson.

---

① 今日は へんな 一日(いちにち)でした。

② わらったり、おこったり、ないたりしました。

③ きょう 七時に おきてから すぐ シャワーを あびました。

④ シャワーを あびているときに、だれかが トイレを ながしました。

⑤ おゆが きゅうに あつくなりました。

⑥ ちょっと！シャワーを あびているときに、トイレを ながさないでよ！

⑦ すごく おこりました。

⑧ そのあと、会社(かいしゃ)の人から でんわが ありました。

⑨ あああ！くびに なりました。

⑩ どうしよう！さみしくて、なきました。

⑫ そのとき「おきて。もう 七時だよ。」と だれかが いいました。

⑬ ああっ！びっくりした。

⑭ じつは まだ ねていました。

⑮ ぜんぶ ゆめでした。

⑯ 七時はんまで わらいました。

9 Lesson Activities

❏ Reading comprehension questions

Answer the following questions about the reading comprehension. Assume the speaker's name is 田中さん.

1. 田中さんは こうこうせいだと おもいますか？ (add the reason in your answer)

    _____

2. 田中さんは いつも 何時ごろ おきると おもいますか。

    _____

3. 田中さんは なぜ おこりましたか。

    _____

4. だれが 田中さんに でんわを しましたか。

    _____

5. 田中さんは なぜ わらいましたか。

    _____

❏ Sentence Jumble

Using ONLY the words and particles provided, create Japanese sentences that match the English translation. You can conjugate adjectives and verbs and reuse items if needed.

1. きたぐち・ひがしぐち・みなみぐち・にしぐち・で・に・しゅうまつ・あう・を
    いう・にじゅうにち・はつか・にじゅういちにち・ようか・よんじ・よじ・しじ

    _____

    Let's meet at the north exit.

    _____

    I want to meet on the 20th.

    _____

    I will meet you at 4 o'clock at the east exit.

2. とても・おもしろい・おかしい・たのしい・へん・おいしい・が・を・で・に
   です・レストラン・ともだち・しゅくだい・きたない・の・パーティー

   _____

   The restaurant was dirty.

   _____

   My friend's party was really fun.

   _____

   It was uninteresting homework.

3. おこる・わらう・なく・シャワーを あびる・下さい・くびに なる・を・が
   かのじょ・かれし・の・わたし・だれか・を

   _____

   Please don't be mad.

   _____

   My girlfriend cried.

   _____

   Somebody didn't flush the toilet!

4. きのう・おととい・あした・えいが・みる・いく・に・おしえる・たべる・かう
   しょくじ・きって・くる・あう・を・ともだち・えいご・あなた

   _____

   I will go see a movie tomorrow.

   _____

   I went and taught English yesterday.

   _____

   I want to go see (meet) you the day after tomorrow.

   _____

   My friend came to eat dinner.

❑ Question and Answer

Answer the following questions using the たり verb form.

1. しゅうまつに 何を しますか。

    _____

2. 学校 / しごとの 休み時間^{じかん}に 何を しますか。

    _____

3. 日本で 何が したいですか。

    _____

4. あなたは ハリウッド・スターです。 どんなことを しますか。

    _____

5. あなたは 無人島^{むじんとう} (a deserted island) に います。 何を しますか。

    _____

❑ Translation

Translate the following sentences into Japanese.

1. I wonder if it is going to be cold tomorrow.

    _____

2. I wonder why I got fired.

    _____

3. I wonder where my cell phone is.

    _____

4. I wonder if I will have enough money this month.

    _____

5. I wonder if I can go to see Mr. Mori tomorrow.

    _____

❏ Short Dialogue

Mrs. Kuroda is complaining about her loud neighbors.

林さん:　　黒田さん、どうしましたか。おこっていますね。

黒田さん:　ええ・・・。近所の人が うるさくて、こまっています。

林さん:　　お子さんが いるからですか。

黒田さん:　いいえ。夜、うるさくて、ぜんぜん ねられません。

夜中の三時に 音楽を かけたり、犬が 外で

ないたりしています。

林さん:　　それは 大変ですね。注意しに 行きましたか。

黒田さん:　はい、もちろんです。でも、自分じゃないと 言ったり、

しょうがないと 言ったり します。

林さん:　　それは ひどいですね。今度は けいさつに 電話して下さい。

黒田さん:　そうですね。じゃあ、そう します。

❏ New Words and Expressions in the dialogue

Progressive	Kanji +	English
こまる	困る	to be troubled
かける	かける	to play (music)
ちゅういする	注意する	to give a warning
しょうがない	しょうがない	It's hopeless.

❏ Short dialogue activities

1. Practice reading the preceding short dialogue in pairs.
2. Play Kuroda san's role and explain why you are upset to your partner.

Kanji Lesson 9

今才作算止市

kanji 129-134

九 **New Kanji あたらしい漢字**

Practice writing each new kanji in the boxes provided. First trace the light gray samples while paying attention to stroke order. Then on a separate piece of paper practice writing the sample kanji words at least five times each.

今	くんよみ	いま	number		129
	おんよみ	コン・キン	meaning	now, immediately	

けさ 今朝	ことし 今年	こんばん 今晩	こんかい 今回	きょう 今日
this morning	this year	this evening	this time	today

4 strokes

丿 𠆢 今 今

今 今 今 今 今

才	くんよみ	–	number		130
	おんよみ	サイ	meaning	wit, talent, ability	

いっさい 一才	さいのう 才能	まんざい 漫才	しゅうさい 秀才	てんさい 天才
one year old	ability	comic backchat	prodigy	genius

3 strokes

一 十 才

才 才 才 才 才

作

| くんよみ | つく（る） | number | | 131 |
| おんよみ | サク・サ | meaning | make, work |

7 strokes

つくかた	さぎょう	さくぶん	さくひん	さっきょく
作り方	作業	作文	作品	作曲
way of making	work	composition, essay	work, production, opus	music composition

ノ イ イ' 作 作 作 作

作 作 作 作 作

算

| くんよみ | – | number | | 132 |
| おんよみ | サン | meaning | count, calculation |

14 strokes

さんすう	けいさん	よさん	かんさん	けっさん
算数	計算	予算	換算	決算
arithmetic	calculation	budget, estimate	conversion	balance sheet

ノ ト ヒ ゲ ゲ ゲ ゲ 筲 筲 筲 筲 算 算

算 算 算 算 算

止

| くんよみ | と（める） | number | | 133 |
| おんよみ | シ | meaning | stop |

4 strokes

ちゅうし	しけつ	ていし	きんし	いど
中止	止血	停止	禁止	行き止まり
cancellation	stop the bleeding	suspension	prohibition	dead end

丨 ト ト 止 止

止 止 止 止 止

市	くんよみ	いち		number		134
	おんよみ	シ		meaning		market, city, municipal

あさいち 朝市	いちば 市場	しやくしょ 市役所	しみん 市民	しえい 市営
morning market	marketplace	city office	citizen	municipal management

5 strokes

丶　亠　亠　市　市

市	市	市	市	市							

九 Kanji Drills 漢字ドリル

❑ Words you can write

Write the following words in the boxes. This is a great way to practice the new kanji and review the words at the same time. For the kanji that hasn't been taught yet, use hiragana.

いま
今
now

今											

こ と し
今年
this year

今	年										

きょう
今日
today

今	日										

ご さい
五才
5 years old

五	才										

てんさい
天才
天才
genius

つく
作る
作る
to make

さくぶん
作文
作文
an essay, composition

けいさん
計算
計算
calculation

よさん
予算
予算
estimate, budget

ちゅうし
中止
中止
cancellation

や
止める
止める
to stop

しりつ
市立
市立
municipal, city

いちば
市場
市ば
market, marketplace (a physical market) "the market" for stocks etc. is 市場 (しじょう)

❏ Fill in the kanji

Fill in the blanks in the following sentences with the appropriate kanji.

1. わたしは＿＿ ＿＿、＿＿ ＿＿ ＿＿ ＿＿に なりました。
   きょう に じゅう ろく さい
   I turned 26 years old today.

2. ＿＿ ＿＿より ＿＿ ＿＿のほうが かんたんです。
   けい さん さく ぶん
   Essays are easier than calculations.

3. この＿＿は＿＿き＿＿りが おおいですね。
   まち い どま
   There are a lot of dead ends in this town.

4. わたしは よく＿＿ばで ＿＿を かいます。
   いち さかな
   I often buy fish at the marketplace.

5. ＿＿で＿＿ ＿＿のゲームが ＿＿ ＿＿に なりました。
   あめ ご ご ちゅう し
   Due to rain the afternoon game got cancelled.

6. ＿＿ ＿＿の ＿＿ 張 の予＿＿を＿＿ ＿＿ しました。
   こん かい しゅっ ちょう よ さん けい さん
   I calculated the budget for the next business trip.

九 Kanji Recognition 漢字にんしき

❏ Individual words

The following words will no longer have any ふりがな (hiragana on top). You might already know some of these words, but don't worry if you can't write them as recognition is the goal.

いま 今 now	こ とし 今年 this year	こんしゅう 今週 this week	こん げつ 今月 this month
ひ 日 day	とし 年 age, year	ちか 近い near, close	つく 作る to make
まえ 前 before	だいじょう ぶ 大丈夫 okay, ok, all right		

❏ Word groups (rank and the hundreds)

The following word groups will no longer have any ふりがな (hiragana on top).

いちばん 一番 number 1, the most	に ばん 二番 number 2	さんばん 三番 number 3	よんばん 四番 number 4
ご ばん 五番 number 5	ろくばん 六番 number 6	ななばん 七番 number7	は ちばん 八番 number 8
きゅうばん 九番 number 9	じゅうばん 十番 number 10	に じゅうばん 二十番 number 20	なんばん 何番 what number?
ひゃく 百 100	に ひゃく 二百 200	さんびゃく 三百 300	よんひゃく 四百 400

ご ひゃく
五百
500

ろっぴゃく
六百
600

ななひゃく
七百
700

はっぴゃく
八百
800

きゅうひゃく
九百
900

❑ Kanji recognition cards

Print and cut out these cards, then write the hiragana and English meaning on the back.
Now you can easily practice your kanji recognition.

今	今年	今週	今月
日	年	近い	作る
前	大丈夫	一番	二番
三番	四番	五番	六番
七番	八番	九番	十番
二十番	何番	百	二百

三百	四百	五百	六百
七百	八百	九百	

Successive Actions and くなる

Before This Lesson

1. Be able to read and write 今才作算止市.

Lesson Goals

1. Learn how to use くなる with adjectives and verbs.
2. Learn how to use て form to describe successive actions.
3. Learn how to use まえ and あと with verbs.

From The Teachers

1. The くなる grammar in this lesson can be used with both adjectives and verbs. This is like learning two grammars in one!

Lesson Highlights

10-9. くなる ("It will become…," or "To get…") used with adjectives

10-10. Using くなる with verbs

10-11. Using the て form to describe successive actions

10-12. Using まえ and あと with verbs

10 New Words あたらしい ことば

日本語	漢字	えいご
ひ	日	day
とし	年	year, age
はつもうで	初詣	a shrine visit on New Year's Day
いずみ	泉	water-spring, fountain
おみやげ	お土産	souvenir
かみのけ	髪の毛	hair
せつめい	説明	an explanation
しんぱい	心配	anxiety, uneasiness
しんぱいごと	心配事	worries, troubles
ダイエット	ダイエット	diet
おしょうがつ	お正月	New Year's Day
ちがい	違い	the difference
ちかく	近く	nearby

10 New Adjectives あたらしい けいようし

日本語	漢字	えいご	タイプ
ほそい	細い	thin	い adjective
ふとい	太い	thick, fat	い adjective
とくべつ	特別	special	な adjective

10 Word Usage ことばの つかいかた

❑ 10-1. ひ (day)

1. さむい日
   a cold day

2. とくべつな日
   a special day

3. なつの日
   a summer day

4. 休みの日
   a vacation day / day off

❏ 10-2. とし (year, age)

1. むずかしい 年です。
It's a difficult age.

2. たいへんな 年でした。
It was a hard year.

3. さいこうな 年でした。
It was a great year.

4. 年は いくつですか。 *
How old are you?

* This literally means, "How many years are there?". This is a very common way to ask someone's age. It is answered the same way that 何さいですか is answered.

❏ 10-3. しんぱい (anxiety, uneasiness, worry)

しんぱい is a noun, but when translated into English it is often translated as if it is a verb. Even though the more accurate translation of しんぱいです is "it's a worry" most of the time you will hear it translated as the more natural "I am worried".

Example sentences
1. おかあさんの ことが しんぱいです。
I am worried about my mother.

2. 明日の テストの ことが しんぱいです。
I am worried about tomorrow's test.

3. しんぱいは いりません。
You don't need to worry. (the verb "to need" is taught in this lesson)

❏ 10-4. しんぱいごと (worries, troubles)

しんぱいごと is a combination of しんぱい and こと and the meaning doesn't change from しんぱい at all. You might see in a dictionary that しんぱいごと is "worries" and しんぱい is "a worry" but in Japanese most nouns can be singular OR plural so this distinction doesn't really help. In most cases the usage of しんぱいごと is the same as しんぱい.

Example sentences
1. しんぱいごとが ありますか。
Do you have any worries?

2. 私の しんぱいごとは 主人の しごとです。
   My worry is my husband's job.

3. しんぱいごとを 思い出したくない。
   I don't want to remember my worries.

10 New Verbs あたらしい どうし

どうし	えいご	た form	タイプ
取る	to take an item	とった	regular
しゃしんを 撮る	to take a picture	とった	regular
年をとる	to age, to get old	としを とった	regular
しんぱいする	to worry	しんぱいした	する
せつめいする	to explain	せつめいした	する
要る	to need	いった	いる/え exception

10 Verb Usage どうしの つかいかた

❑ 10-5. 取る (to take) 撮る (to take [a picture], make [a film])

Both 取る and 撮る are used in the same way. The only difference in usage is the which kanji is used. The item that you are "taking" is marked with the object marker を.

> **Example sentences**
>
> 1. 休みを 取りたいです。
>   I want to take a day off.
>
> 2. 今、日本語の クラスを 取っています。
>   I am taking Japanese class now.
>
> 3. しおを 取って下さい。
>   Please pass me the salt.
>
> 4. しゃしんを 撮って下さい。
>   Please take a photo.
>
> 5. しゃしんを 撮らないで下さい。
>   Please don't take any pictures.
>
> 6. 紙を 2まい 取りました。
>   I took 2 pieces of paper.
>
> 7. しゃしんを 撮るのが じょうずです。
>   I am good at taking photos.
>
> 8. しゃしんの 撮りかたが しりたいです。
>   I want to know how to take photos.

❑ 10-6. 年を取る (to age, get old)

In this lesson you will learn how to say "to get old" with the adjective ふるい by dropping the い and adding くなる. It is VERY easy to assume that ふるくなる is used to say "getting older in age". However, when you want to say "getting old" for a person or living thing you must use the verb phrase としをとる.

> **Example sentences**
> 1. 年を 取りたくないです。
>   I don't want to get old.
>
> 2. 私の おばあちゃんは年を 取っているけど、元気です。
>   My grandmother is getting on in years, but she is fine.
>
> 3. 年を 取ることは たのしくないです。
>   Getting older is not fun.

❑ 10-7. しんぱいする (to worry)

In this lesson you have already learned to say you are worried about something using しんぱい。しんぱい can also be used as a verb by adding する. The thing you are worried about is marked with を.

> **Example sentences**
> 1. 私のことを しんぱいしないで下さい。
>   Please don't worry about me.
>
> 2. おとうさんは いつも 私の ことを しんぱいしています。
>   My father is always worrying about me.
>
> 3. 今年の しゃしんが だめだったから、来年のしゃしんも しんぱいしています。
>   Because this year's picture wasn't good, I'm worried about next year's picture also.
>
> 4. 今週のテストのことを しんぱいしたけど、大丈夫でした。
>   I was worried about this week's test, but it was okay.

❑ 10-8. せつめいする (to explain)

The thing you are explaining is marked with the object marker を.

Example sentences

1. ちゃんと せつめいして下さい。
   Please explain properly.

2. 後^{あと}で せつめいしますね。
   I will explain it to you later.

3. 日本と ヨーロッパの ちがいを せつめいして下さい。
   Please explain the differences between Japan and Europe.

---

10 Grammar ぶんぽう

❑ 10-9. くなる ("It will become…," or "To get…") used with adjectives

By changing the last い of any い adjective into く and then adding なる, you can say things
like "it has become hot." Changing the tense of なる also changes the overall tense.

い adjective minus い + く+なる

it will become / it will get (adjective)

Example conversations
1. Polite conversation between wives.

A: これは だれが 作ったりょうりですか。

B: 主人^{しゅじん}が 作りました。

A: りょうりが うまくなりましたね。

A: Whose cooking is this?

B: My husband made it.

A: His cooking has gotten good!

2. Polite conversation between students.

A: 日本語は むずかしいですか。

B: さいしょは かんたんだったけど、さいきん むずかしく なりました。

A: Is Japanese difficult?

B: It was easy at first, but recently it has gotten difficult.

3. Polite conversation between friends.

A: 今、日本の 天気は どうですか。

B: よるは ちょっと さむくなります。

A: What is Japan's weather like now?

B: It gets a little cold at night.

4. Informal conversation between friends.

A: 昨日 あたらしい コンピューターを かった。

B: いくら だったの？

A: ７まん円ぐらい だった。

B: コンピューターは やすくなったね。
どこでかったの？

A: <u>近く</u>の みせで かった。

> ちかく is rarely used alone to say "nearby". It is normally connected with の to a noun like this sentence.

A: I bought a new computer yesterday.

B: How much did it cost?

A: It was about 70,000 yen.

B: Computers have sure gotten cheap.
Where did you buy it?

A: I bought it at a nearby store.

5. Informal conversation between friends.

A: 今年は 去年より あつくなったの かな.
きょねん

B: そう おもわないです。今年のほうは さむくなった とおもいます。

A: そうかな。。。

A: I wonder if this year it's gotten hotter than last year.

B: I don't think so. I think this year it's gotten colder.

A: I wonder if that's so...

❑ 10-10. Using くなる with verbs

The trick of changing the い to a く then adding なる that you just learned for い adjectives can be used with any verb form that ends in い, including たい, たくない, and ない.

> **い ending verb form minus い + く+なる**

A phrase like いきたくなる can be made with this pattern. However, the phrase does not translate into English very well. It's a nuance that can only be found in Japanese. When you say いきたくなりました, you mean, "I want to go." But the phrase implies that you did not want go before. The くなりました implies that something has changed and you now want to go. Instead of just "I want to go" it really means "NOW, I want to go."

> **Example sentences (using たい forms)**
>
> 1. えいがを 見たくなりました。
>   Now I want to see a movie.
>
> 2. 日本にいるともだちと はなしてから 日本に もどりたくなりました。
>   After talking with my friend in Japan I want to return to Japan.
>
> 3. テレビで 見てからは あたらしい トヨタを かいたくなりました。
>   After seeing it on TV I wanted to buy a new Toyota.

When くなる is used with negative verbs, it tends to be the equivalent of "no longer."

Or instead of saying "I don't want to" you are saying "now I don't want to".

Example sentences

Look at the following example sentences to see how くなる is used with a variety of verb forms. The first sentence implies that you used to be able to buy a car, but now you cannot.

1. くびに なったから 車が かえなくなりました。
   Because I got fired now I can't buy a car.

2. 昨日のパーティーで ケーキが <u>なくなりました</u>。
   At the party yesterday the cake disappeared.

> This sentence is made with ない (to not have). It makes sense to translate なくなる as "to disappear".

3. ともだちは てんきんで <u>いなくなります</u>。

My friend will be gone due to a transfer.

> Literally you are saying that your friend will become いない (not there).

❑ 10-11. Using the て form to describe successive actions

In book 3 you learned how to say one action after another using て form and から.

> **Example sentences**
>
> 1. 勉強してから あそびます。
>   I will play after studying.
>
> 2. バスにのってから タクシーにのります。
>   After I ride a bus I will take a taxi.

If you have more than one action you can simply string the て forms together without using から until you come to the last action. The last verb decides the tense of the entire sentence. The verbs should be in the order of occurrence.

> **Example sentences**
>
> 1. シャワーを あびて、あさごはんを たべて、学校に 行きました。
>   I took a shower, ate breakfast and went to school.
>   * Since the final verb is past tense, every other verb in the string is past tense.
>
> 2. 七時に おきて、四時間ぐらい 勉強して、ひるごはんを たべます。
>   I will wake up at seven, study for about four hours, and then eat lunch.
>   * The last verb is future tense, so every other verb in the string is also future tense.
>
> 3. 左に まがって、つぎの こうさてんで まがらないで、まっすぐ いって下さい。
>   Please turn left, then don't turn at the next intersection and go straight.
>   * The last verb is command form, so every other verb is also command form.

❑ 10-12. Using 前 (まえ) and 後 (あと) with verbs

前 (before) and 後 (after) can be placed after verbs to indicate that something was done before or after another action. When using 前, the verb that comes before it MUST be the dictionary form (う form).

> **う form + 前**
> before [*verb phrase*]

When using 後, the verb must be the informal past tense form (た form), because the action has already taken place.

た form verb phrase + 後
after [*verb phrase*]

Examples

1. 行く前
    before (I,you,he,she etc.) go

    行った後
    after (I,you,he,she etc.) went

2. たべる前
    before (I,you,he,she etc.) eat

    たべた後
    after (I,you,he,she etc.) eat

3. うる前
    before (I,you,he,she etc.) sell

    うった後
    after (I,you,he,she etc.) sell

4. くる前
    before (I,you,he,she etc.) come

    きた後
    after (I,you,he,she etc.) came

5. しる前
    before (I,you,he,she etc.) knew

    しった後
    after (I,you,he,she etc.) knew

Since adding 前 and 後 transforms the sentence into a time you can add the time marker に after them. NOTE: You can also use は instead of に.

Example sentences (using 前)

1. テレビを 見るまえに べん強します。
    Before I watch TV I will study.

2. テレビを 見るまえに べん強しました。
    Before I watched TV I studied.

    > Notice how the tense of the final verb in #2 and #4 changes the tense of the verb in the English translation.

3. 日本に 行くまえに 日本語学校に 行きます。
    Before I go to Japan, I will go to a Japanese language school.

4. 日本に 行くまえに 日本語学校に 行きました。
    Before I went to Japan, I went to a Japanese language school.

Example sentences (using 後)

1. テレビを 見た後に、勉強しました。
   After I watched TV, I studied.

2. 日本に 行った後に、大学に もどりました。
   After I went to Japan, I went back to college.

3. こうえんに 行った後に たべました。
   I ate after going to the park.

4. あした、がっこうから かえった後に べんきょうしたいです。
   Tomorrow, after I return from school I want to study.

10 Mini Conversations ミニ かいわ J→E

1. Casual conversation between husband and wife.

A: ゆかり、明日 帰れないよ。

B: ええ！ なんで？

A: しごと！ しごと！

B: どんな しごと？ せつめいして！

A: ごめん。みんなと のみに 行きたかったけど、早く 帰るよ。

A: Yukari, I can't come home tomorrow.

B: What! Why?

A: Work! Work!

B: What kind of work? Explain!

A: Sorry. I wanted to go drinking with everyone, but I'll come home early.

2. Polite conversation between friends.

A: おばあさんは 元気に なりましたか。

B: はい、もう 一人で あるけます。

A: よかったですね。 まだ びょういんに 行っていますか。

B: いいえ、もう 行っていません。

A: Has your grandmother gotten better?
B: Yes, she can already walk by herself now.
A: That's good. Is she still going to the hospital?
B: No, she is not going anymore.

3. Polite conversation between Japanese friends.

A: 今、イギリスから おねえさんが あそびに きています。

B: おねえさんは イギリスで 何を していますか。

A: 英語の 勉強を しています。

A: My sister is visiting from England. (Literally: "Coming to play")
B: What does your sister do in England?
A: She is studying English.

4. Polite conversation between a first timer to a Japanese restaurant and a friend.

A: 右と 左が わかりません。

B: 何のことを いっていますか。

A: おはしの もちかたの ことです。

A: I don't know right and left.
B: What are you talking about?
A: About the way to hold chopsticks.

5. Polite conversation between a cell phone company clerk and a customer.

A: いらっしゃいませ。何を さがしていますか。

B: けいたいでんわです。

A: こちらのは 一番 あたらしくて、とても べんりです。いかがですか。

B: いくらですか。

A: 三百ユーロと ぜいきんです。

B: わかりました。じゃあ それを 下さい。つかいかたを せつめいして 下さい。

A: Welcome to the store. What are you looking for?
B: A cellular phone.
A: This is the newest and most convenient one. What do you think?
B: How much is it?
A: €300 and tax.
B: Okay. Then give me this one. Please explain how it is used.

10 Mini Conversations ミニ かいわ E→J

1. Polite conversation between friends.

A: It has been decided that we will take a trip to America.
Is it all right if I come to your house, Mr. Smith?
B: When?
A: I think it will be around September.
B: That's fine. Please come.

A: アメリカに 旅行^{りょこう}することに なりました。スミスさんの 家に 行っても いいですか。
B: いつですか。
A: 九月ごろに なると おもいます。
B: いいですよ。きて下さい。

2. Polite conversation between neighbors.

A: It sure has become cold outside.
B: It is still October right?
A: This year it's been getting hot and getting cold.
B: It sure is strange.

A: そとは さむく なりましたね。
B: まだ 十月ですよね。
A: 今年は あつくなったり、さむくなったりしています。
B: へんですね。

3. Casual conversation between friends whom haven't met for a few months.

A: Masahiro kun got big didn't he.
B: It's true! (you're right). I wonder why he got so big!
A: He eats 4 times a day!
B: Well then he is going to get bigger!
A: I am scared.

A: まさひろくんは 大きくなった でしょう。

B: 本当だ！なんで こんなに 大きくなったの！？

A: 一日に 4回 たべます。

B: じゃ、もっと 大きくなるね。

A: こわいです。

4. Polite conversation between long time friends.

A: Your Japanese has gotten better. I am surprised.

B: Thank you.

A: When I met you before, you could only say "Good Afternoon."
 How much are you studying?

B: I study for about an hour every day.

A: 日本語が うまく なりましたね。びっくりしました。

B: ありがとうございます。

A: 前に会ったときは 「こんにちは」しか いえませんでしたね。
 どれぐらい 勉強していますか。

B: 毎日 一時間ぐらい 勉強しています。

5. Polite conversation between two girls in gym class.

A: I want to be thin.

B: Me too. I have been dieting since Spring.

A: What kind of diet are you doing?

B: It's a diet in which I only eat bananas.

A: I don't think that I could do it.

A: ほそく なりたいです。

B: 私も。はるから ダイエットを しています。

A: どんな ダイエットを していますか。

B: バナナしか たべない ダイエットです。

A: 私には できないと おもいます。

10 Reading Comprehension どっかい

Read the sentences below. If you don't understand them, you should review the grammar in this lesson until you do. After you have understood everything, complete the reading comprehension questions in the *Activities* section of this lesson.

① あついなつの日でした。とても 年を とった おじいさんが 山を あるいていました。

② おじいさんは のどが とても かわいていたので、水を さがしました。

③ ちかくて きれいな いずみを 見つけました。

④ 水を のんだ後、おじいさんは とても 元気に なりました。

⑤ ずっと いたかった こしも よくなりました。

⑥ 家に帰った時、おばあさんは おじいさんの かみのけが 黒くなっていたので、とても びっくりしました。

⑦ おじいさんは わかくなりました。

⑧ おじいさんは おばあさんに いずみのことを せつめいしました。

⑨ おばあさんは おじいさんを 見て、「私も わかくなりたい」と おもいました。

⑩ おばあさんは 一人で 水を のみに 行きました。

⑪ でも、おばあさんは 家に 帰ってきませんでした。

⑫ おじいさんは しんぱいして、おばあさんを さがしに 行きました。

⑬ いずみの 近くで ないている 赤ちゃんが いました。

⑭ それは おばあさんでした。

10 | Lesson Activities

❏ Reading comprehension questions

Answer the following questions about the reading comprehension in this lesson.

1. おじいさんの どこが いたかったですか。

   _____

2. おじいさんは どうやって 元気に なりましたか。

   _____

3. おばあさんは 何に びっくりしましたか。

   _____

4. おじいさんが いずみに もどったとき、近くに何が いましたか。

   _____

5. おばあさんは 何で 赤ちゃんに なりましたか。

   _____

6. あなたなら (if it were you) いずみの 水を のみますか。

   _____

❏ Sentence Patterns

Modify the sentence by adding the parts listed. You can add and remove parts as needed so that the final sentence makes sense.

> Ex. 今日、しごとを したくないです。
>
> → don't want to study   今日、勉強したくないです。
>
> → tomorrow   明日、しごとを したくないです。
>
> → last week, didn't want to 先週、しごとを したくなかったです。

1. しんぱいしたことが ありません。

   → have never explained _____

   → have never bought a souvenir _____

   → have been on a diet _____

   → have been in Japan on New Year's Day _____

2. 昨日は たいへんな日でした。

   → a special day   _____

   → a lonely day   _____

   → last year / busy year _____

   → last year / quiet year _____

3. あつくなりましたね。

   → became cold   _____

   → became bright   _____

   → became warm   _____

   → didn't become warm   _____

4. コーヒーを のみたくなりました。(use the くなる form)

   → no longer able to drink _____

   → no longer want to drink _____

   → no longer drink   _____

   → tastes good now   _____

❑ Practice 1

Look at Mr. Yokota's daily routine and answer the following questions.

7:00a.m.	get up	4:30p.m.	go home
7:15a.m.	take a shower	5:00p.m.	go to play tennis
7:30a.m.	eat breakfast	7:30p.m.	dinner with his family
8:00a.m.	go to work	8:00p.m.-9:30p.m.	watch TV
8:30a.m.- 12:00p.m.	work	11:00p.m.	go to bed
12:00p.m.-1:00p.m.	lunch break		

1. よこたさんは あさ おきてから、何を しますか。(*List two activities.*)

   _____

2. 何時に 家を 出ますか。

   _____

3. 昼休みを とる 前に、どれぐらい、しごとを しますか。

   _____

4. 家に 帰った 後に、何を しますか。 (*List three activities.*)

   _____

5. 何時間ぐらい、ねますか。

   _____

❑ Practice 2

Write about your daily routine by using the grammar in this lesson. Make at least three sentences in Japanese.

1. _____

2. _____

3. _____

❏ Short Dialogue

Two Japanese college students are talking about how they are doing.

しゅん： ひろし！久しぶりだね。

ひろし： 本当だね。高校を卒業してから、会ってないね。

今は何をしてるの？

しゅん： 卒業した後は、しばらく バイトだけしていたよ。

でも、大学に入ってからは勉強とバイトの毎日だね。

ひろし： そうか。ぼくも 一日に四つ以上、授業があって、

バイトも 二つ してるから、大変だよ。

しゅん： 高校を出る前は よかったよね。

ひろし： うん。学校に行って、四時には家に帰って、

ビデオゲームしてたからね。

しゅん あの頃が なつかしいね。

❏ New Words and Expressions in the dialogue

Progressive	Kanji +	English
そつぎょうする	卒業する	to graduate
あのころ	あの頃	those days
なつかしい	懐かしい	to feel nostalgic
バイト	バイト	part-time job
		(short for アルバイト)

❏ Short dialogue activities

Practice reading the preceding short dialogue in pairs.

Talk about your good old days and current life with your partner.

Kanji Lesson
10

思紙自寺時室

kanji 135-140

✚ **New Kanji** あたらしい漢字

Practice writing each new kanji in the boxes provided. First trace the light gray samples while paying attention to stroke order. Then on a separate piece of paper practice writing the sample kanji words at least five times each.

思	くんよみ	おも（う）	number		135
	おんよみ	シ	meaning	think, thought, idea	
9 strokes	おも 思う to think	おも　で 思い出 memories	い　し 意思 willingness, intention	おも 思いやり consideration	し　こう 思考 thought, thinking

｜ 冂 冂 用 田 田 思 思 思

思 思 思 思 思

紙	くんよみ	かみ	number		136
	おんよみ	シ	meaning	paper	
10 strokes	しんぶんし 新聞紙 newspaper	て　がみ 手紙 letter	し　へい 紙幣 paper money	お　がみ 折り紙 origami	かべがみ 壁紙 wallpaper

く 乡 幺 幺 糸 糸 紅 紙 紙 紙

紙 紙 紙 紙 紙

自

くんよみ	みずか（ら）	number		137
おんよみ	ジ・シ	meaning		oneself

6 strokes

じたく	じゆう	しぜん	じてんしゃ	じぶん
自宅	自由	自然	自転車	自分
home	freedom	nature	bicycle	myself

゛丨 门 自 自 自

自　自　自　自　自

寺

くんよみ	てら	number		138
おんよみ	ジ	meaning		temple

6 strokes

てら	じいん	やまでら	ぜんでら	あまでら
お寺	寺院	山寺	禅寺	尼寺
temple	temple	mountain temple	zen temple	nunnery

一 十 士 寺 寺 寺

寺　寺　寺　寺　寺

時

くんよみ	とき	number		139
おんよみ	ジ	meaning		time, hour, occasion

10 strokes

じかん	じきゅう	じさ	ときどき	とけい
時間	時給	時差	時々	時計
time	hourly pay	time difference	sometimes	watch

丨 冂 冂 日 日 日 時 時 時 時

時　時　時　時　時

室	くんよみ	むろ		number		140
	おんよみ	シツ		meaning	room	

9 strokes

しつない	ちかしつ	しつおん	きょうしつ	しちゃくしつ
室内	地下室	室温	教室	試着室
inside the room	basement	room temperature	classroom	dressing room

" " 宀 宀 宀 宀 宁 室 室 室

室 室 室 室 室

✛ Kanji Drills 漢字ドリル

❑ Words you can write

Write the following words in the boxes. This is a great way to practice the new kanji and review the words at the same time. For the kanji that hasn't been taught yet, use hiragana.

おも
思う
to think

思	う									

おも　で
思い出
memories

思	い	出								

かみ
紙
paper

紙										

て　がみ
手紙
letter

手	紙									

じ ぶん
自分
myself, * sometimes "you" (in Kansai area)

自	分								

みずか
自ら
for oneself

自	ら								

やまでら
山寺
mountain temple

山	寺								

じ かん
時間
time

時	間								

と けい
時計
watch, clock

時	計								

きょうしつ
教室
classroom

教	室								

むろまち
室町
the Muromachi period

室	町								

❏ Fill in the kanji

Fill in the blanks in the following sentences with the appropriate kanji.

いま　　　なん　　じ
1. ＿＿＿、＿＿＿ ＿＿＿ですか。
What time is it now?

じ ぶん　　じ かん
2. ＿＿＿分の＿＿＿ ＿＿＿が ほしいです。
I want some of my own time.

3. きょう しつ　　て がみ
   ___ ___で___ ___を かきました。
   I wrote a letter in the classroom.

4. しょう がつ　　　てら
   お ___ ___にお___に いきました。
   I want to a temple on New Year's day.

5. みずか　　ちから
   ___ らの ___で がんばりました。
   I did my best with my own power.

6. なつ やす　　おも　で　さく ぶん
   ___ ___みの___い ___を___ ___に しました。
   I put my summer vacation memories into a composition.

7. き いろ　しろ　　　がみ　つく
   ___色と___のおり___を ___ります。
   I will make yellow and white Origami.

✚ Kanji Recognition 漢字にんしき

❑ Individual words

The following words will no longer have any ふりがな (hiragana on top). You might already

know some of these words, but don't worry if you can't write them as recognition is the goal.

ちゅうごく	せんしゅう	せんげつ	きょねん
中国	先週	先月	去年
China	last week	last month	last year

とき	じかん	じぶん	あ
〜時	時間	自分	合う
when〜	time, hour	one's self; myself	to match

<ruby>え<rt></rt></ruby>
絵
painting, drawing

中田
common last name

寺田
common last name

❏ Kanji recognition cards

Print and cut out these cards, then write the hiragana and English meaning on the back.

Now you can easily practice your kanji recognition.

中国	先週	先月	去年
〜時	時間	自分	合う
絵	田中	寺田	

IF-THEN and WHEN statements

Before This Lesson

1. Be able to read and write 思紙自寺時室.

Lesson Goals

1. Learn how to make *if-then* statements using なら and the たら verb forms.
2. Learn how to say something should or should not be done.

From The Teachers

1. IF-THEN statements are very common in everyday language. Pay extra attention to learning how they work because you will be using them a lot.

Lesson Highlights

11-8. You should…

11-9. You shouldn't…

11-10. If-then statements

11-11. If-then statements using なら

11-12. If-then statements using the たら verb form

11-13. Using たら verb form to mean "when"

11-14. Using "or" with verb phrases

11 New Words あたらしい ことば

日本語	漢字	えいご
もし	もし	if
いつでも	いつでも	anytime
テキサス	テキサス	Texas
ほうげん	方言	dialect
かんさいべん	関西弁	Kansai dialect
とうほくべん	東北弁	Touhoku dialect
ひょうじゅんご	標準語	standard Japanese
でんき	電気	electricity, lights
こくばん	黒板	black board

11 Word Usage ことばの つかいかた

❏ 11-1. もし (if)

もし means "if," but is rarely used alone. It is used together with a verb conjugated into one of the various *if-then* conjugations which will be discussed in this and future lessons. Although it seems like you could just say もし いく to mean "If you go.", unfortunately this just doesn't work. いく must be conjugated into one of the "if" forms.

NOTE: You will see もしも also to mean "if..." and it is often used alone such as in the title of a poem or story.

11 New Adjectives あたらしい けいようし

日本語	漢字	えいご	タイプ
けんこうてき	健康的	healthy	な adjective
ヘルシー	ヘルシー	healthy	な adjective

11　Culture Clip カルチャー　クリップ

Japan was not always the linguistically unified country that it is today. Before there was a standard Japanese, language, geography and walls isolated many Japanese towns from each other. There were different styles of speaking from area to area, such as different sentence endings, varied intonations, and even totally unique words.

Even after unification, the different styles of speaking remained then and even in modern Japan. The Tokyo dialect, which is considered to be "standard Japanese" (ひょうじゅんご), is the official language of Japan. The most well-known dialect in Japan is probably the Kansai dialect (かんさいべん). かんさいべん is spoken in the western area of Japan, or as the Japanese call it, the "Kansai area." かんさいべん is typically associated with おおさか which is in the middle of the Kansai area. The surrounding cities also speak similarly, though there are differences from place to place. The differences between かんさいべん and ひめじべん (just one hour apart by train) might be hard for the novice Japanese speaker to notice, but there are quite a few.

11　New Verbs あたらしい　どうし

どうし	英語	た form	タイプ
借りる	to borrow, rent	かりた	いる/える
貸す	to loan, lend	かした	regular
返す	to return (pay back)	かえした	regular
夜ふかしする	to stay up late	よふかしした	irregular
点ける	to turn on	つけた	いる/える
消す	to turn off, to erase	けした	regular

11　Verb Usage どうしの　つかいかた

❑ 11-2. かりる (to borrow)

The item being borrowed is marked with the direct object marker を. Since money is often borrowed it's important to remember that amounts are NOT considered objects so if you say 100 ドル or 1000 円 remember that you don't need an を.

The person or place that you are borrowing from is marked with に or から. Whether you use に or から the meaning doesn't change.

Example sentences

1. はらさんに 五百ドル かりました。
   I borrowed 500 dollars from Mr. Hara.

2. 雨だったから、ともだちに かさを かりました。
   I borrowed an umbrella from my friend because it was raining.

3. ぎんこうから お金を かりたいです。
   I want to borrow money from the bank.

4. 明日、東京まで 運転するので 田中さんから 車を かりました。
   Since I am going to drive to Tokyo tomorrow I borrowed a car from Tanaka san.

❑ 11-3. かす (to loan)

Just like かりる when you use かす the item being loaned is marked with を and of course the same rules apply for using を when talking about amounts of something. The person that items are being lent is marked with the particle に.

Example sentences

1. 明日、車を かして下さい。
   Please lend me your car tomorrow.

2. もう あなたに お金を かしません。
   I am not going to lend you money anymore.

3. 森さんは 林さんに ３万円 かしました。
   Mori san lent Hayashi san 30,000 yen.

❏ 11-4. かえす (to return, pay back)

It's getting a little bit repetitive... perhaps you see a pattern? The item being returned is marked with を.

Example sentences

1. ちょっと、けいたいでんわを かして下さい。すぐ、かえします。
   Please lend me your cell phone a bit. I will return it right away.

2. 昨日、かりた お金を かえします。
   I will pay you back the money I borrowed yesterday.

3. としょかんに 本を かえしました。
   I returned a book to the library.

4. 中田さんは 先週 かりた さとうを 今日かえしました。
   Nakata san returned the sugar that he borrowed last week today.

❏ 11-5. よふかしする (to stay up late)

In a prior lesson you learned how to say てつや (all-nighter) and you can add する to make it into a verb to say "I stayed up all night". The meaning for よふかしする isn't drastically different, but instead of an "all-nighter" where you don't sleep, よふかしする means you stayed up late. This is similar to saying "I burned the midnight oil".

Example sentences

1. 昨日、よふかししました。

   I stayed up late yesterday.

2. 明日は 早いから、こんばん よふかししたくないです。

   Since tomorrow is early (I have to get up early), I don't want to stay up late tonight.

❏ 11-6. つける (to turn on)

The item being turned on is marked with を. Another way to say "turn on" is でんげんを いれる which means to "add power" or "turn the switch on". でんげんを いれる is normally used for computers and other devices.

Example sentences

1. テレビを つけて下さい。
   Turn the TV on please.

2. くらいから でんきを つけましょうか。
   Since it's dark shall I turn on the lights?

   > でんき means "electricity" but it is often used to mean "lights".

3. けいたいでんわの でんげんを いれて下さい。
   Please turn on the cell phone.

4. 田中さんは コンピューターを つけました。
   Tanaka-san turned on the computer.

5. おとうさんが ねてるから でんきを つけないで下さい。
   Because my father is sleeping, please don't turn on the lights (でんき).

6. だれが 私のモニターを つけたの？
   Who turned on my monitor?

❑ 11-7. けす (to turn off)

The item being turned off or erased is marked with を. Another way to say "turn off" is でんげんを きる which means to "cut power" or "turn the switch off".

Example sentences

1. テレビを けして下さい。
   Turn the TV off please.

2. あかるいから でんきを けしましょうか。
   Since it's bright shall I turn off the lights?

3. けいたいでんわの でんげんを きって下さい。
   Please turn off your cell phone.

4. 田中さんは コンピューターを きりました。
   Tanaka-san turned off the computer.

5. こくばんを けして下さい。
   Please erase the blackboard.

11 Grammar ぶんぽう

❏ 11-8. You should…

By adding ほうがいいです after any た form verb (informal past tense) you can say things like, "You should study," or, "You should go". Don't let the fact that you are using the past tense form of the verb confuse you since it doesn't have any bearing on the meaning.

> **た form verb + ほうが いいです**
> **(person) should (verb)**

Example sentences

1. 日本語を 勉強したほうが いいですよ。
   You should study Japanese.

2. やさいは ヘルシーだから、毎日 たべたほうが いいです。
   Since vegetables are healthy, you should eat them everyday.

3. 車は 高いから 銀行から お金を かりたほうが いいです。
   Since cars are expensive you should borrow money from the bank.

4. びょうきのときは オレンジ・ジュースを のんだほうが いいよ。
   You should drink orange juice when you are sick.

5. 毎日 シャワーを あびたほうが いいです。
   You should take a shower everyday.

❏ 11-9. You shouldn't…

If you want to say phrases like, "You shouldn't go," or, "You shouldn't eat," you can add ほうが いいです after the ない form (informal negative present / future tense).

> **ない form verb + ほうが いいです**
> **[person] shouldn't [verb]**

Example sentences

1. 中田さん、明日は しごとがあるから、よふかし しないほうが いいです。
   Mr. Nakata, you have work tomorrow, so you <u>shouldn't stay up late</u>.

2. 毎日、ポテトを <u>たべないほうが いい</u>ですよ。
   You <u>shouldn't eat</u> french fries every day.

3. このえいがは こわいから <u>見ないほうが</u> いいです。
   You <u>shouldn't watch</u> this movie because it's scary.

4. 田中さんは しごとが ないから、お金を <u>かさないほうが いい</u>です。
   Since Tanaka doesn't a job you <u>shouldn't loan</u> him money.

5. こどもに キャンディーを あまり <u>あげないほうが いい</u>です。
   You <u>shouldn't give</u> that much candy to children.

6. きゅうりょうが いいから、しごとを <u>やめないほうが いい</u>です。
   Because the pay is good, you <u>shouldn't quit</u> your job.

❑ 11-10. If-then statments

In Japanese, there are four types of *if-then* statements. We introduce two in this lesson.

An *if-then* statement is made up of two parts, the "condition" (IF) and the "result" (THEN). As in English, the condition is usually the first part of the sentence, and the result is the second part. For example, in the sentence, "<u>If</u> I have work tomorrow, <u>then</u> I won't be able to go to the party," the condition is, "If I have work tomorrow," and the result of the condition is, "I won't be able to go to the party."

❑ 11-11. If-then statements using なら

This is a very simple way to create an if-then statement in Japanese. All you have to do is add もし and なら. When using the なら if-then statement, any verb in the condition must be in the informal form. The tense of the verb in the result decides the formality of the sentence.

> **もし (informal verb / verb phrase) + なら + result**
> **If [condition], then [result]**

Example sentences

1. もし 今年 日本に 行か<u>ない</u>なら、たぶん 来年(らいねん) 行きます。
   If I don't go to Japan this year, I will probably go next year.

2. もし 今 時間(じかん)が ない<u>なら</u>、後(あと)で 会いましょう。
   If you don't have time right now, let's meet later.

3. 出口さんが 行か<u>ない</u>なら、私も 行きません。
   If you (Deguchi san) isn't going, I won't go either.

   > もし is not required for an IF statement.

4. ゆかりも 行く<u>なら</u>、私も 行きたいです。
   If Yukari is going to the party, then I also want to go.

The second part of the if-then statement is not limited to being just a result. It can be a request, command, suggestion or even a question.

Example sentences

1. もし スーツケースを かう<u>なら</u>、はんきゅうデパートが やすいですよ。
   If you are going to buy a suitcase, the Hankyu Department store is cheap.

2. もし 山田さんが 行け<u>ない</u>なら、私が かいに 行きましょうか。
   If you (Yamada san) are unable to go, shall I go to buy it?

3. もし 今日 家に くる<u>なら</u>、五時ごろ きて下さい。
   If you are coming to my house today, please come around five o'clock.

4. お金が ある<u>なら</u>、かった ほうが いいと おもう。
   If you have the money, I think you should buy it.

Of course, なら can also be used with adjectives, including すき and きらい. When the condition is an い or な adjective, です should be removed.

Example sentences

1. もし その みせが やすい<u>なら</u>、そこで かいましょう。
   If that store is cheap, let's buy it there.

2. イタリアりょうりが きらい<u>なら</u>、フランスりょうりは どうですか。
   If you don't like Italian cooking, how about French cooking?

3. もし おすしが すき<u>なら</u>、さしみも たぶん すきに なりますよ。
    If you like sushi, you will probably come to like sashimi too.

4. もし 日本語が すき<u>なら</u>、たぶん かんこくごも すきです。
    If you like Japanese, you will probably like Korean.

5. 昨日 着た スーツが まだ きれい<u>なら</u> 今日も 着ます。
    If the suit I wore yesterday is still clean, I will wear it today also.

6. その レストランが 高い<u>なら</u> ちがう レストランを さがしましょう。
    If that restaurant is expensive, let's find a different restaurant.

❑ 11-12. If-then statements using the たら verb form

The たら "if-then" verb form is made by adding a ら to the た form (informal past tense).

The た form verbs are covered in Course 2, Lesson 9 of Japanese From Zero!.

> **[informal past tense] + ら**
>
> **た form + ら**

> **Examples**
>
> | 行ったら | if (you) go |
> | のんだら | if (you) drink |
> | たべたら | if (you) eat |
> | かったら | if (you) buy |
> | 元気に なったら | if (you) get better |

The if-then statement using たら verb form is made similarly to the なら *if-then* statement.

> **もし [たら verb form] + result**
>
> **If [condition], then [result]**

> **Example sentences**
>
> 1. もし お金が <u>なかったら</u>、かしますよ。
>   If you don't have money, I will loan some to you.
>
> 2. もし わたしが 家を <u>かったら</u>、見に きて下さい。
>   If I buy a house, please come to see it.

3. よふかし したら、つぎの日に しごとが できないですよ。
   If you stay up late, you can't work the next day.

4. 6時までに 家に かえったら、わたしの すきな テレビばんぐみが 見れます。
   If I return home by 6 o'clock, I can watch my favorite TV show.

❑ 11-13. Using たら verb form to mean "when"

The たら verb form is a super-common form because it can also be used in a way similar to how とき is used. There is no easy way to tell when the たら form means "when" and when it means "if" beyond the context of the conversation. You will also find out that most of the time that whether you translate it as IF or WHEN, that the meaning doesn't change.

If もし is at the beginning of the if-then statement, then it will certainly be an if-then statement rather than a "when" statement.

Example sentences

1. ばんごはんを たべたら、出かけましょう。
   Let's go out when I finish eating dinner.

2. ともだちの 家に 行ったら、いつも 映画を 見ます。
   When I go to my friend's house, we always watch movies.

3. そうじを していたら、ともだちが きました。
   When I was cleaning, my friend came over.

4. もし 日本に 行ったら、絵はがきを 下さい。
   If you go to Japan, please send me a postcard.

5. おとうさんが きたら、でんわを 下さい。
   When Dad comes, call me.

❏ 11-14. Using "or" with verb phrases

In Japanese From Zero! Book 3 Lesson 5 you learned how to say a list of items with "or" using か with nouns. Remember it is optional to have か after the last item.

Example sentences

1. 犬か ねこか どっちが すきですか。
   Which do you like, dogs or cats?

2. 来年 日本か 中国に 行きたいです。
   <ruby>来年<rt>らいねん</rt></ruby>
   Next year I want to go to Japan or China.

You can also do this very same list with verb phrases. The verb phrases must be in the informal form. The final verb in the sentence determines the politeness of the entire statement. You can take ANY sentence and add it to the か list. Examples 4-7 are examples of more complicated combinations.

Example sentences

1. 東京に 行くか、大阪に 行くか まよっています。
   I am considering whether to go to Tokyo or Osaka.

2. たべるか、ねるか わからないです。
   I don't know if I am going to sleep or eat.

3. 車を かうか かわないか おしえて下さい。
   Tell me if you are going to buy a car or not.

4. 今、ねたほうがいいのか、よふかしして、勉強したほうがいいかわからないです。
   I don't know if it would be better to sleep now or stay up late and study.

5. 電車で 行きたいか、あるきたいか きめて下さい。
   <ruby>電車<rt>でんしゃ</rt></ruby>
   Please decide if you want to go by train or walk.

6. 明日、しごとが あるか、ないか わかりません。
   I don't know if I have or don't have work tomorrow.

7. この魚は たべたほうが いいのか、すてたほうが いいのか わかりません。
   I don't know if I should eat this fish, or if I should throw it away.

11 | Mini Conversations ミニ かいわ J→E

1. Polite conversation between Japanese friends.

A: もし アメリカに 行くなら、英語を 勉強したほうが いいですよ。

B: はい、私も そう 思います。いい 英語の本が ありますか。

A: ありますよ。今度、いいのを かしますね。

B: ありがとう ございます。

A: If you are going to go to America, you should study English.

B: Yes, I think so too. Do you have any good English books?

A: Yes, I do. I will loan you a good book next time, okay.

B: Thank you.

2. Polite conversation between a boyfriend and girlfriend.

A: 来月 ロンドンに てんきんに なります。

B: そうですか。さびしくなりますね。いつ 帰れますか。

A: 月曜日に わかります。もし てんきんが ながかったら、けっこんして下さい。

A: I am being transferred to London next month.

B: I see. I will be sad. When will you be able to return?

A: I will know on Monday. If the transfer is long, please marry me.

3. Polite conversation between friends.

A: アフリカに 旅行したいです。

B: もし アフリカに 行くなら、くすりを 沢山 かったほうが いいですよ。

A: どんな くすりが いいですか。

B: いろいろです。

A: I want to travel to Africa.

B: If you go to Africa, you should buy a lot of medicine.

A: What kind of medicine?

B: Various.

4. Polite conversation between friends.

A: もし 十万ドルあったら、何を しますか。

B: ボートを かって、ハワイに 行きたいです。

A: すごい ゆめですね。

A: If you had 100,000 dollars, what would you do?

B: I want to buy a boat and go all the way to Hawaii.

A: That's an amazing dream.

11 Mini Conversations ミニ かいわ E→J

1. Casual conversation between classmates.

A: I always want to hear Mai's voice.

B: Why?

A: Because I like her.

B: If you really like Mai, you should not call her in the middle of the night.

A: You're right. I won't do it anymore.

A: いつも まいさんの こえが ききたい。

B: なんで？

A: すきだから。

B: もし まいさんの ことが 本当に すきなら 夜中に でんわを しないほうが いいよ。

A: そうだね。 もう しないよ。

2. Informal conversation between someone who borrowed money and a friend.

A: If you see (meet) Tanaka, return this money to him, will you?

B: What!? How come you are not going to return it yourself?

A: Since I am borrowing a lot of money (owe a lot of), I don't want to (see) meet him.

B: I think you should return it yourself.

A: もし 田中さんに 会ったら、このお金を かえして。

B: ええ、なんで 自分で かえさないの？

A: たくさん かりているから、会いたくない。

B: 自分で かえしたほうが いいと 思うよ。

3. Informal conversation between sisters A: is the younger sister

A: Where are you going (older sister)?

B: I am going to buy clothing.

A: If you buy some, loan them to me.

B: Again!? Buy your own clothes!

A: おねえちゃん、どこに 行くの？

B: ふくを かいに 行く。

A: もし かったら、 かしてね。

B: また！ 自分の ふくを かってよ。

4. Informal conversation between sisters A: is the younger sister

A: You are sure not eating much.

B: Yeah, because I want to be thin.

A: If you get thin, what do you want to do?

B: I want to eat chocolate.

A: That is strange!

A: あまり たべないね。

B: うん、ほそくなりたいから。

A: もし ほそくなったら、何が したい？

B: チョコレートが たべたい。

A: それは おかしい！

11 | Reading Comprehension どっかい

Read the sentences below. If you don't understand them, you should review the grammar in this lesson until you do. After you have understood everything, complete the reading comprehension questions in the *Activities* section of this lesson

① ちかさんは ハワイの 大学に 行っています。

② 昨日から かれが テキサスから あそびに きています。

③ 二人は 五年前に 日本で 会いました。

④ ちかさんは 今年 大学を そつぎょうします。

⑤ 今日 ちかさんは 「もし わたしがテキサスに行ったら、
いっしょにすんでもいい？」 と ききました。

⑥ かれは 「いつでも きてよ。」 と いいました。

⑦ でも ちかさんは とても しんぱいしています。

⑧ 日本人の ともだちに テキサスに テキサスべんが あると
きいたからです。

⑨ ちかさんは今、日本に帰るか、ハワイにいるか、
テキサスに行くか、まよっています。

⑩ ともだちは 「もし テキサスに いくなら、
テキサスべんを 勉強したほうが いい」 と いいました。

⑪ けっきょく、ちかさんは かれのことが 大好きだから
テキサスに行くことに しました。

⑫ かれに 「テキサスに 行くから、テキサスべんを 教えて。」 と
いいました。

⑬ かれは 十分ぐらい わらっていました。そして、いいました。
「テキサスべんはないよ。」

⑭ ちかさんは はずかしくなりました。

11 Lesson Activities

❑ Reading comprehension questions

Answer the following questions about the reading comprehension on the previous page.

1. ちかさんの 大学は どこに ありますか。

   _____

2. ちかさんの かれは どこに すんでいますか。

   _____

3. ちかさんは 何を しんぱいしていますか。

   _____

4. けっきょく、どうしましたか。

   _____

5. ちかさんは どうして はずかしくなりましたか。

   _____

❑ Sentence Patterns

Modify the sentence by adding the parts listed. You can add and remove parts as needed so that the final sentence makes sense.

> Ex. けさ、テレビを たくさん 見ました。
>
> → a little   けさ、テレビを <u>すこし</u> 見ました。

1. 日本には 富士山が あります。
   ^{ふ じ さん}

   → healthy food   _____

   → dialects   _____

   → convenient trains   _____

   → beautiful temples   _____

2. 一万円、かりてもいいですか。
　　　　<small>まん</small>

　　→ Can I lend?　　　　_____

　　→ Can I return?　　　_____

　　→ Can I pay?　　　　_____

　　→ I have lost　　　　_____

3. 毎日 漢字を れんしゅうしたほうが いいですよ。

　　→ throw away garbage　_____

　　→ quit your current job　_____

　　→ You shouldn't　　　_____

　　→ stay up late　　　　_____

4. 時間が あるなら、映画を見ましょう。
　　　　　　　　　　　<small>えい が</small>

　　→ go to buy souvenirs　_____

　　→ rent a DVD　　　　_____

　　→ If you are tired　　　_____

　　→ If you want to stay home　_____

5. 日本に 行ったら、毎日 雨が ふりました。

→ I spoke nothing but Kansai dialect_____

→ I used a lot of money _____

→ when I took time off work_____

→ buy me some anime DVD _____

❑ Question and Answer

Answer the following questions in Japanese.

1. 道^{みち}に まよったら、どうしますか。

_____

2. 東京に てんきんになったら、そこで 何を しますか。

_____

3. 病気^{びょうき}に なったら、何を しますか。

_____

4. ギャンブルで 五百万円^{まん} かったら、何を かいますか。

_____

❏ Practice 1

Read each sentence on the left and select an appropriate sentence that matches up from those in the box.

Ex. 日本に行くなら、   (C)   A. あのみせが いいですよ。

1. 今日、いそがしいなら、   (   )   B. 元気に なりますよ。

2. ステーキを たべるなら、   (   )   **C. おみやげを かって下さい。**

3. たん生日プレゼントを かうなら、 (   )   D. 赤ワインが 合いますよ。

4. このくすりを のんだら、   (   )   E. 明日、おきられませんよ。

5. お金が なかったら、   (   )   F. 明日、会いませんか。

6. こんばん、よふかししたら、   (   )   G. 私が かしますよ。

❏ Practice 2

Look at the pictures below and make suggestions using ～ほうがいいです.

1. _____

2. _____

3. _____

4. _____

5. _____

❑ Short Dialogue

Miss Mori and Mr. Terada are talking about their ideal match.

森_{もり}さん	寺田くんは 結婚_{けっこん}するなら、どんな人としたい？
寺田_{てらだ}くん	そうだなあ。ぼくは きれいで、明_{あか}るくて、 料理上手_{りょうり}な人がいいな。
森さん	ふ～ん。私は やさしくて、男らしい人が いいな。
寺田くん	それだけ？ 森さんは 理想_{りそう}が 高いから、もっとあるでしょう？
森さん	失礼_{しつれい}だね！でも、私は何もできないから、器用_{きよう}な人がいい。
寺田くん	じゃあ、仕事_{しごと}も 家事_{かじ}も 日曜大工_{にちようだいく}も できる人？
森さん	うん。そんな人がいたら、いいな。
寺田くん	ちょっと、難_{むずか}しいと思うけど、がんばって。 見つかったら、教_{おし}えてね。

❑ **New Words and Expressions in the dialogue**

Progressive	Kanji +	English
おとこ 男 らしい	男らしい	manly, manlike
りそう	理想	ideal, dream,
きよう	器用	skilled in using one's hands
にち　　だいく 日よう大工	日曜大工	do-it-yourself (carpenter)
な (particle)	–	used to show envy (end of sentence)

❑ **Short dialogue activities**

Practice reading the preceding short dialogue in pairs.

Talk about your ideal match with your partner.

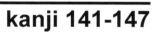

Kanji Lesson 11

社弱首秋春書少
kanji 141-147

＋一 New Kanji あたらしい漢字

Practice writing each new kanji in the boxes provided. First trace the light gray samples while paying attention to stroke order. Then on a separate piece of paper practice writing the sample kanji words at least five times each.

社

くんよみ	やしろ	number	141
おんよみ	シャ	meaning	shrine, company, society

7 strokes

しゃかい 社会	しょうしゃ 商社	じんじゃ 神社	かいしゃ 会社	しゃいん 社員
society	trading company	Shinto shrine	company	company employee

゛ ラ ネ ネ ネ ネー 社 社

社 社 社 社 社

弱

くんよみ	よわ（い）	number	142
おんよみ	ジャク	meaning	weak

10 strokes

じゃくてん 弱点	よわね 弱音	よわむし 弱虫	きょうじゃく 強弱	ひんじゃく 貧弱
weak point	negative thoughts, complaint	coward	strength and weaknesses	poor (physically)

ヲ コ 弓 弓 弓 弓゛ 弓゛ 弱 弱 弱

弱 弱 弱 弱 弱

首	くんよみ	くび	number	143
9 strokes	おんよみ	シュ	meaning	neck, head, first, chief

しゅしょう 首相	しゅい 首位	あしくび 足首	くびわ 首輪	しゅと 首都
Prime Minister	head position	ankle	collar	capital city

首 首 首 首 首

秋	くんよみ	あき	number	144
9 strokes	おんよみ	シュウ	meaning	fall, autumn

あきば 秋晴れ	しゅうぶん 秋分	しゅうき 秋季	ばんしゅう 晩秋	りっしゅう 立秋
fine autumn day	autumnal equinox	autumn season	late autumn	the first day of autumn

秋 秋 秋 秋 秋

春	くんよみ	はる	number	145
9 strokes	おんよみ	シュン	meaning	spring

せいしゅん 青春	ししゅんき 思春期	はるま 春巻き	はるいちばん 春一番	はるひ 春の日
youth	puberty	spring roll	first storm of spring	a spring day

春 春 春 春 春

書	くんよみ	か（く）	number		146
	おんよみ	ショ	meaning	write, book	

しょてん 書店	としょかん 図書館	しょどう 書道	かきとめ 書留	しょるい 書類
bookstore	library	calligraphy	registered mail	documents

10 strokes

ー マ ユ ヨ ヨ 聿 書 書 書 書

書　書　書　書　書

少	くんよみ	すく（ない）・すこ（し）	number		147
	おんよみ	ショウ	meaning	few, young	

すく 少ない	たしょう 多少	しょうしょく 少食	しょうしょう 少々	しょうねん 少年
few	more or less, somewhat	light eating	just a little	boy

4 strokes

ノ 丿 小 少

少　少　少　少　少

十一 Kanji Drills 漢字ドリル

❑ **Words you can write**

Write the following words in the boxes. This is a great way to practice the new kanji and
review the words at the same time. For the kanji that hasn't been taught yet, use hiragana.

かいしゃ
会社
company

| 会 | 社 | | | | | | | | |

しゃかい
社会
society

| 社 | 会 | | | | | | | | |

よわ
弱い
weak

| 弱 | い | | | | | | | | |

よわむし
弱虫
coward, weakling

| 弱 | 虫 | | | | | | | | |

くび
首
neck

| 首 | | | | | | | | | | |

あしくび
足首
ankle

| 足 | 首 | | | | | | | | | |

あしくび
足首
to mix, to blend

| 交 | ぜ | る | | | | | | | |

あき
秋
fall, autumn

| 秋 | | | | | | | | | | |

りっしゅう
立秋
the first day of autumn

立秋 ☐ ☐ ☐ ☐ ☐ ☐ ☐ ☐

はる
春
spring (season)

春 ☐ ☐ ☐ ☐ ☐ ☐ ☐ ☐

せいしゅん
青春
youth

青春 ☐ ☐ ☐ ☐ ☐ ☐ ☐

か
書く
to write

書く ☐ ☐ ☐ ☐ ☐ ☐ ☐

しょどう
書道
calligraphy

書どう ☐ ☐ ☐ ☐ ☐ ☐

すこ
少し
a little bit

少し ☐ ☐ ☐ ☐ ☐ ☐ ☐

しょうねん
少年
boy, juvenile, young boy

少年 ☐ ☐ ☐ ☐ ☐ ☐ ☐

❑ Fill in the kanji

Fill in the blanks in the following sentences with the appropriate kanji.

　　こ　とし　　あき
1. ___ ___の___は さむかったです。
Fall this year was cold.

　　あし　くび　　すこ
2. ___ ___が___し、いたいです。
My ankle hurts a little.

3. ___ ___みに___ ___を___きました。
<small>はる　やす　　　さく　ぶん　　　か</small>

I wrote an essay on spring vacation.

4. ___く、___ ___に___た ほうがいいですよ。
<small>はや　　　しゃ　かい　　　で</small>

You should enter society soon.

5. わたしは___ ___に___いです。
<small>けい　さん　　　よわ</small>

I am weak with calculations.

十一 Kanji Recognition 漢字にんしき

❏ Individual words

The following words will no longer have any ふりがな (hiragana on top). You might already

know some of these words, but don't worry if you can't write them as recognition is the goal.

はる	ともだち	えいが	こんかい
春	友達	映画	今回
spring	friend	movie	this time

ぜんかい	はい	こども	かしゅ
前回	入る	子供	歌手
last time	to enter, to go into	child, children	a singer

❏ Kanji recognition cards

Print and cut out these cards, then write the hiragana and English meaning on the back.

Now you can easily practice your kanji recognition.

春	友達	映画	今回
前回	入る	子供	歌手

Specific periods and amounts

12

Before This Lesson

1. Be able to read and write 社弱首秋春書少.

Lesson Goals

1. Learn how to say something was accomplished within a certain amount of time or with a specific quantity of item.
2. Learn how to use まで with verbs to define a period of time.

From The Teachers

1. You have learned that particle で can be a "by which means" marker. Now you will learn how to use it with time and amounts, but it is still just a "means" marker.

Lesson Highlights

12-8. いる (to need)

12-10. Using まで with verbs

12-11. Using で with amounts

12 New Words あたらしい ことば

日本語	漢字	えいご
じゅんび	準備	preparations
ワイシャツ	ワイシャツ	dress shirt
たいわん	台湾	Taiwan
ぜんかい	前回	the last time
こんかい	今回	this time
はいたつ	配達	delivery
けんか	喧嘩	a fight
のりもの	乗り物	a ride, a mode of transportation
シリコンバレー	シリコンバレー	Silicon Valley
ゆうごはん	夕ご飯	dinner
ベビーシッター	ベビーシッター	baby sitter
あい	愛	love
ほか	他	other, another
はんそで	半袖	short-sleeved shirt
カラオケ	カラオケ	karaoke
さん エルディーケー ３ＬＤＫ	3LDK	3 LDK three bedrooms, a living room, dining room, and kitchen

12 Word Usage ことばの つかいかた

❑ 12-1. じゅんび (preparations)

じゅんび can be made into the verb じゅんび(を)する (to prepare). The item being prepared is connected to じゅんび with a の. In these examples の means "for".

Example sentences

1. 明日の じゅんびを しましょう。
   Let's prepare <u>for</u> tomorrow.

2. けっこんしきの じゅんびは たいへんです。
   It's hard to prepare <u>for</u> a wedding ceremony.

3. しごとの じゅんびを しています。
I am preparing <u>for</u> work.

❏ 12-2. あい (love)

あい also can be made into the verb あいする (to love). The person being loved is marked with the the direct object marker を. Note that since "love" is an ongoing action ています form is used.

> **Example sentences**
>
> 1. むかしから あなたを あいしています。
> I have loved you from a long time ago.
>
> 2. かぞくを あいしています。
> I love my family.

❏ 12-3. ほか (other, another)

ほか is connected to words with a の.

> **Examples**
>
> ほかの人   another person, other people
> ほかの日   another day, other days

> **Example sentences**
>
> 1. 今日の パーティーに <u>ほかの人</u>が きますか。
> Will <u>other people</u> be coming to today's party?
>
> 2. ほかの ペットを かっていますか。
> Are you raising any <u>other pets</u>?

❏ 12-4. 3 LDK (three rooms: living room, dining room and kitchen)

This is the standard way Japanese classify apartments and houses. If the house had five rooms it would be a 5 LDK. Some apartments may not have a dining room or kitchen, so this is how this classification came about: L = Living, D = Dining, K = Kitchen

12 | New Verbs あたらしい どうし

どうし	えいご	た form	タイプ
頼む (たの)	to request,(order) ask for	たのんだ	regular
用意する (よう い)	to prepare, to fight	ようい した	する
喧嘩する (けん か)	to have a fight	けんか した	する
要る (い)	to need, exc.	いった	いる/える exception
貯める (た)	to save (money), to collect	ためた	いる/える

12 | Verb Usage どうしの つかいかた

❏ 12-5. たのむ (to request, ask for)

The direct object marker を is used to mark the thing that is requested. And the person / place to which the request was made is marked with に.

> **Example sentences**
> 1. ピザの はいたつを たのみました。
>   I ordered a pizza delivery.
>
> 2. ジョージさんに たのみました。
>   I asked George to do it.

It's common that the speaker includes the actual words used to make a request when using たのむ. The words are quoted with the quotation marker と.

> **Example sentences**
> 1. いっしょに たべてと たのんだ。
>   I asked (him/her) to eat with (me/us).
>
> 2. 子どもを 見て下さいと たのみました。
>   I asked (him/her) to watch the children.

❑ 12-6. ようい(を)する (to prepare)

The direct object marker を is used to mark the thing being prepared. The usage of ようい and じゅんび are identical.

Example sentences

1. 明日の 旅行の よういを しています。

   I am preparing for tomorrow's trip.

2. おなかが 空いた。夕ご飯の よういを しましょう。

   I am hungry. Let's prepare dinner.

❑ 12-7. けんか(を)する (to fight, to have a fight)

The person that is being fought is marked with と.

Example sentences

1. 私は よく おとうさんと けんかを します。

   I often fight with my father.

2. もし おにいさんと けんかしたら、たぶん まけます。

   If I fight with my brother, maybe I will lose.

The reason for the fight can be indicated by から, ので, and the くて form.

Example sentences

1. お金が なくて、けんかしました。

   Without any money, we fought. / We fought because we didn't have any money.

2. みちこさんは ジェフさんと けんかを したから、パーティーに こなかった。

   Since Michiko had a fight with Jeff, she didn't come to the party.

To say you fought about something you can use のことで or について, which means, "concerning". More about について is covered later in this lesson.

Example sentences

1. お金についてのけんかは おおいと 思います。

   I think there are many fights <u>about</u> money.

2. わたしたちは よく お金のことで けんかを します。

   We often fight <u>about</u> money.

❏ 12-8. いる (to need)

The item that is needed is marked by the subject marker が. The dictionary form of this verb is exactly the same as いる (to be, to exist); however, it is important to note that this new verb you are learning is NOT conjugated in the same way. This verb is an いる / える exception verb, which means you conjugate it as if it was a regular verb.

Example sentences

1. 私は もっと 時間が いります。
   I need more time.

2. 今日、私は 車が いらないから、つかっても いいよ。
   I don't need the car today, so you can use it.

❏ 12-9. ためる (to save, to collect)

The thing being saved or collected is marked with the direct object particle を.

Example sentences

1. 来年 ヨーロッパに 行きたいから、今日から お金を ためます。
   <ruby>来年<rt>らいねん</rt></ruby>

   Since I want to go to Europe next year, I am going to save money starting today.

2. 今、お金を ためています。
   I am saving money now.

---

12 | Grammar ぶんぽう

❏ 12-10. Using まで with verbs

まで can be attached to a positive informal verb to say things like, "until I [verb]." When using まで, the verb that comes before it must be the dictionary form. After the [verb] + まで combination, an action is normally described.

> **[dictionary form verb] + まで + action**
> **until I [verb] + action**

IMPORTANT: Remember that the resulting combination is a time reference. Look at the following series of similar examples using time references in them:

Example sentences

1. ねむくなるまで 勉強を しました。

   Until I got sleepy, I studied. / I studied until I got sleepy.

2. 日本に 行くまで お金を ためます。

   Until I go to Japan, I will save money. / I will save money until I go to Japan.

3. 日本に 行きたいけど、大学を そつぎょうするまで 行けません。

   I want to go to Japan, but until I graduate from college I can't go.

4. けっこんするまで、いつも 一人でした。

   Until I got married, I was always alone.

❏ 12-11. Using で with amounts

で is used with time spans and quantities. It can mean for, per, in, within, or with, depending on the context. It's used in sentences like 五ふんで ばんごはんを たべました。"I ate dinner in five minutes." Look at the following sentences to see how it can be used:

IMPORTANT: Remember that a time span is *not* itself a time. 一時間 (one hour) is very different from 一時 (one o'clock). Make sure that you are using a time span and *not* a time in your sentences.

> ### [time span] + で + [action]
> ### to do [action] within [time span]

Example sentences (using time spans)

1. 私は 一時間で 百ページの 本が よめます。
   I can read a 100-page book in one hour.

2. スミスさんは 日本語を 勉強して、三年で ペラペラに なりました。
   Mr. Smith studied Japanese and became fluent in three years.

3. 五分で もどります。
   I will be back in five minutes.

4. この クラスは 二週間で おわります。
   This class will end in two weeks.

5. 昨日 かったアイス・クリーム一日で ぜんぶ たべました。
   I ate all the ice cream I bought yesterday in one day.

Example sentences (using amounts and quantities)

1. この CD は 六枚で 三千円 です。
   These CDs are 3000 yen for six.

2. 今、七百ドルで 日本までの こうくうけんが かえます。
   Now you can buy an airline ticket to Japan for 700 dollars.

3. 一ドルで ここまで バスで こられます。
   You can come here by bus for one dollar.

4. 五人で カラオケに 行くと 思います。
   I think I will go to karaoke with five people.

5. 七月は あついから、Tシャツ 一枚で いいです。
   Since July is hot, you only need one T-shirt. (with one shirt, it is good)

12 Q&A しつもんと こたえ J→E

1. ロサンゼルスまで 何時間で 行けますか。
In how many hours can you go to Los Angeles?

四時間ぐらいで 行けると 思います。
I think you can you go in about four hours.

車で 二時間で 行けます。
I can go in two hours by car.

2. いくらで アイスクリームが かえますか。
For how much can you buy ice cream?

一ドル 五十セントで かえます。
You can buy it for $1.50.

二ドルで 大丈夫です。
Two dollars would be fine. (You can buy it with two dollars.)

3. そつぎょうするまで 後 何年ですか。
How many years until you graduate?

後 二年です。
Two more years.

去年の 春に そつぎょうしました。
I graduated last spring.

4. いつまで ここに いますか。
How long will you be here?

くらくなるまで いるよ。
I will be here until it gets dark.

出口さんが 車で います。
I will be here until Mr. Deguchi comes.

12 Q&A しつもんと こたえ E→J

1. **How many people will you go with?**
   何人で 行きますか。

   I will go with three people.
   三人で 行きます。

   I will go alone.
   一人で 行きます。

2. **What are you going to do today?**
   今日、何を しますか。

   I am going to study until school starts.
   学校が はじまるまで 勉強します。

   After I go to school, I am going to see my friends.
   学校に 行ってから、友達に 会います。

3. **What are you doing after work tomorrow?**
   明日、しごとの後 何を しますか。

   I might go see a movie with my aunt.
   おばさんと 映画を 見に行きます。

   I am going to watch a movie by myself.
   一人で 映画を 見に行きます。

12 Mini Conversations ミニ かいわ J→E

1. **Polite conversation between friends**
   A: 何が ほしいですか。
   B: 車が ほしいけど、お金を ためるまで かえないです。
   A: お金が いくら いりますか。
   B: 百万円ぐらいです。

A: What do you want?
B: I want a car, but I can't buy one until I save some money.
A: How much money do you need?
B: About one million yen.

2. Polite conversation between neighbors

A: 子供が 大きくなるまでに 家を かいたいです。
B: どんな家が ほしいですか。
A: ３LDKの 学校に 近い 家が いいですね。
B: もし かったら、あそびに 行っても いいですか。
A: いつでも きて下さい。

A: I want to buy a house by the time the children get big.
B: What kind of house do you want?
A: I would like a three-bedroom house that is close to school.
B: If you buy one, is it all right if I come over and play? (hang out)
A: Please come any time.

3. Polite conversation between company workers

A: 今回の 出張_{しゅっちょう} は どこに 行くことに なりましたか。
B: また、シリコンバレーですよ。
A: ええ、またですか。前回も そうでしたよね。
B: はい。前回 ホテルだいが 高かったから、今回 やすいアパートを かりることに なりました。

A: Where are you being sent on this business trip?
B: Silicon Valley again.
A: What! Again? It was same last time, right?
B: Yes. Since the cost of the hotel was expensive last time, this time it has been decided to rent a cheap apartment.

4. **Conversation between a parent and child. Which speaker is the child?**
Look at the formality to find out.

A: どうしたの？ 元気が ないね。

B: おにいちゃんと けんか した。

A: どうして？ また、おにいちゃんの へやに 入ったの？

B: うん。テレビが 見たかったから...

A: What happened? (What's the matter?) You are not fine. (You don't look good.)

B: I had a fight with my brother.

A: Why? Did you go into his room again?

B: Yeah. Because I wanted to watch TV...

12 Mini Conversations ミニ かいわ E→J

1. **Informal conversation between a married couple**

A: Have you prepared for tomorrow?

B: I haven't done it yet.

A: You should do it before you get sleepy.

B: I am not a child anymore, so don't say anything.

A: Fine. Then don't ask me to do anything tomorrow.

A: 明日の よういを したの？

B: まだ していない。

A: ねむくなる前に したほうが いいよ。

B: もう 子供じゃないから 何も いわないで。

A: わかった。 じゃあ、明日 何も たのまないでね。

2. **Polite conversation between friends with kids**

A: Hasn't the babysitter come yet?

B: No, she hasn't come yet. When did you request (him / her)?

A: I requested them 2 hours ago. Normally she comes in 30 minutes.

B: Call one more time please.

A: ベビーシッターは まだ きませんか。

B: まだ こないですね。 いつ たのみましたか。

A: 二時間前に たのみました。ふつうは 三十分で きますが...

B: もう一度 でんわして下さい。

3. Informal conversation between sisters A: is the younger sister

A: I need a car tomorrow, so please loan it to me.

B: Okay, but how come you don't (ask) request your dad?

A: Because I have been fighting with him since the day before yesterday,
I can't request to him.

A: 明日、車が いるから かして 下さい。

B: いいけど、なんで おとうさんに たのまないの？

A: おとといから けんか しているから とのめないです。

4. Polite conversation between two people

A: How much yen can I buy with 100 dollars?

B: Since the yen is becoming cheap now, about 12,000 yen.

A: 百ドルで 円が どれくらい かえますか。

B: 今、円が やすくなってるから、一まん二千円ですね。

12 Reading Comprehension どっかい

Read the sentences below. If you don't understand them, you should review the grammar in this lesson until you do. After you have understood everything, complete the reading comprehension questions in the *Activities* section of this lesson.

① ジムさんは 日本語と 英語の つうやくです。

② あさってから 五日間、しごとで たいわんに 行くことに なりました。

③ ジムさんは ほかの しごとが たくさん あったから、
　出張のじゅんびを おくさんに たのみました。

おくさん：	「しごとは 何日 あるの？」
ジムさん：	「二日間だけだよ。」
おくさん：	「じゃあ ワイシャツは 二まいで いいね。」
ジムさん：	「うん、いいと 思う。それから たいわんは たぶん、
	むしあついから
	はんそでを よういしてね。」
おくさん：	「わかった。あっ、今回 お土産は いらないよ。」
ジムさん：	「うん。ほしいものが あるけど、かってもいい？」
おくさん：	「何なの？」
ジムさん：	「たいわんの 歌手の CDだよ。」
おくさん：	「いいよ。」

④ おくさんは じゅんびを 一時間ぐらいで おわりました。

⑤ けっきょく ジムさんは しごとが いそがしくて、
　CDが かえませんでした。

⑥ でも、空港で おくさんの おみやげを かいました。

12　Lesson Activities

❑ Reading comprehension questions

Answer the following questions about the reading comprehension in this lesson. These questions are asked in order so make sure you follow the context.

1.　ジムさんは どれぐらい、たいわんに いますか。

_____

2.　つうやくの しごとは 何日間ですか。

_____

3.　きせつ (season) は いつだと おもいますか。

_____

4.　おくさんは たいわんで 何か ほしいですか。

_____

5.　ジムさんは たいわんで 時間が ありましたか。

_____

❑ Sentence Jumble

Using ONLY the words and particles provided, create Japanese sentences that match the English translation. You can conjugate adjectives and verbs and reuse items if needed.

1.　日本・まで・なんにち・かう・行く・を・に・ためる・いくら・か
　　お金・ある・いる

_____

How much money will you save until you go to Japan?

_____

How many days until you go to Japan?

_____

Until what day will you be in Japan?

2.   で・５ふん・この・これ・を・が・は・に・できる・たべる・なに・か
　　　ばんごはん・しゅくだい・なんじかん・しごと

_____

I was able to do my homework in 5 minutes.

_____

Can you eat dinner in 5 minutes?

_____

How many hours were you able to do this work?

3.   要る・明日・しお・まで・に・を・が・がっこう・３時・４時・から・もっと
　　　この・スープ・は・ある・車

_____

This soup needs more salt.

_____

Because I have school at 4 o'clock, I need the car at 3 o'clock.

_____

I don't have school until tomorrow.

4.   を・たのむ・何・が・かどうか・ピザ・わかる・だれ・に・か・おいしい

_____

Who asked for (ordered) pizza?

_____

I don't know if I will order or not.

_____

The pizza that I asked for wasn't delicious.

❏ Practice 1

Complete the following sentences with what best matches for you in Japanese.

1. 高校を そつぎょうするまで、 _____

2. けっこんするまで、 _____

3. 日本語が うまくなるまで、 _____

4. _____まで、 日本語を勉強しませんでした。

5. _____まで、 ねられません。

6. _____まで、 海外に行ったことがありません。

❏ Practice 2

Fill in the appropriate particles when required to complete the sentences.

1. この本は むずかしい (   ) 、 一日 (   ) よめませんでした。

2. 夕ご飯のよういをする (   ) 、 ちょっと、 まって下さいね。

3. ロサンゼルス (   ) 日本 (   ) 、 ひこうき (   ) 十一時間ぐらいですよ。

4. 近所の人 (   ) しずかにして下さい (   ) たのみました。

5. ぼくは 彼女 (   ) いつも けんか (   ) しています。

6. 後、四週間（　　　）学校（　　　）おわります。

7. 私は ときどき（　　　）電車（　　　）友達（　　　）会い（　　　）行きます。

❏ Question and Answer

Answer the following questions using the words and patterns in this lesson.

1. 今、あなたに 何が いりますか。

_____

2. 家族と けんかを しますか。

_____

3. 何LDK に すんでいますか。

_____

_____

4. 夕ご飯の じゅんびは だれが しますか。

_____

5. いくらで 日本までの こうくうけんが かえますか。

_____

6. いつまで 日本語を 勉強したいですか。

_____

_____

❑ Short Dialogue

Sakuta-san is in trouble with his mother.

作田さん　　昨日、お母さんと すごいけんかをした。

山本さん　　そう。 今回はどっちが悪いの？

作田さん　　多分、私かな・・・。

山本さん　　何をしたの？ 家のことを 手伝わないとか？

作田さん　　う～ん。それも ある。期末試験の成績もよくなかった。

山本さん　　何点だったの？

作田さん　　五十点以下だったよ。 お母さんは再テストに

　　　　　　合格するまで、私に口をきかないと思う。

山本さん　　点テストは いつなの？

作田さん　　実は、後五時間で始まる・・・ どうしよう。

❑ New Words and Expressions in the dialogue

日本語	漢字	えいご
てつだう	手伝う	to help out, to give some help
きまつしけん	期末試験	term-end exam, final exam
さいテスト	再テスト	makeup exam
ごうかくする	合格する	to pass
くちをきかない	口を利かない	will not talk to me/someone
どうしよう	どうしよう	What shall I do?

❑ Short dialogue activities

Practice reading the preceding short dialogue in pairs.

Play each role with your partner. If you play Sakuta san's role, explain why you had an argument with your mother and how you will reconcile with her.

Kanji Lesson
12

場色食心新親図

kanji 148-154

十二 New Kanji あたらしい漢字

Practice writing each new kanji in the boxes provided. First trace the light gray samples while paying attention to stroke order. Then, on a separate piece of paper practice writing the sample kanji words at least five times each.

場	くんよみ	ば	number		148
	おんよみ	ジョウ	meaning	place	

ばしょ 場所	かいじょう 会場	あなば 穴場	こうじょう 工場	ばめん 場面
place	assembly hall	little-known good place	factory	scene

12 strokes

一 十 土 ±゛ 圤 坍 垌 垸 場 場 場 場

場	場	場	場	場							

色	くんよみ	いろ	number		149
	おんよみ	ショク, シキ	meaning	color	

しきし 色紙	かおいろ 顔色	いろいろ 色々	さんしょく 三色	きいろ 黄色
colored paper	complexion	various	three-color	yellow color

6 strokes

ノ ク タ 勺 乌 色

色	色	色	色	色							

食

9 strokes

くんよみ	く・た	number	150
おんよみ	ショク・ジキ	meaning	eat

しょくじ	た ほうだい	え じき	がいしょく	く に
食事	食べ放題	餌食	外食	食い逃げ
meal	all you can eat	prey	eating out	leaving without paying

ノ 人 へ 今 今 今 食 食 食

食 食 食 食 食

心

4 strokes

くんよみ	こころ	number	151
おんよみ	シン	meaning	heart, mind

こころづよ	しんぞう	ちゅうしん	あんしん	こころ が
心強い	心臓	中心	安心	心掛け
feel confident; supportive	heart (medical name)	center	relief	mind-set

ノ 心 心 心

心 心 心 心 心

新

13 strokes

くんよみ	あたら・あら・にい	number	152
おんよみ	シン	meaning	new, fresh, novel

あら	しんねん	しんぶん	にいがたけん	さいしん
新たに	新年	新聞	新潟県	最新
newly	new year	newspaper	Niigata prefecture	latest

亠 亠 亠 立 立 立 辛 辛 亲 亲 新 新 新

新 新 新 新 新

親	くんよみ	おや・した		number	153
	おんよみ	シン		meaning	parent, intimate

おやゆび 親指	しんせき 親戚	しんゆう 親友	しんせつ 親切	りょうしん 両親
thumb	relative	close friend	kind	parents

16 strokes

親 指 親 戚 親 友 親 切 両 親

` ` 亠 六 产 立 立 辛 亲 亲 耕 親 親 親 親 親 親

親 親 親 親 親

図	くんよみ	はか		number	154
	おんよみ	ズ・ト		meaning	figure, drawing

ずこう 図工	いと 意図	ちず 地図	あいず 合図	としょけん 図書券
drawing and manual arts	intention, purpose	map	sign	book certificate

7 strokes

｜ 冂 冂 図 図 図 図

図 図 図 図 図

十二　Kanji Drills 漢字ドリル

❑ Words you can write

Write the following words in the boxes. This is a great way to practice the new kanji and review the words at the same time. For the kanji that hasn't been taught yet, use hiragana.

かいじょう
会 場　会場
assembly hall, meeting place

ば あい
場 合　場合
case, situation

みょう じ
名 字　名字
last name

いろ
色　色
color

さんしょく
三 色　三色
three-color

き いろ
黄 色　黄色
yellow

た
食 べる　食べる
to eat

がいしょく
外 食　外食
eating out

こころづよ
心強い　心強い
supporting, reassuring

ちゅうしん
中心　中心
center, middle

あたら
新しい　新しい
new

しんねん
新年　新年
new year

おや
親　親
parents

しんゆう
親友　親友
best friend

した
親しい　親しい
intimate, close

はか
図る　図る
to plan

あいず
合図　合図
sign, signal

ちず
地図　ち図
map

❑ **Fill in the kanji**

1. わたしの すきな＿＿は ＿＿と＿＿と＿＿です。
<small>いろ　　あか　くろ　しろ</small>

My favorite colors are red, black, and white.

2. ＿＿が いるから ＿＿ ＿＿いです。
<small>おや　　　　　こころ づよ</small>

Because my parents are around I am reassured.

3. ＿＿べる＿＿しょを きめましたか。
<small>た　　　ば</small>

Have you decided the place to eat?

4. ＿＿ ＿＿に＿＿い お＿＿に ＿＿きました。
<small>しん ねん　ふる　　てら　い</small>

In the new year I went to some old temples.

5. ＿＿ ＿＿は＿＿ ＿＿で はたらいています。
<small>しん ゆう　こう じょう</small>

My friend works at a factory.

6. わたしが＿＿ ＿＿を するまで、まって＿＿さい。
<small>あい　ず　　　　　　　　　　くだ</small>

Until I make a signal, please wait.

7. ＿＿ ＿＿ ＿＿ ＿＿に あの＿＿ ＿＿でコンサートがある。
<small>しち がつ よっ か　　　かい じょう</small>

On July 4th, there is a concert in that meeting hall.

8. ＿＿ ＿＿さん、ちょっと＿＿ ＿＿が わるいですね。
<small>たに ぐち　　　　　　　　かお いろ</small>

Taniguchi-san, you look a bit pale.

The giving and receiving verbs

13

Before This Lesson

1. Be able to read and write 場色食心新親図.

Lesson Goals

1. Learn how and when to use the various giving and receiving verbs.

From The Teachers

1. Memorize the verbs in this lesson. They are very important in the next lesson.

Lesson Highlights

13-1. いただく
(to receive)

13-2. もらう
(to receive)

13-3. くれる
(to be given)

13-4. あげる (to give)

13-5. やる (to give)

13-7. Saying "I want you to…"

13-8. Saying "I don't want you to…"

13 New Words あたらしい ことば

日本語	漢字	えいご
あかの たにん	赤の他人	a complete stranger
えさ	餌	food for animals; bait
よみち	夜道	a street at night

13 New Phrases あたらしい かいわ

1. けっこうです。   No thank you.
2. どうしよう。/ どうしましょう。   What shall I do?

13 New Verbs あたらしい どうし

どうし	えいご	た form	タイプ
いただ 頂く	to receive (from superior or equal)	いただいた	regular
もら 貰う	to receive (from equal or inferior)	もらった	regular
くれる	to be given (from equal or inferior)	くれた	いる/える
あげる	to give (to equal or inferior)	あげた	いる/える
やる	to give (to inferior, animals or plants)	やった	regular
てつだ 手伝う	to help out	てつだった	regular

13 Verb Usage どうしの つかいかた

❑ 13-1. いただく (to receive)

The direct object marker を is used to mark the item that is being received. The person from whom the item is received can be marked with から or に. いただく is very polite and is usually used when something is received from someone older or higher in status, but can also be used to simply be polite.

> (もの) を いただく
> **to recieve (thing)**

> (ひと) に いただく
> (ひと) から いただく
> **to receive from a (person)**

Example sentences

1. 先生から 新しい本を いただきました。
   I received a new book from a teacher.

2. 社長に プレゼントを いただきました。
   I received a present from the president (of the company).

3. いただいても いいですか。
   Is it okay if I receive this?

4. 林さんから このおさらを いただきました。
   I received this plate from Ms. Hayashi.

❑ 13-2. もらう (to receive)

もらう follows the same rules as いただく. The direct object marker を is used to mark the item that is being received. The person from who the item is received can be marked with から or に. もらう is not as polite as いただく. It should be used when receiving things from people of equal or lower status or age. It is also used in neutral situations.

> ### [もの] を もらう
> **to recieve [*item*]**

> ### [ひと] に もらう
> ### [ひと] から もらう
> **to receive from [*person*]**

Example sentences

1. 去年の 誕生日に 友達<u>から</u> ワンピースを もらいました。

   On my birthday last year, I received a dress from my friend.

2. 明日、はじめての うんてんめんきょしょ<u>を</u> もらいます。

   Tomorrow I am going to receive a driver's license for the first time.

3. 赤の 他人から ものを<u></u> もらわないで。

   Don't receive things from a complete stanger.

4. クリスマスに いいもの<u>を</u> もらえると 思ったけど、ぜんぜん もらえなかった。

   On Christmas I thought I would (be able to) receive something good,

   but I didn't (wasn't able to) receive anything at all.

❑ 13-3. くれる (to be given)

The direct object marker を is used to mark the item that is being given. The person who gives the item is marked with が. In modern Japan、くれる is used when something has been given to someone who is of lower, equal and higher status. Normally when a person of higher status has given you something, いただく (receive) is used for politeness.

IMPORTANT NOTE: Even though くれる means "give," it can only be used when discussing things that have been given *to* you. If you are talking about something you gave to someone else, then あげる or やる must be used.

> **[もの] を くれる**
> **to be given [*item*]**

> **[ひと] が くれる**
> **[*person*] gives**

> **Example sentences**
> 1. わたなべさんが コンサートのチケットを くれました。
>   Watanabe gave me some concert tickets.
>
> 2. 友達が わたしに でんわを くれた。
>   My friend gave me a call.
>
> 3. そのゆびわを くれたら うれしいです。
>   If you give me that ring, I will be happy.
>
> 4. 石田さんが 古い車を くれると いいました。
>   Ms. Ishida said she would give me (her/an) old car.

❑ 13-4. あげる (to give)

In the past, あげる was used when giving something to someone of the same level or above, but in modern Japan あげる is used when giving to people of any status. The direct object marker を is used to mark the object being given.

> **[もの] を あげる**
> **to give [*thing*]**

> **[ひと] が あげる**
> **[*person*] gives**

> ## (ひと) に あげる
> **to give to [person]**

Example sentences

1. 誕生日に おにいさんに ネクタイを あげました。
   On his birthday, I gave a necktie to my older brother.

2. この花を リサちゃんに あげて下さい。
   Please give these flowers to Lisa.

3. あなたが くれた おかしを いもうとに あげても いいですか。
   Is it okay if I give the snacks that you gave me to my little sister?

4. ほしかったら、この本を あげます。
   If you want it, I will give you this book.

5. あげなかったの？
   You didn't give it? / Didn't you give it?

❑ 13-5. やる (to give)

In the past, やる was used when giving something to someone of lower status, but in modern Japan やる can be considered rude, and あげる is now more commonly used. やる is used when giving things to animals or watering plants.

> ## [もの] を やる
> **to give [*thing*]**

> ## (ひと) が やる
> **[*person*] gives**

> ## (ひと、どうぶつ) に やる
> **to give to [person, animal]**

Example sentences

1. パンダに えさを やらないで下さい。
   Please don't give food to the panda. / Don't feed the panda.

2. この えさを 犬に やって下さい。
   Please give this food to (your) dog.

3. 毎日、花に 水を やります。
   I water the flowers everyday.

❑ 13-6. てつだう (to help out)

The direct object marker を is used to mark the person or task being helped with.

> [もの] を てつだう
> **to help with [thing]**

Example sentences

1. 今日 せんたくを 手伝って下さい。
   Help me with the laundry today.

2. わたしは よく おとうさんの しごとを手伝います。
   I often help my father with his work.

3. 昨日は 手伝えなくて、ごめんなさい。
   I'm sorry that I couldn't help you yesterday.

13 Grammar ぶんぽう

❑ 13-7. Saying "I want you to…"

When saying you want someone to do something – for example, "I want you to buy it" – the て form plus ほしい is used. You simply add ほしい after any verb in the て form.

> ## [て *form verb*] + ほしい
> ## to want someone to [*verb*]

The person you want to have do the action is marked with the particle に, but as you already know, in Japanese sentences you don't have to say the obvious. If I am looking directly at you and say してほしい (I want you to do it), it is obvious that I am talking about you, so I don't have to add あなたに in front. It is also obvious that I am the one that wants you to do the action, and I therefore do not need to add わたしは either.

Example sentences

1. 日本の映画は いいから、見てほしいです。
   Japanese movies are good, so I want you to watch them.

2. おばあさんに 早く 元気に なってほしいです。
   I want my grandmother to get better soon.

3. このしゅくだいは むずかしいから、手伝_{てつだ}ってほしいです。
   I want you to help me, since this homework is difficult.

4. ごめん。ちょっと、しずかに してほしい。
   Sorry, but I want you to be quiet a little.

❑ 13-8. Saying "I don't want you to…"

There are a couple of ways to say "I don't want you to go." These are いかないでほしい and いってほしくない. By changing the tense of ほしい, you can also say いってほしかった, "I wanted you to go," and いってほしくなかった, "I didn't want you to go."

> ## [ないで form verb] + ほしい
> ## [て form verb] + ほしくない
> ## I don't want you to [verb]

Example sentences

1. ジェレミーは まだ 小さいから、こわい映画を 一人で 見てほしくないです。
   Since Jeremy is still small, I don't want him to see scary movies by himself.

2. はずかしいから 見ないでほしい。
   Since I am shy, I don't want you to look.

3. その 牛乳 は 古いから、のまないでほしいです。
   I don't want you to drink that milk because it's old.

4. くらい よみちは あぶないから、一人で あるかないでほしい。
   I don't want you to walk on the street at night because it's dangerous.

13 Mini Conversations ミニ かいわ J→E

1. Informal conversation between a mother and son

A: 今朝、犬に えさを やった？

B: あっ！昨日から やってない。どうしよう。

A: だから、昨日の よる、すごく うるさかったね。

B: ごめんなさい。今すぐ やります。

A: 今度から 気を つけてね。

A: Did you feed the dog this morning?

B: Ah! I haven't fed him since yesterday. What'll I do?

A: That's why he was noisy last night.

B: I'm sorry. I will feed him right away.

A: Be careful next time.

2. Informal conversation between school friends

A: 見て！どう、わたしの 新しい くつ？

B: かわいいね。どうしたの？

A: おとうさんから もらった。

B: いい おとうさんだね。

A: Look. What do you think of my new shoes?

B: They're cute. How did you get them?

A: I got them from my father.

B: What a nice father.

3. Informal conversation between a boy and a girl

A: ちょっと きて。

B: どうしたの？

A: このソファーが おもくて、自分で もてない。手伝ってほしいの。

B: いいよ。いくら くれるの？

A: 何も あげないよ。

A: Come here for a second.

B: What's up?

A: This sofa is heavy, so I can't carry it by myself. I want you to help me.

B: Okay. How much are you going to give me?

A: I'm not going to give you anything!

13 Mini Conversations ミニ かいわ E→J

1. Informal conversation between boyfriend and girlfriend

A: I don't want to make dinner today.

B: Well then, what are you going to do?

A: I want someone to make it.

B: Who is going to make it?

A: I want "Ken" (you) to make it.

A: 今日は ばんごはんを 作りたくないな。

B: じゃあ、どうするの？

A: だれかに 作ってほしいな。

B: だれが 作るの？

A: けんちゃんに 作ってほしいな。

> Adding な to the end of the sentence shows desire and longing. It is often a long sound written as なぁ with a small あ.

> It is very common for Japanese people to use a person's name in place of あなた for "you". Also added ちゃん after a boy's name is done to show affection.

2. Formal conversation between friends

A: Have you ever been to Europe?

B: No, I haven't. But I want to go to France.

A: I went there twice already. I have so many places I want you to see.

B: Well then, shall we go together next time?

A: ヨーロッパに 行ったことが ありますか。

B: いいえ、ありません。 でも、フランスに 行きたい ですね。

A: わたしは もう 二回、行きました。見てほしいところが たくさん あります。

B: じゃあ、こんど いっしょに 行きましょうか。

3. Informal conversation between a mother and a daughter

A: Hiroko-chan, did you water the flowers? (did you give water?)

B: Not yet.

A: I told you to do it every morning, right?

B: Yes, sorry. I'll do it after I do my homework.

A: Please.

A: ひろこちゃん、花に 水を やった？

B: ううん、まだ。

A: まいあさ、やってと いったでしょう。

B: うん、ごめん。しゅくだいを したあとに やるよ。

A: おねがいね。

13 Reading Comprehension どっかい

Read the sentences below. If you don't understand them, you should review the grammar in this lesson until you do. After you have understood everything, complete the reading comprehension questions in the *Activities* section of this lesson.

① おかあさん	けんちゃん。もうすぐ、誕生日だね。何が ほしい？	
② けんちゃん	うーん…何が いいかな。	
③ おかあさん	きょ年は ロボットを あげたでしょう。 今年は ちがうものがいいね。	
④ けんちゃん	うん。じゃあ、自転車が ほしい。	
⑤ おかあさん	自転車は 一年前に おばあちゃんから もらったでしょう。	
⑥ けんちゃん	でも、もう 古くなったから。	
⑦ おかあさん	だめです。ほかに 何が いいの？	
⑧ けんちゃん	もし、ぼくが 何か いったら、ほんとうに くれる？	
⑨ おかあさん	あまり 高く なかったら、 いいよ。	
⑩ けんちゃん	じゃあ、子犬を かってほしい。	
⑪ おかあさん	えっ、子犬？ それは おとうさんに きいた ほうが いいね。	

13 Lesson Activities

❑ Reading comprehension questions

Answer the following questions about the reading comprehension on the previous page.

1. けんちゃんは 今まで 何を もらいましたか。

    _____

2. それは だれから もらいましたか。

    _____

3. おかあさんは けんちゃんに どんなものを あげられませんか。

    _____

4. プレゼントの けっていけん (decision power) は だれに ありますか。

    _____

5. あなたなら、けんちゃんに 何を あげますか。

    _____

❑ Sentence Jumble

Using ONLY the words and particles provided, create Japanese sentences that match the English translation. You can conjugate adjectives and verbs and reuse items if needed.

1. を・ほしい・のむ・行く・に・くすり・この・ほっかいどう

_____

I don't want you to go to Hokkaidou.

_____

I want you to take (drink) this medicine.

_____

I don't want to drink this medicine.

2. あげる・くれる・もらう・に・が・は・を・えんぴつ・たんじょうび・やる
   えさ・友達・犬・私・から・先生・の・プレゼント

_____

My friend gave me a pencil.

_____

I gave my teacher a present on their birthday.

_____

I gave my dog food.

3. てつだう・の・赤のたにん・が・に・を・せんたく・下さい・ある・時間
   私・えさ・です・なら

_____

I don't want to help with the laundry since I don't have any time.

_____

I helped a complete stranger.

_____

If you have time, please help me.

4. しゅくだい・毎日・みる・ほしい・勉強する・てつだう
    を・日本語・私・です・の

    _____

    I want you to study Japanese everyday.

    _____

    I don't want you to look at me.

    _____

    I want you to help me with my homework.

❑ Practice

What do they want the other person to do? Make sentences using one of the following:

～てほしいです　　　　　　～てほしくないです　　　　　～ないでほしいです

Ex. <u>しずかに なってほしいです。</u>

<u>**She wants him to be quiet**</u>

1. _____

   _____

2. _____

   _____

3. _____

   _____

4. _____

   _____

❑ **Translation**

Translate the following sentences into Japanese.

1. I want you to call me this afternoon.

   _____

2. I want my children to help me with laundry.

   _____

3. I don't want you to receive anything from a complete stranger.

   _____

4. I don't want you to become famous.

   _____

5. I don't want my husband to go on a business trip more than twice a month.

   _____

❏ **Question and Answer**

Answer the following questions using the words and patterns in this lesson.

1. かぞくの 誕生日に 何を あげますか。
   _{たんじょうび}

   _____

2. よく だれに 何を もらいますか。

   _____

3. 友達に 何を してほしいですか。

   _____

4. パートナーに 何を してほしいですか。

   _____

5. だれに 何を してほしくないですか。

   _____

❏ Short Dialogue

Mr. Kuroda is having an interview with a landlord of the house where he wants to stay.

黒田さん	はじめまして。黒田ともうします。
	よろしくおねがいします。
家主	こちらこそ。 黒田さんは学生なの？
黒田さん	はい、東京大学の三年生です。アルバイトもしています。
家主	そう。 アルバイトは夜、遅い？
黒田さん	そうですね。 だいたい、夜七時から十一時までしています。
家主	それは遅いね。 うちは夜十時には寝るから、
	帰るときは静かにしてほしいけど、できる？
黒田さん	はい、もちろんです。
家主	後、友達もつれて来ないでほしいけど、いいかな？
黒田さん	はい、つれて来ません。
家主	うちは規則がきびしいけど、家賃が安いから がまんしてね。
黒田さん	家賃の安さには勝てません。 よろしくおねがいします。

❏ New words and expressions in the dialogue

Progressive	Kanji +	English
しずかにする	静かにする	to be quiet
つれて来る	連れて来る	to bring along, to bring around
きそく	規則	rules, regulations
きびしい	厳しい	strict

❏ Short dialogue activities

Practice reading the preceding short dialogue in pairs.

Play the landlord's role and give your partner your house rules.

Kanji Lesson 13

数西声星晴切
kanji 155-160

十三　New Kanji あたらしい漢字

Practice writing each new kanji in the boxes provided. First trace the light gray samples while paying attention to stroke order. Then, on a separate piece of paper practice writing the sample kanji words at least five times each.

数					number	155
	くんよみ	かず・かぞ			meaning	number, count
	おんよみ	スウ				

にんずう	すうかげつ	かいすう	すうじ	かず かぞ
人数	数ヶ月	回数	数字	数を数える
number of people	several months	number of times	number	to count how many

13 strokes

｀　　丶　　⺌　　半　　米　　米　　半　　娄　　娄　　娄　　数　　数　　数

数	数	数	数	数					

西			number	156
	くんよみ	にし	meaning	west
	おんよみ	セイ, サイ		

にし	たいせいよう	かんさい	にしび	にしかいがん
西	大西洋	関西	西日	西海岸
west	Atlantic Ocean	the Kansai region	the setting sun	west coast

6 strokes

一　　丆　　冇　　西　　西　　西

西	西	西	西	西					

声	くんよみ	こえ	number		157
	おんよみ	セイ	meaning		voice, reputation

	うたごえ	せいえん	かんせい	おおごえ	はなごえ
7 strokes	歌声	声援	歓声	大声	鼻声
	singing voice	cheering	a shout of joy	large voice	nasal voice

一 十 吉 吉 吉 吉 声

声　声　声　声　声

星	くんよみ	ほし	number		158
	おんよみ	セイ	meaning		Star

	ほしぞら	なが ぼし	かせい	せいざ	えいせいほうそう
9 strokes	星空	流れ星	火星	星座	衛星放送
	starry sky	shooting star	Mars	constellation	satellite broadcasting

丿 口 日 日 尸 早 昇 星 星

星　星　星　星　星

晴	くんよみ	は	number		159
	おんよみ	セイ	meaning		Clear

	せいてん	すば	はぎ	きば	みは
12 strokes	晴天	素晴らしい	晴れ着	気晴らし	見晴らし
	fine weather	wonderful	one's best clothes	recreation	a view

丿 冂 月 日 日﹃ 日艹 日圭 晴 晴 晴 晴

晴　晴　晴　晴　晴

切	くんよみ	き		number	160
	おんよみ	セツ・サイ		meaning	Cut

きって	いっさい	たいせつ	ふ き	しめ き
切手	一切	大切	踏み切り	締切り
postage stamp	not...at all	important	railway crossing	deadline

4 strokes

二　七　切切

切	切	切	切	切								

十三　Kanji Drills 漢字ドリル

❑ Words you can write

Write the following words in the boxes. This is a great way to practice the new kanji and review the words at the same time. For the kanji that hasn't been taught yet, use hiragana.

かず
数
numbers, amount

数											

にんずう
人数
number of people

人	数										

かぞ
数える
to count

数	え	る								

にし
西
west

西										

にし び
西日
west sun

西	日									

かんさい
関西
かん西

Kansai area, south western Japan

うたごえ
歌声
歌声

singing voice

おおごえ
大声
大声

large / loud voice

ほしぞら
星空
星空

starry sky

かせい
火星
火星

Mars

は
晴れ
晴れ

clear weather

せいてん
晴天
晴天

fine weather

き
切る
切る

to cut

きって
切手
切手

postage stamp

❏ **Fill in the kanji**

Fill in the blanks in the following sentences with the appropriate kanji.

1. ＿＿ ＿＿を＿＿さないで＿＿さい。
   <small>おお ご え　だ　　　く だ</small>
   Please don't speak in a loud voice.

2. ＿＿ ＿＿は＿＿ケ＿＿ ＿＿、＿＿れています。
   <small>かん さい　すう か げつ かん　は</small>
   The Kansai area has has been sunny for several months.

3. ＿＿ ＿＿、＿＿ ＿＿を＿＿枚、かいました。
   <small>こん げつ　　き っ て　　ろく まい</small>
   This month I bought six stamps.

4. ここは＿＿ ＿＿らしがいいから、＿＿ ＿＿がよく＿＿える。
   <small>み　は　　　　　　　　ほし ぞ ら　　　　み</small>
   Because the view is good here, you can see the starry sky very well.

5. ＿＿ ＿＿に＿＿ ＿＿なのは、きれいな＿＿ ＿＿です。
   <small>か しゅ　た い せつ　　　　　　　　うた ご え</small>
   For a singer, the important thing is a pretty singing voice.

十三　**Kanji Recognition** 漢字にんしき

❏ **Individual words**

The following words will no longer have any ふりがな (hiragana on top). You might already

know some of these words, but don't worry if you can't write them as recognition is the goal.

食べる　　　お母さん　　　お父さん　　　音
<small>た</small>　　　　　　<small>か あ</small>　　　　　　<small>とう</small>　　　　　<small>おと</small>
to eat　　　　mother　　　　　father　　　　　sound

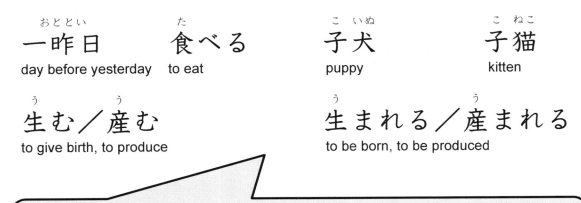

おととい
一昨日
day before yesterday

た
食べる
to eat

こ いぬ
子犬
puppy

こ ねこ
子猫
kitten

う　　　　う
生む／産む
to give birth, to produce

う　　　　　　　　　う
生まれる／産まれる
to be born, to be produced

生む and 生まれる are written with kanji you learned in book 3. But since there are slight differences in meaning, you should know both kanji versions for these "birth" related verbs. Although Japanese people even mix up these kanji, officially 産 is used for the birth of people and animals, and 生 is used for the birth of ideas and products etc.

❑ Kanji recognition cards

Print and cut out these cards, then write the hiragana and English meaning on the back. Now you can easily practice your kanji recognition.

食べる	お母さん	お父さん	音
一昨日	食べる	子犬	子猫
生む	生まれる	産む	産まれる

The power of the て form

Before This Lesson

1. Be able to read and write 数西声星晴切.

2. Know the giving and receiving verbs taught in the prior lesson.

Lesson Goals

1. Learn how to combine the various giving and receiving verbs with other verbs.

From The Teachers

1. The verbs taught in the prior lesson are used in new ways in this lesson. Make sure that you understand how they are used before you start this lesson.

Lesson Highlights

14-5. The power of て

14-6. The difference between ていただく and てもらう

14-7. The difference between てくれる and てあげる

14 New Words あたらしい ことば

日本語	漢字	えいご
かびん	花瓶	flower vase
ロボット	ロボット	robot
アイディア	アイディア	idea
なにか	何か	something
なきごえ	鳴き声	chirp, howl, etc. (animal cry)
なきごえ	泣き声	crying voice (human cry)
せき	席	seat
しりあい	知り合い	acquaintance
かご	籠	basket
こむぎ	小麦	wheat
かってに	勝手に	without permission

14 New Phrases あたらしい かいわ

1. いいな (sometimes written いいなぁ or いいな~ to show the trailing sound)
This implies a feeling of envy. Perhaps your friend has bought a new car and you are slightly jealous, you could say いいな.

14 New Verbs あたらしい どうし

どうし	えいご	た form	タイプ
聞こえる (き)	to be able to hear	きこえた	いる/える
壊す (こわ)	to break, destroy, ruin	こわした	regular
壊れる (こわ)	to be broken	こわれた	いる/える
産まれる (う)	to be born (people, animals)	うまれた	いる/える
生まれる (う)	to be born (idea, result, etc.)	うまれた	いる/える

14　Verb Usage　どうしの　つかいかた

❏ 14-1. きこえる (to be able to hear)

The thing that is heard is marked with が.

> ## (もの) が きこえる
> ## to be able to hear (thing)

Example sentences

1. わたしの 声が きこえますか。

   Can you hear my voice?

2. 音がくが うるさいから きこえません。

   I can't hear because the music is loud.

3. おじいさんは 八十才に なってから、耳が きこえなく なりました。

   After my grandfather turned 80, he became hard of hearing.

❏ 14-2. こわす (to break, destroy, ruin) *Active*

The thing that was or will be broken *by somebody* is marked with を. You can even say
おなかを こわす when talking about something you eat that might make you sick.

> ## (もの) を こわす
> ## to break a (thing)

Example Sentences

1. だれが テレビを こわしたと 思いますか。
   Who do you think broke the television?

2. 五才の時、おかあさんの すきな 花びんを こわしました。
   When I was five years old I broke my mother's favorite flower vase.

3. からだを こわしました。
   I broke my body. (I am sick.)

❏ 14-3. こわれる (to be broken) *Passive*

The thing that is or will be broken is marked with が.

> **[もの] が こわれる**
> **[*thing*] broke**

Example Sentences

1. せんたくき（せんたっき）が こわれています。

   The washing machine is broken.

   > こわれています form is used because being "broken" is an ongoing state.

2. ドアの かぎが こわれました。

   The key to the door broke.

3. おととい、けんちゃんに かった ロボットが こわれました。

   The day before yesterday, the robot that I bought for Ken got broken.

❏ 14-4. 産まれる／生まれる (to be born)

The living thing or idea that is being born is marked with が

> **(いきもの、アイディア) が 生まれる**
> **(living thing, idea) being born**

Example Sentences

1. 昨日、会社の会議で、いい アイディアが 生まれました。
   Yesterday I got a good idea during the company meeting.

2. 十月に はじめての 赤ちゃんが 産まれました。
   In October our first baby was born.

   > Notice a different kanji is different when babies are born versus ideas in #1.

3. 赤ちゃんが 産まれたら、しごとを ３か月かん 休みます。
   When the baby is born, I will break from work for 3 months.

14 | Grammar ぶんぽう

❏ 14-5. The power of て

You can use もらう, いただく, くれる, and あげる after any て form to make the following

patterns – for example, if the verb する (to do) is used, it is changed into して (て form).

て form combination	**English meaning**
して もらう	to have (someone) do
して いただく	to have (someone) do
して くれる	to do for (me)
して あげる	to do for (someone)
して ほしい	want (someone) to do it

Examples

ごはんを 作って もらう	to have someone make dinner
日本語を 教えて いただく	to have someone teach Japanese
おかしを かって くれる	to buy snacks for me
本を よんで あげる	to read a book for someone
ごみを すてて ほしい	to want someone to throw the trash away

❏ 14-6. The difference between ていただく and てもらう

てもらう and ていただく mean the same thing, with the exception that ていただく is

humble and is used when the person doing the action is of higher status than the person

receiving the benefit of the action. てもらう is very common in modern Japan.

Example sentences

1. 目が いたかった から、医者さんに 見ていただきました。
   Since my eye was hurting, I had a doctor look at it.

2. 明日、先生に 家に きていただく ことに しました。
   I decided to have my teacher come to my house tomorrow.

3. 私は 漢字が 書けない から、友達に 書いてもらいました。
   Since I can't write kanji, I had a friend write it.

❏ **14-7. The difference between てくれる and てあげる**

てあげる is used when you will do something for some one, as in "I will do it for you".

てくれる is used when some one will do something for you. The use of てくれる and てあげ

る imply that the action was done as a favor to the person receiving the benefit of the

action.

Example Sentences

1. もし、生物（なまもの）が きらいなら、わたしが 食べてあげる。
   If you don't like raw food, I will eat it for you.

2. 親友（しんゆう）は いつも 会いに きてくれます。
   My best friend always comes to see me.

3. 田中さんに 百円 かしてあげた。
   I loaned 100 yen to Tanaka-san.

4. 知り合（し あ）いが 車を うってくれました。
   My acquaintance sold me a car.

---

14 Q&A しつもんと こたえ E→J

1. 何か きこえましたか。
   Did you hear something?

> The が is missing from this sentence. In spoken Japanese は and が are many times dropped from the sentence.

とりの なき声（ごえ）が きこえました。
I heard the chirping of a bird.

ひこうきの 音が きこえました。
I heard the sound of an airplane.

だれかが 家に 入った音が きこえました。
I heard the sound of someone entering the house.

2. 何を こわしましたか。
What did you break?

コンピューターを こわしました。
I broke a computer.

たばこで からだを こわしました。
I ruined my body with cigarettes.

何も こわしていません。
I haven't broken anything. (I didn't break anything.)

3. 何が こわれましたか。
What broke?

コンピューターが こわれました。
The computer broke.

お父さんに かってもらった ピアノが こわれました。
I broke the piano my father bought me.

何も こわれていません。
Nothing is broken.

4. 何が 産まれましたか。
What was born?

さるの 子供が 三匹、産まれました。
Three monkey kids were born.

男の子が 産まれました。
A boy was born.

何も 産まれなかった。
Nothing was born.

5.   何を してもらいたいですか？
What do you want them to do for you?

車を かって もらいたいです。
I want them to buy me a car.

ゆびわを くれたら、うれしいです。
I would be happy if they gave me a ring.

何も してもらわなくても いいですよ。
You don't have to do anything.

6.   何か して ほしいことは ありますか。
Is there anything that you want me to do?

サンドイッチを 作ってほしいです。
I want you to make a sandwich.

昨日、手伝っていただいたので、今日は けっこうです。
Since I had you help me yesterday, I am ok today.

ううん。 大丈夫だよ。
No, I'm fine.

7.   あなたと けっこんしたら、 何を してくれるの？
If I marry you, what will you do for me?

毎日 そうじを してあげる。
I will clean for you everyday.

しゅうに 一回、食事を 作ってあげる。
I will make dinner for you once a week.

きゅうりょうを ぜんぶ あげる。
I will give you all of my pay.

14   Q&A しつもんと こたえ J→E

1. Polite conversation at a concert

A: せきを かわって いただけますか。

B: <u>どうして</u>ですか。

> どうして is another way to say "why". It's usage is similar to なんで and なぜ.

A: あなたの となりの人が 友達だから です。

B: ああ、そう でしたか。いいですよ。

A: Would you mind changing seats?

B: Why?

A: Because the person next to you is my friend.

B: Oh, is that so? Sure.

2. Informal conversation between neighbors

A: 昨日から 子猫の なき声(ごえ)が きこえるけど、どうしたの？

B: 一昨日、おじさんから もらったの。

A: ええ？ いいな！ 今ど 見せてね。ねこが 大好き(だいす)だから。

B: いいよ。かわいいよ。

A: I have heard a kitten crying since yesterday – what's up?

B: I received it from my uncle the day before yesterday.

A: What? I want one too (this is what いいな implies). Show me next time okay.

I love cats!

B: Ok. It's cute.

3. Polite conversation between co-workers

A: 来年(らいねん)の カレンダーを あげましょうか。

B: ありがとう。でも けっこうです。いろいろな人から もらって、

家に たくさん あります。

A: これは いいですよ。 日本の お寺の しゃしんが あって。。。。

B: じゃあ、いただきます。

A: Shall I give you a next year's calendar?

B: Thank you, but no thank you. I received many from various people and have many at my home.

A: This is a good one. There are pictures of Japanese temples and….

B: Well then, I'll take it.

4. Mixed conversation between friends

A: かっている ねずみが かごを こわしました。

B: えさを ちゃんと やっていたの？

A: 毎日、小麦<ruby>こむぎ</ruby>を あげたり, チーズを あげたりしてましたよ。

A: The mouse I am raising broke the basket.

B: Were you feeding it properly?

A: I gave the mouse wheat and cheese everyday.

5. Informal conversation between two girls

A: ここで 何を してるの？

B: 人を まってるの。

A: ちょっと、この にもつを 見てもらえる？

B: いいけど、どれくらい？

A: トイレに 行くだけ。

B: ああ、それだったら、いいよ。

A: What are you doing here?

B: I am waiting for someone.

A: Can I have you watch this luggage just a little while?

B: Okay, but for how long?

A: I am just going to the bathroom.

B: Okay, if it is that long then okay.

14 Mini Conversations ミニ かいわ E→J

1. Sad conversation between friends

A: What's the matter? You don't look good. Is there anything I can do for you?

B: The pig I was raising recently died and…

A: And what else?

B: When I asked my wife she said she ate it. Don't you think that is a horrible story?

A: That is terrible.

A: どうしたの？ 元気が ないね。何か できることが ある？

B: 最近 かっていた ぶたが しんで…
     _{さいきん}

A: うん、うん。それから？

B: 家内に きいたら、食べたと いうんだ！ ひどいはなしだと 思わない？
     _{かない}

A: それは ひどいね。

2. Freaky conversation

A: Can't you hear the cry of a baby?

B: Yes. There isn't anyone in the room next to us, but actually two years ago a
     mother and a baby……

A: That's scary!!! Don't say any more!!!

A: 赤ちゃんの なき声が きこえませんか？

B: はい。 となりの へやには だれも いませんが、じつは、二年まえに おかあさんと
     赤ちゃんが ・・・・・。

A: こわい！！！ それ 以上 いわないで！！！！

3. Mixed conversation between acquaintances

A: Recently six puppies were born. Is there someone who wants them?

B: I want one, but we are in an apartment, so I don't think it would work.

A: Can you please ask your friends for me?

B: Well okay, when I go to school tomorrow I'll ask.

A: 最近 子犬が 六匹 産まれました。 だれか ほしい人が いますか。

B: ほしいけど、家は アパートだから、 だめだと 思う。

A: 友達にも きいてくれませんか？

B: じゃあ、明日 学校に 行った時、ききますね。

4. Polite conversation between friends

A: Can you please hold this for me?

B: This sure is heavy. What is it?

A: It's fifteen kilos of rice.

A: これを もっていただけませんか。

B: おもい ですね。何ですか。

A: おこめが 十五キロです。

14 | Reading Comprehension どっかい

Read the sentences below. If you don't understand them, you should review the grammar in this lesson until you do. After you have understood everything, complete the reading comprehension questions in the *Activities* section of this lesson.

---

①しんじ	どうしよう。コンピューターが こわれた・・・
②おねえさん	えっ、何か したの？
③しんじ	何も しないよ。かってに、こわれたと 思う。
④おねえさん	コンピューターは かってに こわれないよ。
	しんじが こわしたでしょう！
⑤しんじ	ううん。ぼくは こわさないよ！！
⑥おねえさん	じゃあ、どうするの？
⑦しんじ	おねえちゃんは コンピューターに 強いから、
	見てくれるかな？
⑧おねえさん	うーん・・・いいよ。見てあげる。
⑨しんじ	おねえちゃんは いつも うるさいけど、
	よく 手伝ってくれるね。
⑩おねえさん	今度、そんなこと いったら、もう 何も してあげないよ！
⑪しんじ	ごめんなさい・・・

14 Lesson Activities

❏ Reading comprehension questions

Answer the following questions about the reading comprehension in this lesson.

1. しんじくんは コンピューターをこわしたと いいましたか。

   _____

2. あなたは コンピューターが かってに こわれると 思いますか。

   _____

3. 「コンピューターに強い」のいみは何ですか。

   _____

4. おねえちゃんは しんじくんに やさしいですか。

   _____

5. あなたは コンピューターが こわれた時、どうしますか。

   _____

❏ Sentence Patterns

Modify the sentence by adding the parts listed. You can add and remove parts as needed so that the final sentence makes sense.

Ex.	まいあさ、早く おきられます。	
	→ can't get up	まいあさ、早く おきられません。
	→ can eat breakfast	まいあさ、あさごはんが 食べられます。
	→ can't eat breakfast	まいあさ、あさごはんが 食べられません。
	→ can go to work	まいあさ、しごとに 行けます。

1. バイクの音が きこえます。

→ teacher's voice _____

→ crying voice _____

→ singing voice _____

→ can't hear _____

2. れいぞうこを こわしました。

→ flower vase _____

→ a basket _____

→ my body (I got sick.)_____

→ isn't broken _____

3. いいアイディアが 生まれました。

→ baby _____

→ is needed / I need_____

→ I told (taught) _____

→ I received _____

4. お母さんが 毎朝、おこしてくれます。(おこす = to wake someone up)

→ prepares lunch for me _____

→ is worried about me _____

→ will buy a new car for me _____

→ drives for me   _____

5. 私は 親友に でんわを してもらいます。

→ have her teach math _____

→ have my teacher teach history _____

→ have my teacher read my essay _____

→ have my boyfriend carry my bag _____

❏ Question and Answer

Answer the following questions using the words and patterns in this lesson.

1. 何が かってに こわれますか。

_____

2. 何を こわしたことが ありますか。

_____

3. よく、どんな音が きこえますか。

_____

4. かぞくに 何を してもらいますか。

_____

5. ともだちに 何を してあげますか。

_____

❏ Practice

Circle correct words in parentheses and complete the sentences.

1. 先日、子犬が 産まれたので、私は ミルクを (あげました ・ くれました)。
   でも、その子は あまり (のんでくれない ・ のんでもらわない) ので、きんじょの
   動物病院の先生に きいたら、やさしく (教えてくれました ・ 教えてもらいました)。

2. 私のおとうとは、よく 赤の他人から おかしを (くれます ・ もらいます)。
   私は だめだと いいますが、おとうとは (きいてあげません ・ きいてくれません)。

3. もし 彼女と けっこんしたら、ぼくは りょうりを (してほしい ・ してくれる)
   けど、けっきょくは ぼくのほうが (上手 ・ とくい) だから、ぼくが すると
   おもう。

❏ Short Dialogue

Hiroko has just found out that her microwave oven is broken.

ひろこさん	あれ？ 電子レンジが こわれてる！ いつ、こわれたの？
ルームメート	ああ、それ？ 昨日、つかっている時に、こわれた。
ひろこさん	ええっ！ちょっと それは困るよ！
ルームメート	仕方ないでしょう？ わたしは こわしてないよ。
	もう古いからだよ。
ひろこさん	じゃあ、新しいのを かう？
ルームメート	いいよ。 割り勘にする？
ひろこさん	うーん・・・。 私は あんまり つかわないから、
	七割、出してくれる？
ルームメート	だめ。 いつも 私が 料理してあげてるから、
	つかわないだけでしょう。
ひろこさん	分かった・・・。 今月は きついなあ・・・。

❏ New words and expressions in the dialogue

Progressive	Kanji +	English
つかう	使う	to use
こまる	困る	to be troubled
しかたない	仕方ない	can't be helped, have no choice
わりかんにする	割り勘にする	to evenly split a bill
七わり	七割	70%
きつい	きつい	tight, demanding, hard

❏ Short dialogue activities

Practice reading the preceding short dialogue in pairs.

1. Play the roommate's role and tell Hiroko why you think two of you should go halves.

Answer Key

❏ Lesson 1: Fill in the kanji

1. きょうは 何月何日 ですか。
   What is the month and day of the month today?
2. 夏休み に 日本 に いきました。
   I went to Japan on my summer vacation.
3. すきな 科目 は れきしです。
   My favorite subject is history.
4. そのドアを 開いて 下 さい。
   Please open that door.
5. 学校 の ともだちと 遠足 に いきたいです。
   I want to go on an excursion with my school friends.
6. あの 大きい 雨雲 が 見えますか。
   Can you see those big rain clouds?

❏ Lesson 2: Reading comprehension translation

① For me there is my father, mother and older brother.
② But, in our house, there is only one TV.
③ I always watch TV after I get home from school.
④ When I am watching TV, my mother is always making dinner.
⑤ My brother is doing his homework.
⑥ When my father has returned home, he always changes the TV channel.
⑦ I ask (request) to "buy one more TV!" but it's no good.
⑧ Our house needs one more TV.

❏ Lesson 2: Reading comprehension questions

(answers will vary)

1. かぞくは 何人、いますか。
   How many people are in the family?

   四人 かぞくです。   It's a 4 person family.
   かぞくは 四人です。   The family is 4 people.
   かぞくは 四人 います。   There are 4 people in the family.

2. うちに テレビは 何だい、ありますか。
   How many TVs are there in the house?

   一だいしか ありません。   There's only one.
   一だいしか ないです。   There's only one.

3. テレビを 見ているとき、おにいさんは 何を していますか。
   When the TV is being watched, what is the older brother doing?

   しゅくだいを しています。   He's doing homework.
   しゅくだいです。   Homework.

4. 何で おとうさんに おこりますか。
    Why is he mad at his father?

    いつもテレビの チャンネルを かえるからです。   Because he always changes the TV channel.
    テレビが 一だいしかないからです。   Because there is only one TV.

5. かぞくは もう一だい、テレビを かいますか。
    Will the family one more TV?

    いいえ、かいません。   No, they won't.
    いいえ、かわないです。   No, they won't.

❏ Lesson 2: Sentence Patterns

1. この本が おもしろいです。   This book is interesting.

    → necessary   この本は ひつようです。

    → heavy   この本は おもいです。

    → smelly   この本は くさいです。

2. お金が 足りますか。   Is there enough money?

    → Do you have   お金が ありますか。

    → necessary   お金が ひつようですか。

    → 100 dollars   １００ドルで 足りますか。

3. むかしの ともだちを よく おもい出します。   I often remember (recall) my old friends.

    → sometimes remember   むかしの ともだちを ときどき おもい出します。

    → can't remember at all   むかしの ともだちを ぜんぜん おもい出せません。

    → grandmother   おばあさんを よく おもい出します。

4. 車が 二だい あります。   There are 2 cars.

    → three TVs   テレビが 三だい あります。

    → two old telephones   古いでんわが 二だい あります。

    → one ship   ふねが いっき あります。

    → is only one car   車が 一だいしか ありません。

❏ Lesson 2: Translation

1. I only have dollars.   一ドルしか ありません (もっていません)。

2. I only went to Tokyo and Kyoto.   とうきょうと きょうとにしか いきませんでした。

3. I only have one car.   車は 一だい しかありません (もっていません)。

4. I can see only one airplane.   ひこうきは 一だいしか 見えません。

5. I only have one cat.   ねこは いっぴきしか かっていません。(raising)

❏ Lesson 2: Question and answer

1. Are you still friends (in good relations) with your elementary school friends?

   はい、いまでも なかが いいです。　　　　　　Yes, even now we are friendly.

   はい、なかいいです。　　　　　　　　　　　Yes, we are friendly.

   いいえ、なかが よくないです。　　　　　　　No, we aren't in good relations.

2. Do you clean your room by yourself?

   はい、じぶんで そうじを します。　　　　　Yes, I clean it by myself.

   いいえ、おにいさんと そうじを します。　　No, I clean it with my older brother.

3. What are you going to make for dinner?

   なにも つくりません。　　　　　　　　　　I won't make anything.

   カレーを つくります。　　　　　　　　　　I will make Curry.

4. Who do you often remember (recall)?

   おかあさんを おもい出します。　　　　　　I remember my mother.

   おじいさんを おもい出します。　　　　　　I remember my grandfather.

5. How many cars to you have (own)?

   一だい もっています。　　　　　　　　　　I have one.

   もっていません。　　　　　　　　　　　　　I don't have one.

❏ Lesson 2: Fill in the kanji

1. りょこうの 計画 がありますか。
2. 去年、海に 三回 いきました。
3. 先月 、大家 に 家ちんを はらいました。
4. 田中 さんのは 歌声は きれいですね。
5. おととい、画家 に 会いました。
6. 海外で 家が かいたいです。

❏ Lesson 3: Reading comprehension translation

① It was a very cold day.
② A girl, was walking alone.
③ For the girl, her father and mother were already gone.
④ She was a child also without a home.
⑤ She met a man who was hungry.

⑥ The girl gave the bread that she only had one of to an old man.
⑦ To a barefoot child she gave her own shoes.
⑧ To a cold looking old woman she gave her skirt.
⑨ To a child not wearing anything, she gave her own shirt.
⑩ The girl that had become naked looked at the stars.

⑪ She thought "Oh... I want to go to the place of the stars."
⑫ Then, many stars dropped from the sky.
⑬ The stars became the girl's dress.
⑭ The girl became very happy.

❏ Lesson 3: Reading comprehension questions

Actual answers may be worded slightly different for each student.

1. Does the girl have a family?

   いいえ、もう いません。　　　　　　　　　　　No, not anymore.

2. Where is the girl's house?

   家が ありません。　　　　　　　　　　　　　　She doesn't have a house.

3. How come she gave bread to and old man?

   おじいさんが おなかが すいていたから です。　Because the old man was hungry.

4. Why did she give her skirt to an old lady?

   おばあさんが さむそうだったから です。　　　Because the old lady looked cold.

5. What kind of feelings do you think the of the girl that became naked had?

   かなしかったです。　　　　　　　　　　　　　She was sorrowful.

   さみしかったです。　　　　　　　　　　　　　She was lonely / sad.

   しにたかったです。　　　　　　　　　　　　　She wanted to die.

6. When the stars dropped from the sky, what kind of feeling do you think the girl had?

   しあわせ でした。　　　　　　　　　　　　　She was happy.

   うれしかったです。　　　　　　　　　　　　　She was happy.

❏ Lesson 3: Sentence Patterns

1. かいだんから おちました。　　　　　　　　　I fell from the stairs.

   → from the escalator　　　　　　　　　　エスカレーターから おちました。

   → from the ladder　　　　　　　　　　　　はしごから おちました。

   → my father　　　　　　　　　　　　　　　おとうさんが かいだんから おちました。

   　　　　　　　　　　　　　　　　　　　　　おとうさんが おちました。

   → younger sister　　　　　　　　　　　　いもうとが かいだんから おちました。

   　　　　　　　　　　　　　　　　　　　　　いもうとが おちました。

2. ともだちに プレゼントを あげたいです。　　　I want to give a present to my friend.

   → to my girlfriend　　　　　　　　　　　かのじょに プレゼントを あげたいです。

   → a wedding ring　　　　　　　　　　　ともだちに けっこんゆびわを あげたいです。

   → don't want to give　　　　　　　　　　ともだちに プレゼントを あげたくないです。

   → didn't want to give　　　　　　　　　ともだちに プレゼントを あげたくなかったです。

3. いまの しごとは つまらないです。　　　　　My current job is boring.

   → part-time job　　　　　　　　　　　　いまの アルバイトは つまらないです。

   → important　　　　　　　　　　　　　　いまの しごとは だいじです。

   → not difficult　　　　　　　　　　　　いまの しごとは むずかしくないです。

   → dangerous　　　　　　　　　　　　　いまの しごとは あぶないです。

4. おもしろそうな本です。   It's an interesting looking book.
    → uninteresting looking   おもしろくなさそうな本です。
    → person   おもしろそうな ひとです。
    → movie   おもしろそうな えいがです。
    → expensive looking   たかそうな本です。

5. たかそうな 車です。   It's an expensive looking car.
    → cheap looking   やすそうな 車です。
    → seems fast   はやそうな 車です。
    → seems slow   おそそうな 車です。
    → not expensive looking   たかくなさそうな 車です。

❏ Lesson 3: Verb Practice: What are they wearing?

1. (かのじょは) ジャケットを きています。
2. (かれは) スエターを きています。
3. (かれは) ぼうしを かぶっています。
4. (かれは) スーツを はいています。
5. (かれは) くつしたを はいています。
6. (かれは) ジーパンを はいています。

❏ Lesson 3: Modifying with verbs

Hiroshi san: Excuse me, which person is Tom?
Jun san: Tom is the person drinking coffee.
Hiroshi san: Well then, which person is John?
Jun san: John is the _____ person.
Hiroshi san: Is that so? Is Kyle the person _____?
Jun san: Yes, he is. The _____ dog is Max.
Hiroshi san: Sure is cute. Who is the girl _____?
Jun san: That person is Jenny. She is Tom's wife.

Answers
① ジョンさんは ねている人です。   John is the sleeping person.
② カイルさんは ほんをよんでいる人です。   Kyle is the person reading a book.
③ たべている犬は マックすくんですよ。   The dog that is eating is Max.
④ でんわを している 女の人は だれですか。   Who is the lady on the phone?
   でんわで はなしている 女の人は だれですか。   Who is the lady talking on the phone?

❏ Lesson 3: Practice

1. あつそうな コーヒー
2. さむそうな 男 / さむそうな だんせい / さむそうな 男の人
3. つめたそうな ビール
4. あたたかそうな ジャケット / あったかそうな ジャケット
5. おもそうな スーツケース
6. さむそうな サラリーマン

❏ Lesson 3: Fill in the kanji

1. 公園 で 絵本 をよみました。
2. 人 間 は 外見 だけでは はんだんが できません。
3. 顔が 赤くなりました。
4. ヨーロッパで 絵画 が 見たいです。
5. あの 汽車 は 大きくて、古いです。

❏ Lesson 4: Reading comprehension translation

① Yesterday my summer bonus came out.
② This time my bonus was 450,000 yen.
③ With that money and money that I saved since last year, I want to take a trip abroad.
④ I am looking forward to it.
⑤ The place I want to go most is Switzerland.
⑥ My wife has been to Europe, but I have never been.
⑦ When my wife went to Europe, I couldn't go because I was busy at work.
⑧ I want to take a trip every year, but since it costs money I can't.

❏ Lesson 4: Reading comprehension questions

1. When did the speaker's bonus come out?
   きのうでました。　　　　　　　　　　It came out yesterday.

2. What is the speaker looking forward to?
   かいがいりょこうを たのしみにしています。　　He is looking forward to a trip abroad.

3. Where has the speaker's wife been before?
   ヨーロッパにいったことが あります。　　She has been to Europe.

4. Why wasn't the speaker able to go to Europe?
   しごとで いそがしかったからです。　　Because he was busy at work.

5. What is the speaker holding back on?
   まい年 りょこうを することです。　　Going on a trip every year.

6. About how many times a year to Japanaese companies have bonuses?
   一年に ２回くらいです。　　About 2 times a year.
   わかりません。　　I don't know.

❏ Lesson 4: Sentence Jumble

1. せんしゅうまつに うまを はじめて みました。
   せんしゅうまつに はじめて うまを みました。

   よこしまさんは せんしゅうまつまで うまに のったことが ありませんでした。
   よこしまさんは せんしゅうまつまで うまに のったことが なかった。

   よこしまさんは うまに のったことが あると おもいますか。
   よこしまさんは うまに のったことが あると おもう？

2. こんなに おいしい わかめ (は/を) たべたことが ありません。
    こんなに おいしい わかめ (は/を) たべたことが ないです。

    らいしゅうまつまで (に) きゅうりょうが でません。
    きょうりゅうが しんで (い) るから 車の うんてんが できません。

3. あだちさんの おんがく (を・は) きいたこと (が) ありますか。
    あだちさんの おんがく (を・は) きいたこと (が) あう？

    あだちさんは しっていますか。
    あだちさんが あんなに じょうずに おんがくが つくれることを しっていましたか。

❏ Lesson 4: Practice

1. ゆかたは きたことが あります。
2. えいがに でたことが あります。
3. まえに かのじょに ゆびわを あげたことが あります。
4. スキーは したことが ありません。
5. いぬを かったことが ありません。

❏ Lesson 4: Short dialogue translation

田中さん: Have you ever appeared on TV?

トムさん: No, I haven't, what about you?

田中さん: I have. A long time ago, I appeared on a quiz show.

トムさん: What! That's amazing. What type of show was it?

田中さん: It was a show that if you answered every question you would win a trip abroad.

トムさん: And, what happened?

田中さん: Since I didn't know the last question, it was no good…

トムさん: That was unfortunate. Will you challenge again?

田中さん: No. Since I have challenged 5 times already, I have given up.

トムさん: Since I've never been on a TV show, I want to someday.

❏ Lesson 4: Fill in the kanji

1. わたしは 毎日、日記を かきます。
2. 東京 に 日帰り 旅行しましょう。
3. 魚屋で まぐろを 四匹かって 下さい。
4. 先生はどんな 教科を 教えていますか。
5. 家で 牛肉を 食べてから、学校に いきます。
6. ここに 名前を 記入して 下さい。
7. 早く 日本に 帰りたいです。
8. 金魚は 大きいのと 小さいのが います。

❏ Lesson 5: Reading comprehension translation

① Tomorrow Scott will take a business trip to Oosaka for the first time.
② There is a meeting at the Oosaka branch at 1pm.
③ Scott will go to Oosaka after going to the main office in Shinjuku.
④ Scott asked various things to the kindest looking in the company, Mr. Nakamura.

❏ Lesson 5: Dialogue translation

Scott:	Where is the Oosaka branch?
Nakamura:	It's in the building in front of the Umeda station.
Scott:	How do you go there from here?
Nakamura:	After going from Shinjiku station to Tokyo station, you go by bullet train to the Shin Oosaka station.
Scott:	From Shin Oosaka station how do I go to Umeda station?
Nakamura:	You go by train. After turning left at the Umeda station exit, you go straight. You go up to the 2nd floor with the stairway at the end (of the walkway). The branch is there.
Scott:	How long will it take?
Nakamura:	I think from the company it will take about 4 and a half hours.
Scott:	Got it. Thank you. Alright then, I'll go and be back.
Nakamura:	Take care.

❏ Lesson 5: Reading comprehension questions

1. Why do you think Scott asked Nakamura san various things?
   大阪支社に はじめて いくからです。   Because it's the first time he's going to the Oosaka branch.

   （大阪支社への） いきかたが わからなかったからです。
   Because he didn't know the way (to the Oosaka branch).

2. With what and what do you go to the Oosaka branch?
   でんしゃと しんかんせんで いきます。

3. Has Scott ever been to Oosaka?
   いいえ、いったことが ありません。   No, he has never been.
   いいえ、こんかいが はじめてです。   No, this is his first time.

4. How long does it take to get to the branch in Oosaka?
   ４時かんはんぐらいです。   About 4 and a half hours.

5. Do you go by train from Umeda station to the branch in Oosaka?
   いいえ、あるいて いきます。   No, you go by foot.
   いいえ、あるきます。   No, you walk.

❏ Lesson 5: Sentence Jumble

(order can change as long as particles remain attached to the appropriate words)

1. どうやって ここ（まで・に） あるきましたか / あるいたの？。

   エレベーターで よじまで よんかいに あがって下さい。

   エレベーターで よんかいに おりられなかったから、かいだんで おりました。

2. みっつめの こうさてんで ひだりに まがって、それから つきあたりまで まっすぐ いって下さい。

    こうそくどうろを おりてから、つぎの こうさてんで みぎに まがって下さい。

    フロントへ いって、それから ホテルのいりぐちを さがして下さい。

3. 2013 ねんに いっしゅうかん しゅっちょうを しました。

    しゅっちょうが おわってから、まっすぐ いえに いきました。

    この しゅっちょうから いえに かえったとき、フランスに いきたいです。

❑ Lesson 5: Question and Answer

1. How do you study Japanese?
    まいにちべんきょうします。   I study everyday.

    よく 日本のテレビを見ます。   I often watch Japanese TV.

2. How do you go to your company / school?
    でんしゃで いきます。   I go by train.

    バスで いきます。   I go by bus.

    あるいて いきます。   I go by foot.

3. How do you get up to the 3rd floor?
    かいだんで いきます。   I go by the stairs.

    エレベーターで いきます。   I go by elevator.

    エスカレーターで いきます。   I go by escalator.

4. Do you often go on business trips?
    いいえ、いきません。   No, I don't go.

    いいえ、あまり いきません。   No, I don't go that often.

    はい、よく いきます。   Yes, I often go.

❑ Lesson 5: Short Dialogue

ジョンくん：	Excuse me, where is the hospital.
けいさつかん：	There is an intersection there right?
けいさつかん：	① Please turn left at the intersection.
	こうさてんで ひだりに まがって下さい。
	② The hospital is on the left.
	びょういんは ひだりに あります。
ジョンくん：	Ok then, there is the department store?
けいさつかん：	③ Please go straight ahead. It's on the right.
	まっすぐ いって下さい。 みぎに あります。
ジョンくん：	Thank you.

❏ Lesson 5: Fill in the kanji

1. あの 角を 右に まがって 下さい。
2. 田中さんは いつも 強気ですね。
3. おばあさんの 時計は とても ふるいです。
4. 来月、遠足の 計画が あります。
5. 最近、勉強 する 時間が ありません。
6. 早く元気 に なって 下さい。
7. 林さんは 強引なときが あります。

❏ Lesson 6: Reading comprehension translation

① Smith when to Tokyo for the first time.

② Because he has no friends at all in Japan, he went on the trip by himself.

③ On the first day after shopping he entered a coffee shop.

In the coffee shop.

スミスさん:	Excuse me. Coffee please.
ウェイトレス:	Hot or cold?
スミスさん: Hot please.	
ウェイトレス:	Ok, I have understood. (order received)

30 minutes later.

スミスさん: Excuse me can I pay for the coffee here?	
ウェイトレス:	Please settle your bill at the cash register over there.
スミスさん:	Oh, is that so. Got it.

At the register.

ウェイトレス:	It's 350 yen.
スミスさん:	Can I pay the tip here too?
ウェイトレス:	No, because this is Japan, you don't have to pay a tip.

❏ Lesson 6: Reading comprehension questions

1. Has Smith been to Japan a long time ago.
   スミスさんは 日本に いったことが ありません。   Smith has never been to Japan.

   いいえ、いったことが ありません。   No, he has never been.

2. What did he do on the first day?
   かいものを してから、きっさってんに 入りました。   After shopping, he entered a coffee shop.
   かいものを したり、きさってんに いったり しました。 He did things like shop and go to a
                                                        coffee shop.

3. In Japanese coffee shops do you pay money at the table?
   いいえ、レジで はらいます。   No you pay at the register.

   いいえ、はらいません。   No you don't (pay).

4. In your country what person do you pay for tips?

１５パーセント はらいます。   We pay 15%.

チップは はらわなくても いいです。   We don't have to pay tips.

❏ Lesson 6: Sentence Patterns

1. やちんを はらって下さい。   Please pay rent.

    → bill (at a restaurant)   おかんじょうを はらって下さい。

    → Did you pay?   やちんを はらいましたか。

    → I didn't pay.   やちんを はらいませんでした。

    → tip   チップを はらって下さい。

2. うんてんしても いいですか。   Is it okay if I drive?

    → look   みても いいですか。

    → eat   たべても いいですか。

    → turn right   みぎに まがっても いいですか。

    → make dinner   しょくじを つくっても いいですか。

3. 家を 出ます。   I will leave the house.

    → Is it ok if I leave?   家を 出ても いいですか。

    → It is not ok if you leave   家を 出ては いけないです。

    → want to leave   家を 出たいです。

    → at 10 o'clock   家を 十時に 出ます。

❏ Lesson 6: Translation

1. It's ok if you go by the elevator, but it's not ok if you go up by the escalator.
エレベーターで いっても いいけど、エスカレーターで いっては いけないです。

2. I want to drink coffee, but I won't because I can't sleep.
コーヒーをのみたいけど、ねむれないから のみません。

3. There is only one cake (left), but is it ok if I eat it?
ケーキは ひとつしかないけど、たべても いいですか。

4. I always drive, but I will go to school on foot today.
わたしは いつもうんてんするけど、きょうは あるいていきます。

5. You can turn right here, but please be careful.
ここで まがってもいいけど、きをつけて下さい。

❏ Lesson 6: Short Dialogue translation

けん: Yumiko chan. I'm hungry. Whart will we eat?

ゆみこ: Can we eat at that restaurant?

けん:	What? At that high end place?
ゆみこ:	It's almost my birthday right? Let's eat delicious things.
けん:	Ok. Let's go then.

In the restaurant

ゆみこ:	Excuse me. Please show me the wine list.
ウェイター:	Ok. I understand.
けん:	What? Are you going to drink wine in the afternoon.
ゆみこ:	Of course! Can I drink red wine?
けん:	Okay…
ゆみこ:	That and for an appetizer can I eat caviar?
けん:	The wine is okay… but the caviar is a bit…
ゆみこ:	Stingy!
けん:	…

❏ Lesson 6: Practice
Possible Answers

1. なかないで 下さい。 — Please don't cry.
   げんきだして 下さい。 — Cheer up.
   ないては いけません。 — You can't cry. (you shouldn't cry)

2. あまり たべないで 下さい。 — Don't eat so much.
   やせて 下さい。 — Please lose weight.
   そんなに たべては いけません。 — You can't eat that much. (you shouldn't eat that much)

3. さけを のまないで 下さい。 — Don't drink alchohol.
   たくさん のんでは いけません。 — You can't drink a lot. (you shouldn't drink a lot)

❏ Lesson 6: Fill in the kanji

1. 犬は 草原を はしり周りました。
2. この引き戸 は 古いですか。
3. きょう 午後に 会いましょう。
4. 日本語で 歌を 歌いました。
5. わたしは 中古車を うっています。
6. 後ろに 先生が いますよ。

❏ Lesson 7: Reading comprehension translation

① My name is Marina.
② Next year, since I am going to graduate college, I am really looking forward to it.
③ I have decided to go on a graduation trip with my friends.

④ I still haven't decided a place to go.

⑤ There are friends who want to go to Australia.

⑥ There are also friends who want to go to England again.

⑦ Since I have been to Australia and English, I am thinking I want to go to New York.

One year later

⑧ My graduation trip was really fun.

⑨ Everyone hesitated about the place to go, but, in the end we decided to go to New York.

⑩ I heard that New York was a dangerous place, but it was ok.

⑪ I think I want to go again.

❑ Lesson 7: Reading comprehension questions

1. Is Marina a high school student now?

   いいえ、大学生です。　　　　　　　　　　No she is a college student.

2. Does Marina want to go to Australia?

   いいえ、ニューヨークに いきたいです。　No she wants to go to New York.

3. In there end, where did she go?

   ニューヨークに いきました。　　　　　　She went to New York.

4. Was that place dangerous?

   いいえ、だいじょうぶ でした。　　　　　No it was okay.

   いいえ、あぶなくなかったです。　　　　No, it wasn't dangerous.

5. You are going to take a graduation trip. Where do you want to go?

   日本に いきたいです。　　　　　　　　I want to go to Japan.

   _____に いきたいです。　　　　　I want to go to _____.

   どこにも いきたくないです。　　　　　I don't want to go anywhere?

❑ Lesson 7: Sentence Patterns

1. ともだちの家に いきます。　　　　　　I am going to a friend's house.

   → honeymoon　　　　　　　　　　しんこんりょこうに いきます。

   → company trip　　　　　　　　　しゅっちょうに いきます。

   → Is it ok if I ~?　　　　　　　　ともだちの いえに いってもいいですか。

   → It is not good if you~　　　　ともだちの いえに いっては いけないです。

   　　　　　　　　　　　　　　　　　ともだちの いえに いっちゃ だめです。

2. きのう、しごとを しました。　　　　　I did my job yesterday.

   → I quit　　　　　　　　　　　　きのう しごとを やめました。

   → I decided (chose)　　　　　　きのう しごとを きめました。

   → I decided not to go　　　　　きのう しごとに いかないことに しました。

   → I decided to take a day off　きのう やすみことに しました。

3. おちゃが のみたいです。   I want to drink tea.

   → I will have...   おちゃを おねがいします。

   → Is it ok if I drink...?   おちゃを のんでも いいですか。

   → It is not ok if you have...   おちゃを のんでは いけません。

                                         おちゃを のんじゃ だめです。

   → I decided to drink   おちゃを のむことに しました。

   → I have drunk before   おちゃは のんだことが あります。

❏ Lesson 7: Practice

A) 1.   ゴルフを することに しました。

   2.   ひこうきで しゅっちょうを することに しました。

   3.   はやく ねることに しました。

   4.   タバコを やめることに しました。

B) 5.   あした、びょういんに いくことに なりました。

   6.   らいげつ、大学を そつぎょうすることに なりました。

   7.   一日一回 くすりを のむことに なりました。

❏ Lesson 7: Short dialogue translation

面接官: Have you ever done sales?

田中さん: Yes, I have. I was doing it for 5 years at a gas company.

面接官: Do you think you are suited for sales work.

田中さん: Yes I do. Since I am out going, I think sales matches me more than office work.

面接官: Is that so. Well then, Please tell me more of your selling points.

田中さん: Yes. I am aggressive and am good at conversation with people.
          And, I am accurate with time, so I won't miss deadlines.

面接官: Well then, are you also good (strong) with pressure? This field is tough.

田中さん: Yes, I'm good (ok). I request it.

❏ Lesson 7: Question and Answer

Student answers will vary.

1. Where do you want to go on your honeymoon? / Where did you go?
2. After high school graduation, what did you do? / Will you do?
3. Now, are you hestitating with your course in life?
4. Are your days off decided?
5. What are things that you have decided to do everyday?

❏ Lesson 7: Fill in the kanji

1. 大工は雨の日に しごとが できません。
2. あの広い公園で会いましょう。
3. つぎの交差点を右に まがって下さい。
4. 銀行に行ってから、家に帰ります。
5. 考えるとき へんな顔をします。
6. 広間には たくさんの光が入りますね。

❏ Lesson 8: Reading comprehension translation

① Last month Beth came to Japan.

② It was her first time overseas.

③ She homestayed in my home for one week.

④ I was surprised her Japanese was so good. (very skilled)

⑤ Since Beth said she wanted to see a baseball game, we went to the baseball stadium together.

⑥ Since Beth really likes baseball, she was really looking forward to it.

⑦ Beth said that she saw a famous Japanese player called, "Ichirou", one year ago in Seattle.

⑧ At that time, the Seattle Mariner's beat the New York Yankees.

⑨ She said she was surprised that Ichirou was so fast.

⑩ Beth said that in Japan everyone doesn't eat peanuts that much at the baseball stadium.

⑪ I told (taught) Beth that the things that people eat at Japanese and American baseball stadiums are different.

❏ Lesson 8: Reading comprehension questions

1. How long was Beth in Japan?
   いっしゅうかん いました。   She was there for one week.

2. What did Beth want to do in Japan?
   やきゅうの しあいを みたかったです。   She wanted to see a baseball game.

3. What did Beth think of Ichirou?
   あしが はやかったと おもいました。   She thought he was fast.

4. What type of things do Americans eat at baseball stadiums.
   (Note: This answer may vary since the comprehension doesn't give specific answers.)
   ピーナッツを たべます。   They eat peanuts.

5. What type of things do you think they eat in Japanese baseball stadiums.
   おにぎりを たべると おもいます。   I think they eat onigiri (rice balls).

6. Literally: What number time is this for Beth to go overseas?
   はじめて でした。   It was her first time.

   いっかいめです。   It's the first time.

❑ Lesson 8: Sentence Jumble

1. 500円かちました。

   しあいに まけました。

   ともだちに 500円まけました。

2. （あなたは） あんなに じょうず （で / から） びっくりしました。

   むしあつくて びっくりしました。

   あなたの たべかたが へたです。

3. ピザの つくりかたを おしえて下さい。

   （わたしの） アパートの ごみの すてかたが （わかりません / わからないです）。

   いつから はしの つかいかたが わかりますか。

❑ Lesson 8: Practice

Answer is underlined.

1. A: Taguchi san is sure good at tennis.
   B: Yes, I am actually also good at it.

2. A: Teacher, your wife's cooking is delicious.
   B: Thank you, I also think so.

3. A: Tom, tomorrow I'm playing tennis, do you want to come too? (are you coming too?)
   B: Yeah, I'm going. Who else is coming?
   A: John and Kerry also. You will be surprised because John is good at tennis.
   B: Yeah. I am not that good.

❑ Lesson 8: Question and Answer

1. Do you know how to make sushi?

   はい、 （つくりかたを） しってます。

   いいえ、 しらないです。

   いいえ、 しりません。

   はい、 とくい です。

2. Do you know how to go from Tokyo to Oosaka?

   いいえ、 いきかたが わかりません。

   はい、 しんかんせんで いけます。

   はい、 わかります。

3. Who always throws out the garbage?

   おかあさんが すてます。

   わたしが すてます。

   だれも すてません。

4. Which sports are you good at?

サッカーが とくいです。

スポーツが とくい じゃないです。

5. What is your mother good at?

りょうりが 上手です。

そうじが じょうずです。

6. What things are Japanese people surprised at.

いえが おおきくて びっくりします。

ニューヨークのビルが たかくて びっくりします。

アメリカの たべものが にほんの たべものより やすくて びっくりします。

❏ Lesson 8: Short dialogue translation

かの女：   Ken, dinner is ready.

けん：   Wow! It sure looks delicious. Spaghetti is my favorite food.

かの女：   Great. I am good at cooking.

けん：   Ohhh. Well then I will receive. (said before eating)

かの女：   Go ahead. Eat a lot ok.

けん：   ・・・

かの女：   How is the taste? It's delicous right?

けん：   Ummm…. What is this?

かの女：   That is melon. That brown one is nattou.

けん：   What?! You put those type of things in spaghetti?

かの女：   Yeah, I always make unique food. (りょうり can be translated as "food")
I can teach you how to make it.

けん：   That's okay… Ummm sorry.
I am full now.

かの女：   You haven't eaten yet right? What a waste!

けん：   Yes, I know. I will eat it. (I will receive)

❏ Lesson 8: Fill in the kanji

1. 今日は気温が高いです。

2. 黒がすきだけど、黄色は すきじゃないです。

3. きのう日本に帰国しました。

4. アメリカ合衆国は広いですね。

5. 高校生のとき、よく谷でやきゅうを しました。

❏ Lesson 9: Reading comprehension translation

① Today was a strange day.

② I laughed, got made, and cried.

③ Today, after waking up at 7 o'clock, I immediately took a shower.

④ When I was taking my shower, someone flushed the toilet.

⑤ The hot water suddenly got hot.

⑥ Hey! Don't flush the toilet when I'm taking a shower!

⑦ I got really mad.

⑧ After that, I there was a phone call from a person from the company.

⑨ AHHH! I got fired.

⑩ What should I do? I was so sad I cried.

⑫ Then, someone said, "Wake up. It's already 7 o'clock."

⑬ AHH! I was suprised.

⑭ Actually I was still sleeping.

⑮ It was all a dream.

⑯ I laughed until 7:30.

❏ Lesson 9: Reading comprehension questions

1. Do you think Tanaka san is a high school student?

   いいえ、しごとを してるから こうこうせいじゃないと おもいます。
   No, because he is working, I don't think he is a high school student.

2. Around what time do you think Tanaka san always wakes up?
   7じごろに おきると おもいます。   I think he wakes up around 7 o'clock.

3. Why did Tanaka san get mad?
   だれかが トイレを ながしたからです。   Because somebody flushed the toilet.

   だれかが シャワーを あびているときに トイレを ながしたからです。
   Because somebod flushed the toilet when he was taking a shower.

4. Who called Tanaka san?
   会しゃのひとが でんわを しました。   A company person called.

5. Why did Tanaka san laugh?
   ゆめだったからです。   Because it was a dream.

❏ Lesson 9: Sentence Jumble

1. きたぐちで あいましょう。
   はつかに あいたいです。
   ひがしぐちに よじに あいます。

2. レストランが とても きたなかったです。

（わたしの）ともだちの パーティーは とても たのしかったです。

おもしろくない しゅくだいでした。

3. おこらないで 下さい。

わたしの かのじょが なきました。

だれかが トイレを ながさなかった（です）！

4. あした えいがを みに いきます。

きのう えいごを おしえに いきました。

あさって あなたに あいに いきたいです。

ともだちが しょくじを たべに きました。

❑ Lesson 9: Question and Answer
(sample answers)

1. What do you do on the weekend?

テレビを みたり、ともだちと あそんだり します。I will do things like watch TV and play with friends.

2. What do you do on your school / work break time.

ニュースを よんだり、ひるねを したりします。   I do things like reading news, and taking naps.

3. What do you want to do in Japan?

AKB48 の コンサートをみたり、あきはばらに いったり したいです。

I want to do things like go to an AKB48 concert, and go to Akihabara.

4. You are a Hollywood star. What type of things do you do?

たかい車を かったり、いろいろな くにに いったりします。

I buy things like expenseive cars, and go to various countries.

5. You are on a deserted island. What do you do?

たべものを さがしたり、およいだり、ねたりします。

I do things like search for food, swim and sleep.

❑ Lesson 9: Translation

1. あしたは さむい（なの）かな。

2. なぜ / なんで くびに なった（の）かな。

3. わたしの けいたいでんわは どこ（なの）かな。

4. ことしは お金が たりる（の）かな。

5. あした もりさんに あいに いける（の）かな。

❑ Lesson 9: Short dialogue translation

Hayashi san: What happened Kuroda san? You are mad right?

Kuroda san: Yes… A person in the neighborhood is so loud, I am troubled.

Hayashi san:	Is it because they have children?
Kuroda san:	No. They are so loud at night I can't sleep at all.
	The do things like play music at 3 in the middle of the night, and their dog barks outside.
Hayashi san:	That's terrible. Did you go to warn them?
Kuroda san:	Yes, of course. But they say things like, "it isn't me" and "it's hopeless".
Hayashi san:	That's terrible. Next time please call the police.
Kuroda san:	Yes, that's right. Then that is what I will do.

❑ Lesson 9: Fill in the kanji

1. わたしは今日、二十六才にに なりました。
2. 計算より作文のほうが かんたんです。
3. この町は行き止りが おおいですね。
4. わたしは よく市場で 魚を かいます。
5. 雨で午後のゲームが 中止に なりました。
6. 今回の出張の予算を計算しました。

❑ Lesson 10: Reading comprehension translation

① It was a hot summer day. A very old man was walking a mountain.

② The old man was very thirsty so he looked for water.

③ He found a nearby, clean spring.

④ After he drank the water, the old man felt really good.

⑤ The lower back that had always hurt got better.

⑥ After returning home, the old woman was very surprised that the old man's hair had turned black.

⑦ The old man had become young.

⑧ The old man explained about the spring to the old woman.

⑨ The old woman looked at the old man and thought, "I also want to become young."

⑩ The old woman when alone to drink the water.

⑪ But, the old woman did not return home.

⑫ The old man worred and went to look for the old lady.

⑬ Near the spring there was a crying baby.

⑭ That was the old lady.

❑ Lesson 10: Reading comprehension questions

1. Where on the the old man was hurting?
   こしが いたかったです.   His back was hurting.

2. How did the old man feel better?
   いずみの みずを のみました.   He drank the spring water.

3. What was the old lady suprised about?
    おじいさんの かみが くろくなっていた ことに びっくりしました。
    She was surprised that the old man's hair had become black.

4. When the old man returned to the spring, what was nearby?
    あかちゃんが いました。　　　　　　　There was a baby.

5. Why did the old lady become a baby?
    いずみの みずを のんだからです。　　Because she drank the spring water.

6. If it were you, would you drink the spring water?
    はい、のみます。　　　　　　　　　　Yes, I would drink it.

    いいえ、のみません。　　　　　　　　No, I wouldn't drink it.

❑ Lesson 10: Sentence Patterns

1. しんぱいした ことが ありません。　　I have never worried.

    → have never explained　　　　　せつめいした ことが ありません。

    → have never bought a souvenir　おみやげを かった ことが ありません。

    → have been on a diet　　　　　ダイエットを した ことが あります。

    → have been in Japan on New Year's Day　おしょうがつに にほんに いった ことが あります。

2. きのうは たいへんな 日でした。　　Today was an awful day.

    → a special day　　　　　　　きょうは とくべつなひ でした。

    → a lonely day　　　　　　　　きょうは さみしいひ でした。

    → last year / busy year　　　きょねんは いそがしいとし でした。

    → last year / quiet year　　きょねんは しずかなとし でした。

3. あつくなりましたね。　　　　　　It sure got hot.

    → became cold　　　　　　　さむくなりましたね。

    → became bright　　　　　　あかるくなりましたね。

    → became warm　　　　　　あたかくなりましたね。

    → didn't become warm　　あたくなりませんでしたね。

4. コーヒーを のみたくなりました。　I want to drink coffee now.

    → no longer able to drink　コーヒーを のめなくなりました。

    → no longer want to drink　コーヒーを のみたくなくなりました。

    → no longer drink　　　　　コーヒーを のまなくなりました。

    → tastes good now　　　　　コーヒーが おいしくなりました。

❏ Lesson 10: Practice 1

1. When Yokota san wakes up in the morning what does he do?
   シャワーをあびたり、あさごはんを たべたりします。
   He takes showers, and eats breakfast.

2. What time does he leave the house?
   8 じに でます。   He leaves at 8 o'clock.

3. Before he takes his afternoon break how much work does he do?
   3 じかんはん しごとを します。   He works for 3 and a half hours.

4. After he has returned home, what does he do?
   テニスを したり、かぞくと しくじを したり、テレビを みたりします。
   He plays tennis, has dinner with his family, and watches TV.

5. About how many hours does he sleep?
   8 じかん（ぐらい）ねます。   He sleeps (about) 8 hours.

❏ Lesson 10: Short dialogue translation

しゅん：　Hiroshi! It's been a long time huh!?

ひろし：　It really (has been)! We haven't met since graduating high school.
　　　　　What are you doing now?

しゅん：　After I graduated, I was doing a part time job for a while.
　　　　　But, after entering college, it's been study and my job everyday.

ひろし：　I see. It's awful since I have over 4 classes in a day, and 2 part time

しゅん：　It was good before we got out of high school

ひろし：　Yeah. Because we went to school, returned home at 4 o'clock, and played videos.

しゅん　　Those days feel nostalgic.

❏ Lesson 10: Fill in the kanji

1. 今、何時ですか。
2. 自分の時間が ほしいです。
3. 教室で手紙を かきました。
4. お正月にお寺に いきました。
5. 自らの力で がんばりました。
6. 夏休みの思い出を作文にしました。
7. 黄色と白のおり紙を作ります。

❏ Lesson 11: Reading comprehension translation

① Chika san goes to a college in Hawaii.

② Her boyfriend has been visiting her from Texas since yesterday.

③ They met in Japan 5 years ago.

④ Chika san will graduate college this year.

⑤ Today, Chika san asked, "If I go to Texas, can I live with you?".

⑥ Her boyfriend said, "Come any time."

⑦ But, Chika san is very worried.

⑧ It's because she heard from her Japanese friends that there is a Texas dialect in Texas.

⑨ Chika san is deciding on whether to return to Japan, be in Hawaii, or go to Texas.

⑩ Her friend said, "If you go to Texas, you should study Texas dialect".

⑪ In the end, since Chika san really likes her boyfriend, she decided to go to Texas.

⑫ She said to her boyfriend, "I'm going to Texas, so teach me Texas dialect."

⑬ He laughed for about 10 minutes. Then he said. "There isn't a Texas dialect."

⑭ Chika san got embarrassed.

❏ Lesson 11: Reading comprehension questions

1. Where is Chika's college?
   ハワイに あります。

2. Where does Chika's boyfriend live?
   テキサスに すんでいます。

3. What is Chika worried about?
   テキサスに テキサスべんが あると きいたから、しんぱいしています。

   テキサスべんのことを しんぱいしています。

4. In the end, what did she do?
   テキサスに 行くことに しました。

5. Why was Chika embarrassed?
   かれに テキサスべんは ないと きいたからです。

❏ Lesson 11: Sentence Patterns

1. 日本には ふじ山が あります。   In Japan there is Mt. Fuji.

   → healthy food   日本には けんこうてきな たべものが あります。

   → dialects   日本には ほうげんが あります。

   → convenient trains   日本には べんりな でん車が あります。

   → beautiful temples   日本には きれいな お寺が あります。

2. 一まん円、かりてもいいですか。   Can I borrow 10,000 yen?

   → Can I lend?   一まん円、かしてもいいですか。

   → Can I return?   一まん円、かえしても いいですか。

   → Can I pay?   一まん円、はらっても いいですか。

   → I have lost   一まん円、なくしました。

3. まい日 かん字を れんしゅうしたほうが いいですよ。
   You should study kanji everyday.

→ throw away garbage	まい日 ごみを すてたほうが いいですよ。
→ quit your current job	今の しごとを やめたほうが いいですよ。
→ You shouldn't	まい日かん字を れんしゅうしないほうが いいですよ。
→ stay up late	まい日 夜ふかし しないほうが いいですよ。

4. 時間が あるなら、えい画を 見ましょう。
   If you have time, let's see a movie.

→ go to buy souvenirs	時間があるなら、おみやげを かいに いきましょう。
→ rent a DVD	時間があるなら、DVD をかりましょう。/レンタルしましょう。
→ If you don't have time	時間がないなら、えい画を 見ましょう。
→ If you want to stay home	家に いたいなら、えい画を 見ましょう。

5. 日本に 行ったら、まい日 雨が ふりました。   When I went to Japan, it rained everyday.

→ I spoke nothing but Kansai dialect	日本に 行ったら、かんさいべんしか しゃべらなかった。(はなさなかった)
→ I used a lot of money	日本に 行ったら、お金を たくさん つかいました。
→ when I took time off work	しごとを やすんだら、まい日 雨が ふりました。
→ buy me some anime DVD	日本に 行ったら、アニメの DVD をかって下さい。

❑ Lesson 11: Question and Answer

(sample answers)

1. When / If you got lost, what do you do?

だれかに いきかたを ききます。	I ask someone the way (how to go).
だれかに でんわを します。	I call someone.
あるいている人に ききます。	I ask a person walking.

2. If you are transferred to Tokyo, what would you do there?

日本の いろいろな ところに りょこうします。	I would take trips to various places in Japan.
ともだちを 作ります。	I would make friends.

3. If you get sick, what would you do?

くすりを のみます。	I would drink medicine.
ベッドで 休みます。 / しごとを 休みます。	I would rest in bed. / I would take a break from work.

4. If you win 5 million yen by gambling, what would you buy?

いい車を かいます。	I would buy a good car.
休みを とって、りょこうを します。	I would take a vacation and travel.

❏ Lesson 11: Practice 1

Ex. 日本に行くなら、   (C) A.   あの店が いいですよ。

1. 今日、いそがしいなら、   (F) B.   げん気に なりますよ。

2. ステーキを たべるなら、   (D) C.   おみやげを かって下さい。

3. たん生日プレゼントを かうなら、 (A) D.   赤ワインが 合いますよ。

4. このくすりを のんだら、   (B) E.   あした、おきられませんよ。

5. お金が なかったら、   (G) F.   あした、会いませんか。

6. こんばん、よふかししたら、   (E) G.   わたしが かしますよ。

❏ Lesson 11: Practice 2

1. あたらしいテレビを かったほうが いいですよ。

2. わるいことを しないほうが いいですよ。／ おとなしくしたほうが いいですよ。

3. くすりを ぬった(to apply) ほうが いいですよ。／ びょういんに 行ったほうが いいですよ。

4. あんまり のまないほうが いいですよ。／ ベッドで ねたほうが いいですよ。

5. よく ねたほうが いいですよ。／ かぜぐすりを のんだほうが いいですよ。

❏ Lesson 11: Short dialoguq translation

Mori: If you get married, what kind of person would be good, Terada kun?
Terada: Let's see. It would be nice to have someone who is beautiful, cheerful and good at cooking.
Mori: Hmm....I want the person to be sweet and manly.
Terada: That is it? I bet you wish more because you have high expectations.
Mori: That is rude! But I need someone who is handy becaue I can't do anything.
Terada: You mean, a person who is capable of working, doing housework and fixing things around the house?
Mori: That is right. It would be nice if there is someone like that.
Terada: I think it would be a little difficult, but go for it. Tell me if you find one.

❏ Lesson 11: Fill in the kanji

1. 今年の秋は さむかったです。

2. 足首が少し、いたいです。

3. 春休みに作文を書きました。

4. 早く、社会に出た ほうがいいですよ。

5. わたしは計算に弱いです。

❏ Lesson 12: Reading comprehension translation

① Jim is a Japanese and English interpreter.

② For 5 days from the day after tomorrow, it's been decided that he's going to Taiwan for work.

③ Since Jim had a lot of other work, he requested business trip preparations to his wife.

おくさん: How many days do you have work?

ジムさん: It's just 2 days.

おくさん: Then, just 2 business shirts should be fine.

ジムさん: Yeah, I think so. Also, Taiwan is probably humid, so prepare some short sleeves.

おくさん: Got it. Ah, this time I don't need any souvenirs.

ジムさん: Okay. There is a thing I want, can I buy it?

おくさん: What is it?

ジムさん: The CD of a Taiwanese singer.

おくさん: Okay.

④ His wife finished the perparations in about an hour.

⑤ Jim was busy at work and couldn't buy a CD afterall.

⑥ But, he bought his wife a souvenir at the airport.

❑ Lesson 12: Reading comprehension questions

1. How long will Jim be in Taiwan for?
    ５日かん います。

2. How many days is his interpreting work?
    ２日かん です。

3. What season do you think it is?
    なつだと おもいます。

4. What does the wife what in Taiwan?
    何も ほしくないです。

5. Did Jim have time in Taiwan?
    いいえ、なかったです。
    いいえ、ありません でした。

❑ Lesson 12: Sentence Jumble

1. 日本に行くまで、いくら ためますか。
    日本に行くまで、何日ありますか。
    何日まで 日本にいますか。

2. ５ふんで しゅくだいが できました。
    ５ふんで しょくじ (が / を) たべられますか。
    このしごとは 何時間で できましたか。

3. このスープは もっと しおが 要ります。
    がっこうが ４じに あるから、車が ３じに 要ります。
    明日まで がっこうが ないです。

4.　だれが ピザを たのみましたか。

　　たのむかどうかが わかりません。

　　たのんだピザが おいしくなかった。

❏ Lesson 12: Practice 1

(sample answers)

1.　高校を そつぎょうするまで、車を うんてんしたことが ありませんでした。

　　高校を そつぎょうするまで、まい日、べんきょうを がんばります。

2.　けっこんするまで、アパートに すんでいました。

　　けっこんするまで、いろいろな国に 行きたいです。

3.　日本語がうまくなるまで、日本人のともだちを作ったり、大学で日本語のクラスをとったりしました。

　　日本語がうまくなるまで、まい日、たくさん べん強します。

4.　二十二才になるまで、日本語をべん強しませんでした。

　　日本人のかの女とけっこんするまで、日本語をべん強しませんでした。

5.　十二時になるまで、ねられません。

　　しごとがおわるまで、ねられません。

6.　今まで、海外に行ったことがありません。

　　社会人になるまで、海外に行ったことがありませんでした。

❏ Lesson 12: Practice 2

1.　この本は むずかしい(から)、一日(で) よめませんでした。

2.　夕ごはんのよういをする(まで)、ちょっと、まって下さいね。

3.　ロサンゼルス(から)日本(まで)、ひこうき(で) 十一時間ぐらいですよ。

4.　近じょの人(に) しずかにして下さい(と) たのみました。

5.　ぼくは かの女(と) いつも けんか(を) しています。

6.　あと四しゅう間(で) 学校(が) おわります。

7.　わたしは ときどき( )でん車(で) ともだち(に)会い(に)行きます。

❏ Lesson 12: Question and Answer

(sample answers)

1.　What do you need now?

　　休みが いります。 / しごとが いります。 / 何も いりません。

2.　Do you have a fight with your family?

　　あんまり、けんかしません。

　　ときどき、します。

3. How many rooms do you have in your house? (*lit: What LDK are you living in?*)

    3LDK に すんでいます。

    1K に すんでいます。

4. Who prepares for dinner?

    おくさんが します。

    みんなで します。

5. How much does it cost to buy an airline ticket to Japan?

    千ドルぐらいで かえます。

    十万円ぐらいで かえます。

6. Until when do you want to study Japanese?

    ペラペラに なるまで、べん強したいです。

    かんたんな かいわが できるまで、べん強したいです。

❏ Lesson 12: Short dialogue translation

Sakuta	I had a big fight with my mother yesterday.
Yamamoto	Did you? Who is wrong this time?
Sakuta	Maybe me…
Yamamoto	What did you do? You don't help her around the house or something like that?
Sakuta	Umm. That one, too. My final test result wasn't good.
Yamamoto	How many points did you get?
Sakuta	It was less than 50 points. I think my mother won't talk to me until I pass a makeup exam.
Yamamoto	When is your makeup exam?
Sakuta	Actually it is going to start in 5 hours. What shall I do?

❏ Lesson 12: Fill in the kanji

1. わたしのすきな 色は 赤と 黒と 白です。
2. 親がいるから、心強いです。
3. 食べる 場しょを きめましたか。
4. 新年に 古いお寺に 行きました。
5. 親友は 工場で はたらいています。
6. わたしが 合図をするまで、まって 下さい。
7. 七月八日に あの 会場でコンサートがある。
8. 谷口さん、ちょっと 顔色がわるいですね。

❏ Lesson 13: Reading comprehension translation

Mom:	Ken chan, your birthday is coming soon. What do you want?
Ken:	Well... what do I want...
Mom:	I gave you a robot last year, right? It would be better to have a different one this year.
Ken:	Yeah. Well then, I want a bicycle.
Mom:	You got a bicycle from your grandmother one year ago, didn't you?
Ken:	But it became old already, so...
Mom:	No. What else do you want?

Ken: If I say something, will you really give it to me?
Mom: If it is not too expensive.
Ken: Well then, I want you to buy me a puppy.
Mom: What? Puppy? You should ask your dad about it.

❏ Lesson 13: Reading comprehension questions

1. What has Ken received up until now?
   ロボットと 自てん車を もらいました。

2. Who did he receive it from?
   おかあさんと おばあちゃんから もらいました。

3. What kind of things can't Ken's mom give to him?
   高いものを あげられません。

4. Who makes a decision on what to buy for him?
   おとうさんに あります。 / おとうさんが きめます。

5. If it were you, what would you give to Ken?
   子犬を あげます。 / ビデオゲームを あげます。

❏ Lesson 13: Sentence Jumble

1. ほっかいどうに いってほしくないです。 / ほっかいどうに いかないでほしいです。
   このくすりを のんでほしいです。
   このくすりを のまないでほしいです。 / このくするを のんでほしくないです。

2. ともだちが わたしに えんぴつを くれました。
   （わたしの） せんせいに たんじょうびに プレゼントを あげました。
   （わたしの） いぬに えさを やりました。

3. じかんが ないから せんたくを てつだいたくないです。
   あかのたにんを てつだいました。
   じかんがあるなら、（わたしを） てつだって下さい。

4. まいにち 日本ごを べんきょうしてほしいです。
   わたしを みないで ほしいです。 / わたしを みてほしくないです。
   わたしの しゅくだいを てつだってほしいです。

❏ Lesson 13: Practice (sample answers)

1. しずかに してほしいです。 / 音を下げてほしいです。 / とおくに 行ってほしいです。
2. けっこんしてほしいです。 / プロポーズに OK してほしいです。
3. こたえを 教えてほしいです。
4. おかしを かってほしいです。 / 一つ、かってほしいです。
5. ちかくに こないでほしいです。 / せき(cough)を しないでほしいです。

❏ Lesson 13: Translation

1. 今日の午後、でんわしてほしいです。
2. 子どもに せんたくを 手つだってほしいです。
3. 赤のた人 / しらない人から 何も もらわないでほしいです。
4. あなたに ゆうめいに ならないでほしいです。
5. しゅじんに 一か月に 二回いじょう、出ちょうに 行かないでほしいです。

❏ Lesson 13: Question and answer

(sample answers)
1. What do you give on your family's birthday?
   本をあげたり、CD をあげたりします。

2. What kind of things do you receive often and from who?
   よく ともだちに DVD を もらいます。

3. What do you want your friends to do for you?
   ときどき、でんわを してほしいです。 / はなしを きいてほしいです。
4. What do you want your partner to do for you?
   いつも いっしょに いてほしいです。 / ごはんを 作ってほしいです。

5. What kind of things don't you want someone to do and by whom?
   よる、犬に ないてほしくないです。 / かぞくに よふかししないでほしいです。

❏ Lesson 13: Short dialogue translation

Mr. Kuroda:	How do you do. I am Kuroda. Nice to meet you.
Landlord:	Nice to meet you too. Are you a student, Mr. Kuroda?
Mr. Kuroda:	Yes. I am a junior at Tokyo university. I am also doing a part-time
job.	
Landlord:	I see. Is your part-time job late at night?
Mr. Kuroda:	Yes, it is. I usually work from 7 o'clock until 11 o'clock at night.
Landlord:	That is late. We go to bed at 10 o'clock, so I want you to be quiet
when you	
	come home. Can you do it?
Mr. Kuroda:	Yes, of course.
Landlord:	And also, I don't want you to bring your friends here, but is it ok?
Mr. Kuroda:	Yes, I won't bring them.
Landlord:	We have strict rules, but be patient because the rent is cheap.
Mr. Kuroda:	I can't resist the cheapness of the rent. Thank you./Please accept
me.	

❏ Lesson 13: Fill in the kanji

1. 大声を 出さないで 下さい。
2. かん西は 数か月間、晴れていますね。
3. 今月、切手を 六まい、かいました。
4. ここは 見晴らしが いいから、星空がよく 見えます。
5. 歌手に 大切なのは、きれいな 歌声です。

❏ Lesson 14: Reading comprehension translation

Shinji:	What will I do... The computer got broken.
Older sister:	What? Did you do something?
Shinji:	I didn't do anything. I think it just broke.
Older sister:	The computer doesn't just break! You broke it, didn't you!
Shinji:	No, I don't break (computers) !
Older sister:	Well then, what are you going to do?
Shinji:	You are good at computers, so can you take a look at it for me?
Older sister:	Let me see... ok. I will take a look at it for you.
Shinji:	You are always fussy, but you often help me out, don't you?
Older sister:	If you say such a thing next time, I won't do anything for you any more!
Shinji:	Sorry...

❏ Lesson 14: Reading comprehension questions

1. Did Shinji say he broke the computer?

   いいえ、いいませんでした。「かってに こわれた」と いいました。

2. Do you think computers break on their own?

   いいえ、思いません。/ はい、古かったら、こわれると 思います。

3. What does コンピューターに強い mean?

   It means to know computers well.

4. Is Shinji's older sister kind to him?

   はい。うるさいけど、よく 手つだって くれます。

5. What would you do when your computer is broken?

   おみせに もって行きます。/ コンピューターに強いともだちに おねがいします。

❏ Lesson 14: Sentence patterns

1. バイクの音が きこえます。　　　　　　　I can hear the sound of a motorbike.

   → teacher's voice　　　　　　　先生の声が きこえます。

   → crying voice　　　　　　　なき声が きこえます。

   → singing voice　　　　　　　歌声が きこえます。

   → can't hear　　　　　　　バイクの音が きこえません。

2. れいぞうこを こわしました。　　　　　　I broke the refrigerator.

   → flower vase　　　　　　　花びんを こわしました。

   → a basket　　　　　　　かごを こわしました。

   → my body (I got sick.)　　　　　　　からだを こわしました。

   → isn't broken　　　　　　　れいぞうこが こわれていません。

3. いいアイディアが うまれました。　　　　A good idea was born.

   → a baby　　　　　　　赤ちゃんが 生まれました。

   → is needed / I need　　　　　　　いいアイディアが ひつようです / いります。

   → I told (taught)　　　　　　　いいアイディアを 教えました。

   → I received　　　　　　　いいアイディアを もらいました。

4. おかあさんが まいあさ おこしてくれます。   My mother wakes me up every morning.

    → prepares lunch for me   おかあさんが まいあさ、おひるごはん
    （おべんとう）を よういしてくれます
    / 作ってくれます。

    → is worried about me   おかあさんが （わたしを） しんぱいしてくれます。

    → will buy a new car for me   おかあさんが 新車を かってくれます。
    → drives for me   おかあさんが うんてんしてくれます。

5. わたしは 親友に でんわを してもらいます。   I will have my best friend call.
    → have her teach math   わたしは かの女に 数学を 教えてもらいます。
    → have my teacher teach history   わたしは 先生に れきしを 教えていただきます。
    → have my teacher read my essay   わたしは 先生に 作文を よんでいただきます。
    → have my boyfriend carry my bag   わたしは かれに かばんを もってもらいます。

❏ Lesson 14: Question and answer
(sample answers)

1. What breaks on its own?
    れいぞうこや せんたくきが こわれます。

2. What have you broken?
    車のサイドミラーを こわしたことが あります。

3. What kind of sounds can you hear often?
    犬のなき声や、車の音が きこえます。

4. What kind of things does your family do for you?
    たん生日に プレゼントを もらったり、でんわを してもらったりします。

5. What kind of things do you do for your friends?
    しんぱいごとを きいてあげたり、ばんごはんを 作ってあげたりします。

❏ Lesson 14: Practice

1. 先日、犬の赤ちゃんが うまれたので、わたしは ミルクを （あげました）。
    でも、その子は あんまり （のんでくれない）ので、きんじょの動物病院の先生にきいたら、
    やさしく （教えてくれました）。

2. わたしの おとうとは よく 赤のた人から おかしを （もらいます）。
    わたしは だめだと いいますが、おとうとは （きいてくれません）。

3. もし、かの女と けっこんしたら、ぼくは りょうりを （してほしい）けど、
    けっきょくは ぼくのほうが （とくい）だから、ぼくが すると おもう。

❏ Lesson 14: Short dialogue translation

Hiroko	Huh? The microwave oven is broken! When did it break?
Roommate	Oh, that one? It broke when I was using it yesterday.
Hiroko	What?! I don't know what to do without it!
Roommate	We have no choice. I didn't break it. Because it is old.
Hiroko	Well then, are we going to buy a new one?
Roommate	Ok. Are we going to split?
Hiroko	Umm… since I don't use it that often, will you pay 70%?
Roommate	No way. You just don't use it because I always cook for you.
Hiroko	All right… this month is tight…

GLOSSARY: English-Japanese

English 英語	**Japanese** 日本語	**Kanji** 漢字

A

abroad, overseas	かいがい	海外
account (internet account)	アカウント	アカウント
accurate	せいかく	正確
acquaintance	しりあい	知り合い
after that	そのあと	そのあと
aggressive, positive	せっきょくてき	積極的
alcohol, liquor, sake	おさけ	お酒
all	ぜんぶ	全部
all-nighter, sleepless night	てつや	徹夜
almost, very shortly	もうすぐ	もうすぐ
an explanation	せつめい	説明
Android	アンドロイド	アンドロイド
anxiety, uneasiness	しんぱい	心配
anytime	いつでも	いつでも
appetizer	ぜんさい	前菜
Australia	オーストラリア	オーストラリア
awesome, great	さいこう	最高

B

baby sitter	ベビーシッター	ベビーシッター
barefoot	はだし	裸足
baseball stadium	やきゅうじょう	野球場
basket	かご	籠
bill (at a restaurant/store)	おかんじょう	お勘定
black board	こくばん	黒板
bonus	ボーナス	ボーナス
branch office	ししゃ	支社
business field / world	ぎょうかい	業界
business trip	しゅっちょう	出張

C

café, coffee shop	きっさてん	喫茶店
can't be helped, have no choice	しかたない	仕方ない
celebration	おいわい	お祝い

character; personality	せいかく	性格
chirp, howl, etc. (animal cry)	なきごえ	鳴き声
coffee milk beverage	コーヒーぎゅうにゅう	コーヒー牛乳
company trip (for fun)	しゃいん りょこう	社員旅行
complete stranger	あかの たにん	赤の他人
computer software	ソフト	ソフト
corner	かど	角
country	くに	国
course, route, way	しんろ	進路
crying voice (human cry)	なきごえ	泣き声

D

day	ひ	日
daytime, during the day	ひるま	昼間
dead end (of street)	いきどまり	行き止まり
deadline	しめきり	締め切り
definitely, absolutely, positively	ぜったいに	絶対に
delivery	はいたつ	配達
dialect	ほうげん	方言
diet	ダイエット	ダイエット
difference	ちがい	違い
dinner	ゆうごはん	夕ご飯
dirty, disgusting	きたない	汚い
do-it-yourself (carpenter)	にちようだいく	日曜大工
double cheesburger	ダブルチーズバーガー	ダブルチーズバーガー
dress shirt	ワイシャツ	ワイシャツ

E

east entrance/exit	ひがしぐち	東口
electricity, lights	でんき	電気
electronic dictionary	でんしじしょ	電子辞書
end (of street or hallway etc.)	つきあたり	突き当たり
enemy	てき	敵
England	イギリス	イギリス
entrance	いりぐち	入口
even now	いまでも	今でも
everyone	ぜんいん	全員
excercise, motion	うんどう	運動
exit	でぐち	出口

F

favorite food	だいこうぶつ	大好物
fermented soybeans	なっとう	納豆
fight	けんか	喧嘩
first, the beginning)	さいしょ	最初
flavor	あじ	味
flower vase	かびん	花瓶
food for animals; bait	えさ	餌
freeway, highway	こうそくどうろ	高速道路
front desk (hotel)	フロント	フロント
funny, strange	おかしい	おかしい

G

get along	なかが いい	仲がいい
good at	とくい	得意
good at	とくい	得意
grades, standing in class	せいせき	成績
graduation	そつぎょう	卒業
graduation trip	そつぎょう りょこう	卒業旅行
Grand Canyon	グランド・キャニオン	グランド・キャニオン
ground	じめん	地面

H

hair	かみのけ	髪の毛
happiness	しあわせ	幸せ
hard, awful	たいへん	大変
headquaters, home office	ほんしゃ	本社
healthy	けんこうてき	健康的
healthy	ヘルシー	ヘルシー
heavy	おもい	重い
hedgehog	はりねずみ	針鼠
Hey!	おおい！	おおい！
hiccups	しゃくり	しゃくり
high end, high class	こうきゅう（な）	高級（な）
historical play; period drama	じだいげき	時代劇
hole	あな	穴
home page	ホームページ	ホームページ
home, residence	おたく	お宅
honeymoon	しんこん りょこう	新婚旅行
hot water	おゆ	お湯
how is it done, in what way	どうやって	どうやって

I

ice tea	アイスティー	アイスティー
idea	アイディア	アイディア
ideal, dream	りそう	理想
if	もし	もし
if you can answer	こたえられたら	答えられたら
in front of the train station	えきまえ	駅前
in the middle of the night	よなか	夜中
in the store	てんない	店内
intersection	こうさてん	交差点
iPhone	アイフォン	アイフォン
It's hopeless.	しょうがない	しょうがない

J

Japanese pinball game	パチンコ	パチンコ

K

Kansai dialect	かんさいべん	関西弁
karaoke	カラオケ	カラオケ
knowing, having knowledge of	ごぞんじ	ご存知

L

last name (in the bamboo)	たけなか	竹中
last time	ぜんかい	前回
last weekend	せんしゅうまつ	先週末
Let's eat (informal)	たべよう	食べよう
Let's go (informal)	いこう	行こう
light (weight)	かるい	軽い
love	あい	愛
lunch box	おべんとう	お弁当

M

makeup exam	さいテスト	再テスト
manly, manlike	おとこらしい	男らしい
meeting	かいぎ	会議
miso soup	おみそしる	お味噌汁
more	もっと	もっと
morning assembly (meeting)	ちょうれい	朝礼
motorcycle	バイク	バイク
muggy, hot and humid	むしあつい	蒸し暑い

N

necessary, needed	ひつよう	必要
New Year's Day	おしょうがつ	お正月
next weekend	らいしゅうまつ	来週末
no matter how much	どんなに	どんなに
north entrance/exit	きたぐち	北口

O

office work	じむ	事務
oneself, myself	じぶん	自分
oneself, myself	じぶん	自分
order; request	ごちゅうもん	ご注文
order; request	ちゅうもん	注文
other, another	ほか	他
out going, diplomatic	がいこうてき	外交的

P

part-time job	バイト	バイト
person	かた	方
place (same as ところ)	とこ	所
polite version of さん (Mr., Miss, Mrs.)	さま	様
preparations	じゅんび	準備
presently, right now	ただいま	只今

R

real estate office	ふどうさんや	不動産屋
recently	さいきん	最近
register	レジ	レジ
regrettable	くやしい	悔しい
ride, a mode of transportation	のりもの	乗り物
road	みち	道
robot	ロボット	ロボット
roller coaster	ジェットコースター	ジェットコースター
rules, regulations	きそく	規則

S

sales and marketing	えいぎょう	営業
seat	せき	席
seat	せき	席
seaweed	わかめ	わかめ

selling point	セールスポイント	セールスポイント
Shakespeare	シェークスピア	シェークスピア
short-sleeved shirt	はんそで	半袖
shower	シャワー	シャワー
shrine visit on New Year's Day	はつもうで	初詣
Silicon Valley	シリコンバレー	シリコンバレー
silver coin	ぎんか	銀貨
since, because	ので	ので
skilled in using one's hands	きよう	器用
skillful, delicious, tasty	うまい	旨い、美味い
skillful, good at	じょうず	上手
smart phone	スマートフォン	スマートフォン
smelly, bad smelling	くさい	臭い
so sad, pitiful	かわいそう	可哀想
socks	くつ下(した)	靴下
something	なにか	何か
soup	スープ	スープ
south entrance/exit	みなみぐち	南口
souvenir	おみやげ	お土産
special	とくべつ	特別
special	とくべつ	特別
standard Japanese	ひょうじゅんご	標準語
stars	おほしさま	お星様
stingy	けっち	けっち
straight ahead	まっすぐ	真っ直ぐ
strange	へん	変
street at night	よみち	夜道
strict	きびしい	厳しい
strict, tough	きびしい	厳しい

T

Taiwan	たいわん	台湾
take out, to go	もちかえり	持ち帰り
tears	なみだ	涙
television show	テレビばんぐみ	テレビ番組
term-end exam, final exam	きまつしけん	期末試験
Texas	テキサス	テキサス
that much, so ~	そんなに	そんなに
that over there, over there, that person over there		あちら　あちら
that, there, that person	そちら	そちら
then, and then, after that	それから	それから
thick, fat	ふとい	太い
thin	ほそい	細い

this much, so ~	こんなに	こんなに
this time	こんかい	今回
this time	こんかい	今回
this time, next time	こんど	今度
this weekend	こんしゅうまつ	今週末
this, here, this person	こちら	こちら
those days	あのころ	あの頃
tight, demanding, hard	きつい	きつい
tip	チップ	チップ
to age, to get old	としを とる	年をとる
to appear, to come out	でる	出る
to be able to hear	きこえる	聞こえる
to be alive	いきる	生きる
to be born (idea, result, etc.)	うまれる	生まれる
to be born (people, animals)	うまれる	産まれる
to be broken	こわれる	壊れる
to be decided, be settled	きまる	決まる
to be fired	くびに なる	首になる
to be given (from equal or inferior)	くれる	くれる
to be mad or angry	おこる	怒る
to be quiet	しずかにする	静かにする
to be suited for	むく	向く
to be surprised	びっくりする	びっくりする
to be troubled	こまる	困る
to be troubled	こまる	困る
to borrow, rent	かりる	借りる
to break, destroy, ruin	こわす	壊す
to bring along, to bring around	つれて来る	連れて来る
to change	かえる	変える
to cry	なく	泣く
to decide	きめる	決める
to die	しぬ	死(し)ぬ
to do, to play	なさる	なさる
to drive	うんてんした	運転する
to eat, to drink	めしあがる	召し上がる
to evenly split a bill	わりかんにする	割り勘にする
to explain	せつめいする	せつめいする
to fall down, drop	おちる	落ちる
to feel nostalgic	なつかしい	懐かしい
to fit, match	あう	合う
to flush the toilet	トイレを ながす	トイレを 流す
to get lost, be uncertain, to hesitate	まよう	迷う
to get mad, to get upset	おこる	怒る
to give	あげる	あげる

to give (to equal or inferior)	あげる	あげる
to give (to inferior, animals or plants)	やる	やる
to give a warning	ちゅういする	注意する
to give up	あきらめる	諦める
to go down, get off of	おりる	下(お)りる
to go or come up	あがる	上がる
to graduate	そつぎょうする	卒業する
to have a fight	けんかする	喧嘩する
to have enough of	たりる	足りる
to have, to exist	ござる	ござる
to help out	てつだう	手伝う
to help out, to give some help	てつだう	手伝う
to hit, to win	あたる	当たる
to hold, have, carry	もつ	持つ
to know	しる	知る
to laugh	わらう	笑う
to loan, lend	かす	貸す
to lose (opposite "to win")	まける	負ける
to make, to build	つくる	作る
to need	いる	要る
to pass	ごうかくする	合格する
to play (music)	かける	かける
to prepare, to fight	よういする	用意する
to pull an all-nighter	てつやをする	徹夜をする
to quit one's job or responsibility	やめる	辞める
to recall, to remember	おもいだす	思い出す
to receive (from equal or inferior)	もらう	貰う
to receive (from superior or equal)	いただく	頂く
to request,(order) ask for	たのむ	頼む
to return (pay back)	かえす	返す
to ride, to get on, to get in	のる	乗る
to save (money), to collect	ためる	貯める
to say	おっしゃる	仰る
to see	ごらんに なる	ご覧になる
to show	みせる	見せる
to stay up late	よふかしする	夜ふかしする
to stop, to quit	やめる	止める
to take a business trip	しゅっちょうする	出張する
to take a picture	とる	しゃしんを 撮る
to take a shower	シャワーを あびる	シャワーを あびる
to take an item	とる	取る
to teach	おしえる	教える
to that extent, to that degree	あんなに	あんなに
to throw away	すてる	捨(す)てる

to turn	まがる	曲がる
to turn off, to erase	けす	消す
to turn on	つける	点ける
to use	つかう	使う
to walk	あるく	歩く
to wear (hats, things on head)	かぶる	かぶる
to wear (shirts, jackets)	きる	着る
to wear (shoes, pants)	はく	履く
to win, to beat	かつ	勝つ
to worry	しんぱいする	しんぱいする
tool	どうぐ	道具
Touhoku dialect	とうほくべん	東北弁
trip abroad	かいがいりょこう	海外旅行

U

umph!, heave ho	よいしょ	よいしょ
unique, one of a kind	こせいてき	個性的
unskillful, poor	へた	下手
used to show envy	な (particle)	な

V

very	すごく	凄く

W

warm	あたたかい	暖かい
water-spring, fountain	いずみ	泉
web site	ウェブサイト	ウェブサイト
website	ウェッブサイト	ウェッブサイト
weekend	しゅうまつ	週末
west entrance/exit	にしぐち	西口
what a waste	もったいない	もったいない
What shall I do?	どうしよう	どうしよう
wheat	こむぎ	小麦
where, which and who	どちら	どちら
will not talk to me/someone	くちをきかない	口を利かない
without permission	かってに	勝手に
wonder [see Grammar section]	かな	かな
worries, troubles	しんぱいごと	心配事

Y

year, age	とし	年

GLOSSARY: Japanese-English

Japanese 日本語	English 英語	Kanji 漢字

あ

あい	愛	love
アイスティー	アイスティー	ice tea
アイディア	アイディア	idea
アイフォン	アイフォン	iPhone
あう	合う	to fit, match
アカウント	アカウント	account (internet account)
あかの たにん	赤の他人	a complete stranger
あがる	上がる	to go or come up
あきらめる	諦める	to give up
あげる	あげる	to give (to equal or inferior)
あじ	味	flavor
あたたかい	暖かい	warm
あたる	当たる	to hit, to win
あちら	あちら	that over there, over there, that person over there
あな	穴	a hole
あのころ	あの頃	those days
あるく	歩く	to walk
アンドロイド	アンドロイド	Android
あんなに	あんなに	to that extent, to that degree

い

いきどまり	行き止まり	dead end (of street)
イギリス	イギリス	England
いきる	生(い)きる	to be alive
いこう	行こう	Let's go (informal)
いずみ	泉	water-spring, fountain
いただく	頂く	to receive (from superior or equal)
いつでも	いつでも	anytime
いまでも	今でも	even now
いりぐち	入口	entrance
いる	要る	to need
いる	要る	to need, exc.

う

ウェッブサイト	ウェッブサイト	website
ウェブサイト	ウェブサイト	web site
うまい	旨い、美味い	skillful, delicious, tasty
うまれる	産まれる	to be born (people, animals)
うまれる	生まれる	to be born (idea, result, etc.)
うんてんした	運転する	to drive
うんどう	運動	excercise, motion

え

えいぎょう	営業	sales and marketing
えきまえ	駅前	in front of the train station
えさ	餌	food for animals; bait

お

おいわい	お祝い	celebration
おおい！	おおい！	Hey!
オーストラリア	オーストラリア	Australia
おかしい	おかしい	funny, strange
おかんじょう	お勘定	bill (at a restaurant/store)
おこる	怒る	to get mad, to get upset
おこる	怒る	to be mad or angry
おさけ	お酒	alcohol, liquor, sake
おしえる	教える	to teach
おしょうがつ	お正月	New Year's Day
おたく	お宅	home, residence
おちる	落ちる	to fall down, drop
おっしゃる	仰る	to say
おとこらしい	男らしい	manly, manlike
おべんとう	お弁当	lunch box
おほしさま	お星様	stars
おみそしる	お味噌汁	miso soup
おみやげ	お土産	souvenir
おもい	重い	heavy
おもいだす	思い出す	to recall, to remember
おゆ	お湯	hot water
おりる	下(お)りる	to go down, get off of

か

| かいがい | 海外 | abroad, overseas |
| かいがいりょこう | 海外旅行 | a trip abroad |

かいぎ	会議	meeting
がいこうてき	外交的	out going, diplomatic
かえす	返す	to return (pay back)
かえる	変える	to change
かける	かける	to play (music)
かご	籠	basket
かす	貸す	to loan, lend
かた	方	person
かつ	勝つ	to win, to beat
かってに	勝手に	without permission
かど	角	corner
かな	かな	wonder
かびん	花瓶	flower vase
かぶる	かぶる	to wear (hats, things on head)
かみのけ	髪の毛	hair
カラオケ	カラオケ	karaoke
かりる	借りる	to borrow, rent
かるい	軽い	light (weight)
かわいそう	可哀想	so sad, pitiful
かんさいべん	関西弁	Kansai dialect

き

きこえる	聞こえる	to be able to hear
きそく	規則	rules, regulations
きたぐち	北口	north entrance/exit
きたない	汚い	dirty, disgusting
きつい	きつい	tight, demanding, hard
きっさてん	喫茶店	café, coffee shop
きびしい	厳しい	strict, tough
きびしい	厳しい	strict
きまつしけん	期末試験	term-end exam, final exam
きまる	決まる	to be decided, be settled
きめる	決める	to decide
きよう	器用	skilled in using one's hands
ぎょうかい	業界	business field / world
きる	着る	to wear (shirts, jackets)
ぎんか	銀貨	silver coin

く

くさい	臭い	smelly, bad smelling
くちをきかない	口を利かない	will not talk to me/someone
くつ下(した)	靴下	socks

くに	国	country
くびに なる	首になる	to be fired
くやしい	悔しい	regrettable
グランド・キャニオン	グランド・キャニオン	The Grand Canyon
くれる	くれる	to be given (from equal or
inferior)		

け

けす	消す	to turn off, to erase
けっち	けっち	stingy
けんか	喧嘩	a fight
けんかする	喧嘩する	to have a fight
けんこうてき	健康的	healthy

こ

ごうかくする	合格する	to pass
こうきゅう（な）	高級（な）	high end, high class
こうさてん	交差点	intersection
こうそくどうろ	高速道路	freeway, highway
コーヒーぎゅうにゅう	コーヒー牛乳	coffee milk beverage
こくばん	黒板	black board
ござる	ござる	to have, to exist
こせいてき	個性的	unique, one of a kind
ごぞんじ	ご存知	knowing, having knowledge of
こたえられたら	答えられたら	if you can answer
ごちゅうもん	ご注文	order; request
こちら	こちら	this, here, this person
こまる	困る	to be troubled
こまる	困る	to be troubled
こむぎ	小麦	wheat
ごらんに なる	ご覧になる	to see
こわす	壊す	to break, destroy, ruin
こわれる	壊れる	to be broken
こんかい	今回	this time
こんかい	今回	this time
こんしゅうまつ	今週末	this weekend
こんど	今度	this time, next time
こんなに	こんなに	this much, so ~

さ

| さいきん | 最近 | recently |
| さいこう | 最高 | awesome, great |

さいしょ	最初	first, the beginning)
さいテスト	再テスト	makeup exam
さま	様	polite for Mr., Miss, Mrs.

し

しあわせ	幸せ	happiness
シェークスピア	シェークスピア	Shakespeare
ジェットコースター	ジェットコースター	roller coaster
しかたない	仕方ない	can't be helped, have no choice
ししゃ	支社	branch office
しずかにする	静かにする	to be quiet
じだいげき	時代劇	historical play; period drama
しぬ	死(し)ぬ	to die
じぶん	自分	oneself, myself
じむ	事務	office work
しめきり	締め切り	deadline
じめん	地面	the ground
しゃいん りょこう	社員旅行	company trip (for fun)
しゃくり	しゃくり	the hiccups
シャワー	シャワー	shower
シャワーを あびる	シャワーを あびる	to take a shower
しゅうまつ	週末	the weekend
しゅっちょう	出張	business trip
しゅっちょうする	出張する	to take a business trip
じゅんび	準備	preparations
しょうがない	しょうがない	It's hopeless.
じょうず	上手	skillful, good at
しりあい	知り合い	acquaintance
シリコンバレー	シリコンバレー	Silicon Valley
しる	知る	to know
しんこん りょこう	新婚旅行	honeymoon
しんぱい	心配	anxiety, uneasiness
しんぱいごと	心配事	worries, troubles
しんぱいする	しんぱいする	to worry
しんろ	進路	course, route, way

す

スープ	スープ	soup
すごく	凄く	very
すてる	捨(す)てる	to throw away
スマートフォン	スマートフォン	smart phone

せ

せいかく	正確	accurate
せいかく	性格	character; personality
せいせき	成績	grades, standing in class
セールスポイント	セールスポイント	selling point
せき	席	seat
せき	席	seat
せっきょくてき	積極的	aggressive, positive
ぜったいに	絶対に	definitely, absolutely, positively
せつめい	説明	an explanation
せつめいする	せつめいする	to explain
ぜんいん	全員	everyone
ぜんかい	前回	the last time
ぜんさい	前菜	appetizer
せんしゅうまつ	先週末	last weekend
ぜんぶ	全部	all

そ

そちら	そちら	that, there, that person
そつぎょう	卒業	graduation
そつぎょう りょこう	卒業旅行	graduation trip
そつぎょうする	卒業する	to graduate
そのあと	そのあと	after that
ソフト	ソフト	computer software
それから	それから	then, and then, after that
そんなに	そんなに	that much, so ~

た

ダイエット	ダイエット	diet
だいこうぶつ	大好物	favorite food
たいへん	大変	hard, awful
たいわん	台湾	Taiwan
たけなか	竹中	last name (in the bamboo)
ただいま	只今	presently, right now
たのむ	頼む	to request,(order) ask for
ダブルチーズバーガー	ダブルチーズバーガー	double cheesburger
たべよう	食べよう	Let's eat (informal)
ためる	貯める	to save (money), to collect
たりる	足りる	to have enough of

ち

ちがい	違い	the difference
チップ	チップ	tip
ちゅういする	注意する	to give a warning
ちゅうもん	注文	order; request
ちょうれい	朝礼	morning assembly (meeting)

つ

つかう	使う	to use
つきあたり	突き当たり	end (of street or hallway etc.)
つくる	作る	to make, to build
つける	点ける	to turn on
つれて来る	連れて来る	to bring along, to bring around

て

てき	敵	enemy
テキサス	テキサス	Texas
でぐち	出口	exit
てつだう	手伝う	to help out, to give some help
てつや	徹夜	all-nighter, sleepless night
てつやをする	徹夜をする	to pull an all-nighter
でる	出る	to appear, to come out
テレビばんぐみ	テレビ番組	a television show
でんき	電気	electricity, lights
でんしじしょ	電子辞書	electronic dictionary
てんない	店内	in the store

と

トイレを ながす	トイレを 流す	to flush the toilet
どうぐ	道具	tool
どうしよう	どうしよう	What shall I do?
とうほくべん	東北弁	Touhoku dialect
どうやって	どうやって	how is it done, in what way
とくい	得意	good at
とくい	得意	good at
とくべつ	特別	special
とくべつ	特別	special
とこ	所	place (same as ところ)
とし	年	year, age
としを とる	年をとる	to age, to get old
どちら	どちら	where, which and who

とる	取る	to take an item
とる	しゃしんを 撮る	to take a picture
どんなに	どんなに	(no matter) how much

な

な (particle)	な	used to show envy
なかがいい	仲がいい	get along
なきごえ	鳴き声	chirp, howl, etc. (animal cry)
なきごえ	泣き声	crying voice (human cry)
なく	泣く	to cry
なさる	なさる	to do, to play
なつかしい	懐かしい	to feel nostalgic
なっとう	納豆	fermented soybeans
ななわり	七割	70%
なにか	何か	something
なみだ	涙	tears

に

| にしぐち | 西口 | west entrance/exit |
| にちょうだいく | 日曜大工 | do-it-yourself (carpenter) |

の

ので	ので	since, because
のりもの	乗り物	a ride, a mode of transportation
のる	乗る	to ride, to get on, to get in

は

バイク	バイク	motorcycle
はいたつ	配達	delivery
バイト	バイト	part-time job
はく	履く	to wear (shoes, pants)
はだし	裸足	barefoot
パチンコ	パチンコ	Japanese pinball game
はつもうで	初詣	a shrine visit on New Year's Day
はりねずみ	針鼠	hedgehog
はんそで	半袖	short-sleeved shirt

ひ

| ひ | 日 | day |
| ひがしぐち | 東口 | east entrance/exit |

びっくりする	びっくりする	to be surprised
ひつよう	必要	necessary, needed
ひょうじゅんご	標準語	standard Japanese
ひるま	昼間	daytime, during the day

ふ

ふとい	太い	thick, fat
ふどうさんや	不動産屋	real estate office
フロント	フロント	front desk (hotel)

へ

へた	下手	unskillful, poor
ベビーシッター	ベビーシッター	baby sitter
ヘルシー	ヘルシー	healthy
へん	変	strange

ほ

ほうげん	方言	dialect
ボーナス	ボーナス	bonus
ホームページ	ホームページ	home page
ほか	他	other, another
ほそい	細い	thin
ほんしゃ	本社	headquaters, home office

ま

まがる	曲がる	to turn
まける	負ける	to lose (opposite "to win")
まっすぐ	真っ直ぐ	straight ahead
まよう	迷う	to get lost, be uncertain, to hesitate

み

みせる	見せる	to show
みち	道	road
みなみぐち	南口	south entrance/exit

む

むく	向く	to be suited for
むしあつい	蒸し暑い	muggy, hot and humid

め

めしあがる	召し上がる	to eat, to drink

も

もうすぐ	もうすぐ	almost, very shortly
もし	もし	if
もちかえり	持ち帰り	take out, to go
もつ	持つ	to hold, have, carry
もったいない	もったいない	what a waste
もっと	もっと	more
もらう	貰う	to receive (from equal or inferior)

や

やきゅうじょう	野球場	baseball stadium
やめる	辞める	to quit one's job or responsibility
やめる	止める	to stop, to quit
やる	やる	to give (to inferior, animals or plants)

ゆ

ゆうごはん	夕ご飯	dinner

よ

よいしょ	よいしょ	umph!, heave ho
よういする	用意する	to prepare, to fight
よなか	夜中	in the middle of the night
よふかしする	夜ふかしする	to stay up late
よみち	夜道	a street at night

ら、り、れ、ろ、わ

らいしゅうまつ	来週末	next weekend
りそう	理想	ideal, dream
レジ	レジ	register
ロボット	ロボット	robot
ワイシャツ	ワイシャツ	dress shirt
わかめ	わかめ	seaweed
わらう	笑う	to laugh
わりかんにする	割り勘にする	to evenly split a bill

Japan
日本

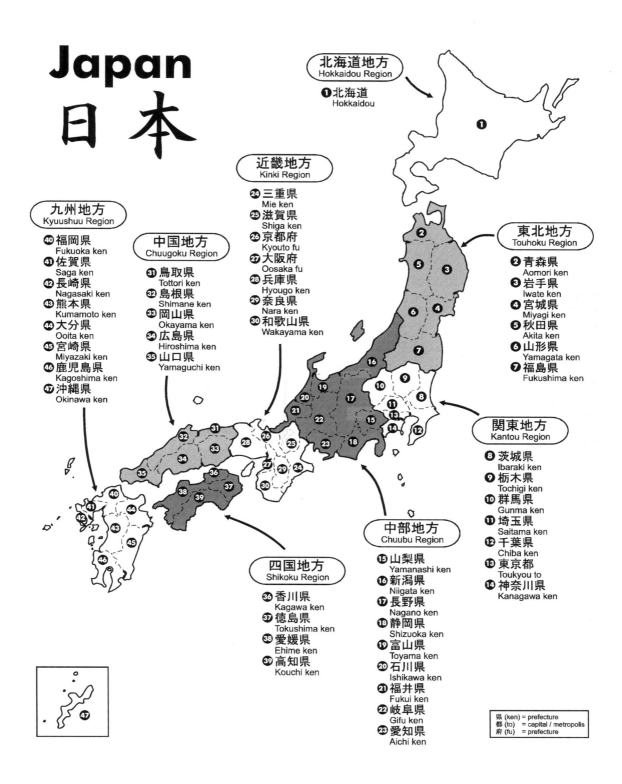

北海道地方
Hokkaidou Region
❶ 北海道
Hokkaidou

近畿地方
Kinki Region
㉔ 三重県
Mie ken
㉕ 滋賀県
Shiga ken
㉖ 京都府
Kyouto fu
㉗ 大阪府
Oosaka fu
㉘ 兵庫県
Hyougo ken
㉙ 奈良県
Nara ken
㉚ 和歌山県
Wakayama ken

東北地方
Touhoku Region
❷ 青森県
Aomori ken
❸ 岩手県
Iwate ken
❹ 宮城県
Miyagi ken
❺ 秋田県
Akita ken
❻ 山形県
Yamagata ken
❼ 福島県
Fukushima ken

九州地方
Kyuushuu Region
㊵ 福岡県
Fukuoka ken
㊶ 佐賀県
Saga ken
㊷ 長崎県
Nagasaki ken
㊸ 熊本県
Kumamoto ken
㊹ 大分県
Ooita ken
㊺ 宮崎県
Miyazaki ken
㊻ 鹿児島県
Kagoshima ken
㊼ 沖縄県
Okinawa ken

中国地方
Chuugoku Region
㉛ 鳥取県
Tottori ken
㉜ 島根県
Shimane ken
㉝ 岡山県
Okayama ken
㉞ 広島県
Hiroshima ken
㉟ 山口県
Yamaguchi ken

関東地方
Kantou Region
❽ 茨城県
Ibaraki ken
❾ 栃木県
Tochigi ken
❿ 群馬県
Gunma ken
⓫ 埼玉県
Saitama ken
⓬ 千葉県
Chiba ken
⓭ 東京都
Toukyou to
⓮ 神奈川県
Kanagawa ken

四国地方
Shikoku Region
㊱ 香川県
Kagawa ken
㊲ 徳島県
Tokushima ken
㊳ 愛媛県
Ehime ken
㊴ 高知県
Kouchi ken

中部地方
Chuubu Region
⓯ 山梨県
Yamanashi ken
⓰ 新潟県
Niigata ken
⓱ 長野県
Nagano ken
⓲ 静岡県
Shizuoka ken
⓳ 富山県
Toyama ken
⓴ 石川県
Ishikawa ken
㉑ 福井県
Fukui ken
㉒ 岐阜県
Gifu ken
㉓ 愛知県
Aichi ken

県 (ken) = prefecture
都 (to) = capital / metropolis
府 (fu) = prefecture

☺ KANJI: Lesson Reference

2   引雲遠何科夏

3   家歌画回会海

4   絵園外間顔汽

5   記帰牛魚京教

6   強角近形計元

7   原戸古午後語

8   工広交光行考

9   高黄合谷国黒

10   今才作算止市

11   思紙自寺時室

12   社弱首秋春書少

13   場色食心新親図

14   数西声星晴切

☺ KANJI: Kanji Recognition Words

Lesson 1	九つ	海外
漢字	十個	一回
お金	十一個	二回
車	十二個	三回
円	Lesson 2	四回
日本	毎日	五回
日本語	毎月	六回
日本人	毎年	七回
下さい	今年	八回
一月	下手	九回
二月	上手	十回
三月	一年	十一回
四月	二年	十二回
五月	三年	Lesson 4
六月	四年	先生
七月	一ヶ月	右
八月	二ヶ月	左
九月	三ヶ月	上
十月	四ヶ月	上がる
十一月	Lesson 3	中村
十二月	今日	田中
一つ	昨日	下
二つ	明日	手
三つ	私	人
四つ	大きい	大阪
五つ	小さい	東京
六つ	赤い	出口
七つ	青い	入り口
八つ	白い	一つ目

二つ目	天気	八時
一回目	木	九時
二回目	名前	十時
一ヶ月目	大学	十一時
二ヶ月目	教える	十二時
一年目	雨	一分
二年目	一歳	二分
Lesson 5	一才	三分
気	十歳	四分
家	十才	五分
休み	十五歳	六分
休む	15 才	七分
水	100 歳	八分
犬	何歳	九分
京都	何才	十分
勉強	Lesson 7	十五分
足	英語	三十分
帰る	～語	Lesson 8
月曜日	古い	沢山
火曜日	人生	山田
水曜日	小林	村田
木曜日	小学校	高い
金曜日	本当	赤ちゃん
土曜日	行く	後
日曜日	一時	一人
何曜日	二時	二人
Lesson 6	三時	三人
生きる	四時	四人
金魚	五時	何人
早く	六時	一日
早い	七時	二日

三日	五番	Lesson 11
四日	六番	春
五日	七番	友達
六日	八番	映画
七日	九番	今回
八日	十番	前回
九日	二十番	入る
十日	何番	子供
十一日	百	歌手
十二日	二百	Lesson 12 (none)
十三日	三百	Lesson 13
十四日	四百	食べる
十五日	五百	お母さん
十八日	六百	お父さん
二十日	七百	音
何日	八百	一昨日
Lesson 9	九百	食べる
今	Lesson 10	子犬
今年	中国	子猫
今週	先週	生む
今月	先月	生まれる
日	去年	産む
年	～時	産まれる
近い	時間	
作る	自分	
前	合う	
大丈夫	絵	
一番	田中	
二番	寺田	
三番		
四番		

Other From Zero! Books

Made in United States
Orlando, FL
20 March 2022

15941752R00239